D0962480

What the experts are saying about
MICHAEL SIVY'S RULES OF INVESTING . . .

MICHAEL SIVY'S
RULES
OF
INVESTING

HOW TO PICK STOCKS
LIKE A PRO

MICHAEL SIVY

WARNER BOOKS

A Time Warner Company

Warner Books, Inc., 1271 Avenue of the Americas, New York, NY 10020

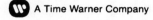 A Time Warner Company

Printed in the United States of America
First Printing: May 1996
10 9 8 7 6 5 4 3 2 1

ISBN: 0-446-72907-8

Book design and composition by L&G McRee

ACKNOWLEDGMENTS

I would like to thank **MONEY** Managing Editor Frank Lalli for all his encouragement and assistance. Without his support, this book would not have been possible. I would also like to thank **MONEY** Book Editor Dan Green and **MONEY** Assistant Managing Editor Richard Eisenberg for their many thoughtful suggestions. Thanks also to Senior Editor Rick Wolff and Executive Managing Editor Harvey-Jane Kowal at Warner Books.

John Markese, President of the American Association of Individual Investors, James R. Solloway, Director of Research at Argus Research, and Richard C. Young, President of Young Research & Publishing, read sections of this book and suggested improvements, for which I am most grateful. **MONEY** Reporters Karen Hube, Jeanhee Kim, Leslie M. Marable, and Duff J. McDonald helped enormously in double-checking the facts in this book. Ibbotson Associates, the Institute for Econometric Research, InvesTech Market Analyst, the Leuthold Group, and Value Line generously provided research. Whatever errors exist are my own.

Finally, I would like to thank Donna Torrance, Adriane Stark, and Elizabeth Gilbert for their invaluable counsel.

CONTENTS

CONTENTS

MICHAEL SIVY'S
RULES
OF
INVESTING

HOW THIS BOOK CAN HELP YOU BECOME A BETTER INVESTOR

The past 10 years have been a very happy decade for small investors. Safe blue-chip stocks have turned in gains averaging 14.5% a year, and more volatile growth stocks have posted even better results. Returns that high will double your money every five years or so.

Some experts believe that this stock boom is nearly over. They say that the fantastic profits shareholders earned in the 1980s were the result of a onetime drop in inflation and interest rates from the almost unprecedented levels reached early in the decade. But though that inflation decline was one reason for the bull market that carried the Dow industrials from 1400 in 1985 to more than 5000 today, there's a lot more to the story.

The key to the stock market's recent gains has been a global economic boom that began in the '80s and that will continue into the twenty-first century—even if it is occasionally disrupted by events like the collapse of the Mexican peso. And an expanding world economy will create plenty of exceptional opportunities for U.S. investors.

The goal of this book is to help you cash in on those opportunities, particularly by selecting safe, high-quality U.S. stocks that can beat the market by a healthy margin if you hold them for five years or longer.

If you're like most people, you've probably had some investing experience already. After all, small investors like you poured more than $100 billion into stock mutual funds each year from 1993 through 1995. Even if you haven't invested in mutual funds on your own, you've probably still had to make some decisions about where to put money that's in a 401(k) retirement account at work or some other tax-deferred retirement account such as an IRA, a Keogh, or a 403(b). You may also have bought individual stocks or bonds directly—at least once in a while.

Few people, however, know the basic principles for building a portfolio and picking safe, undervalued stocks. Those principles aren't hard to grasp or difficult to put into practice. But you do have to understand them to be a successful individual investor. And that's exactly what this book will cover.

In the chapters that follow, I'll tell you what you need to know about setting your goals and gauging risk; managing a portfolio of stocks and bonds; spotting the best picks for growth or income; and using some of the sophisticated investing techniques that the pros know and small investors don't.

If this sounds complicated, don't worry. Once you know the essentials, the rest is common sense. Even if you take only a couple of key ideas away with you after reading this book, they could improve your investing performance greatly. For example, if you had bought any reasonably well-chosen portfolio of blue-chip stocks in 1985, you would have more than tripled your money since then and earned at least two and a half times as much as if you had kept your money in bank certificates of deposit.

TRUE FACT

Since 1926, blue-chip stocks have returned an average of 10.2% a year.

Source: Ibbotson Associates

Beginners who buy and hold a solid portfolio of high-quality stocks and don't even try to do anything fancy are likely to earn almost as much as most sophisticated investors do. I can vouch for this. Over the past 18 years, in addition to being a financial journalist, I've worked as a Wall Street research director and an analyst for a stock trading desk. I've tried most of the stock investing techniques you read about in books—as well as a few that you have to be affiliated with a trading desk to consider. I can tell you from my own experience which strategies actually pay off for small investors and which sound good in theory but don't really work in practice.

Here's the surprise. With a few specific exceptions that I'll discuss in this book, most of the complicated stuff you read about usually doesn't succeed in practice—at least not if you're a small investor getting information late and paying relatively high commissions. By contrast, some of the simplest investing moves you can make will work out spectacularly well.

Of course, I don't mean to say that investing is easy. It isn't. For starters, you have to overcome natural psychological obstacles. If you give way to greed or fear—the two central emotions that drive the stock market—you'll be a loser. But the confidence you need to be a winner comes from knowledge. If you're forearmed with historical data and a sound understanding of the cycles that rule the stock and bond markets, you can scoop up bargains when other investors are dumping securities and take your profits when others are naively jumping in at a market top.

To select promising growth stocks, you don't have to have a

lot of secret information. But you do need to understand what makes a promising company sizzle—or fizzle. To earn high income without taking big risks, you should be able to check that a company's dividends are secure and that they can grow faster than inflation. Similarly, to discover great bargains that other investors have overlooked, you must be able to size up a company's value and have confidence in your own calculations when other investors—and many analysts—are convinced that the stock is a loser.

Assessing growth, income, and value investments doesn't require high-powered calculators or abstruse mathematics. All you need is simple arithmetic, a few basic reference books, and an understanding of the techniques professional investors use to size up a stock.

When it comes to more aggressive investments, there are ways that small investors can win like the pros. I'll tell you how to select promising little growth companies, how to score with new issues, and how to invest in gold without being a patsy.

There are even a few ways that little guys can profit from the options market. Most small investors who buy stock options are almost guaranteed to be losers, but there are one or two ways that stock options can boost your profits by 25% or so with little or no risk.

Don't be concerned if some of the strategies I'll tell you about seem confusing or hard to implement. Once you've mastered the basics, you'll be 90% of the way to maximum profits. The sophisticated tactics I'll talk about could help you earn even more, but if they make you uncomfortable, forget about them.

The crucial fact for you to remember as you read this book is that the stock market isn't a zero-sum game. Every long-term investor can be a winner for the simple reason that in the long run stocks return more than almost any other investment you can make. So as you read the chapters that follow, take whatever you can use. The important thing is to be in the market and be comfortable with what you are doing. That alone will be enough to earn you double-digit annual profits as the global economy enters what could well prove to be the biggest boom of your lifetime.

THE 12 RULES OF INVESTING

1. On average, you can't lose with blue-chip stocks if you plan to hold them for 20 years.

2. Diversification is the only free lunch.

3. Use a discount broker whenever possible.

4. Buy stocks after a recession has gone on for six months.

5. Sell stocks if the Federal Reserve raises short-term interest rates above long-term rates.

6. Revenue growth is the only true growth.

7. Staying ahead of inflation is more important than earning the highest possible yield.

8. A good stock at a small discount is a better buy than a lousy stock at a big discount.

9. When it comes to trading deal stocks, small investors can't beat the pros.

10. Small investors who buy stock options generally end up losers.

11. You make money by participating in the stock market's major moves, not by fighting them.

12. Anything reported in the news is already reflected in a company's share price.

PART I

MANAGING YOUR MONEY

CHAPTER 1

BEFORE YOU BEGIN:

How to Set Your Goals, Gauge Your Risks, and Master the Psychology of Investing

W ithout question, the most difficult challenge you'll face as an investor is controlling your own emotions. The stock market ought to be a feast for small investors. Because the economy grows over time—at an average rate of 2% or 3% a year after inflation is taken into account—corporate profits continue to increase, and stocks offer superb returns, on average. In fact, since 1926 equities have always posted gains over any 20-year period. If you hold a diversified assortment of stocks long enough—for your retirement, say—it's virtually impossible to lose money.

RULE NO. 1 OF INVESTING:
ON AVERAGE, YOU CAN'T LOSE WITH BLUE-CHIP
STOCKS IF YOU PLAN TO HOLD THEM FOR
20 YEARS.

The only catch is in the words "on average." If you pick just one or two stocks, you could be unlucky and suffer irretrievable losses.

Also, over a short time frame such as a year you could see enormous volatility in the value of your shares. In a full-fledged bear market, for instance, stocks can easily drop 20% or 30%. If you panic and sell at that point, you would miss out on the chance to make back your losses and go on to big profits.

It's worth noting that in terms of risk, stocks and bonds are the exact opposite of savings such as bank accounts and certificates of deposit. With savings accounts and CDs, there's a guarantee that you won't lose any principal, but after taxes you'll earn so little that you won't keep up with inflation. With stocks and bonds, on the other hand, you're virtually certain to come out ahead in the long run, but you could face hair-raising setbacks in the short term.

Think about this. The true risks are exactly the opposite of what they appear. Seemingly safe investments such as CDs are sure to be relative losers over a 20-year period, while stocks are almost certain to be winners. Bonds are likely winners, too. All you need to do is make sure that you are in the market for a long enough time.

The two keys to successful investing, then, are to diversify your holdings, so that you would not be irreparably hurt by a loss on any single stock, and to hang on throughout the ups and downs so that you are fully invested during the periods when the stock market sprints to big gains. Better yet, you should buy more stocks when the market is depressed and lighten up when prices are peaking. Or, as the old saying goes, "Buy low, sell high."

That's where the psychology comes in. To buy and sell at the right time, you will have to do the exact opposite of what your instincts tell you to do. You will have to sell just when everything seems to be breaking your way and buy when you feel totally bummed out.

The funny thing is, even after you have accepted this idea intellectually, you'll find yourself making the wrong choice because emotions are so hard to resist. When stocks are soaring, you'll get giddy and want to wait and sell just a little bit higher.

Then, once you've missed the peak, you'll get angry at yourself and hope for a second chance to sell at the top. Conversely, when stocks have drifted to a bottom you'll feel vaguely depressed and lose interest in the market. If you do buy something, you'll tell your friends and then immediately see the stock you bought go even lower. They'll laugh at you and tell you you're a jerk.

Let them laugh. The way to become a great investor is to make independent decisions and analyze the mistakes you make. Only by coming to terms with your own psychological drives will you be able to start to separate what you think and know from how you feel—and the ability to do that is the hallmark of a winner.

If you don't have much experience investing, you should recognize that you are almost certain to make common mistakes over the course of your first stock market cycle. Such cycles typically last five or six years. So start off with small amounts of money and stick with very conservative choices for the first few years. The important thing is to participate, not to become an instant master of the universe.

Before I get into the essentials of investing—portfolio management, economics, stock selection, and sophisticated analysis—it's worth spending a little time on the psychological background to the stock market. That consists of four subjects: setting sensible investing goals, gauging your true appetite for risk, understanding the way psychology affects share prices, and avoiding the most common money mistakes.

WHAT IS A STOCK OR BOND REALLY WORTH?

What do you actually own when you own a stock or bond? And what should you expect to get out of it? Those may sound like silly questions. But the more you think about them, the more you'll realize how puzzling they really are.

Legally, of course, when you own a stock you own a share of a company. But unless you own a very big slice, your votes will

11

hardly count for anything at the company's annual meeting; and although you would have a claim on the company's assets if it were liquidated, it probably won't be. For all practical purposes, what you really own is the right to receive the company's dividends for as long as you own your shares. And in the case of a growth stock that pays no current dividend, you have the right to any future dividends it might start paying.

Sounds pretty airy, doesn't it?

Bonds are a little more solid. When you buy a bond you are lending money to a company in exchange for a series of promised interest payments and the return of your principal at some time in the future. Just as with stocks, though, you are receiving a stream of promised payments that could continue for a decade or more. The worst of it is that you don't have the faintest idea what future economic conditions will be like. Will inflation soar? Will higher interest rates be available elsewhere? Will corporate profits—and dividends—rise quickly or slowly? No one knows.

To make sense out of this, economists have devised a scheme for valuing stocks and bonds called the **dividend-discount model**, which I'll explain over the next three pages. If you find the discussion boring or hard to follow, feel free to skip to the next section, "Choosing Sensible Investing Goals."

Let's start by talking about the time value of money. When you buy a one-year certificate of deposit, the bank is promising to pay you, say, $1,050 in a year if you give up the use of $1,000 until that time. In other words, a borrower who needs your money for a year is willing to pay you $50, or 5%, to delay using it. That's all an interest rate is—it's a payment to put off enjoying your money today in exchange for more money to spend tomorrow.

What determines the price of delaying your spending? Partly it depends on how badly the money is burning a hole in your pocket; if you really want your money now, you'd charge a lot to lend it to someone. The price also reflects how many people want to borrow your money, what they're willing to pay, and whether there's any risk you won't be paid back on time.

The dividend-discount model is based on this commonsense thinking. While the mathematics gets complicated, the principles are simple. The model says that the value of a stock or a bond today is the sum of the payments the security will make in the future. If someone agreed to pay you $1 this year and $1 next year, you'd figure that was worth a little less than $2.

The reason it's less than $2 is that the value of payments has to be adjusted to reflect the time value of money. The further away a payment is, the less it will be worth. And the higher interest rates are, the less a future payment will be worth. For example, $1 a year from now is worth $.95 today if interest rates are 5%, but only $.91 if interest rates are 10%.

Investors also take points off the present value of future payments if the size and timing of the payments are likely to be erratic or if there is a danger that the payments will fail to keep up with inflation. And investors discount future payments especially severely if there is any chance of a default.

Throughout the rest of this book you'll see these basic ideas occurring over and over again. Here's what the dividend-discount model boils down to in the most practical terms:

■ The higher the growth rate of a company's profits, the pricier its stock will be. (This is measured by the **price/earnings ratio,** known as the P/E.) That's why Microsoft trades at 38 times earnings, while Con Edison goes for 10 times earnings. If investors think the growth rate is about to speed up, they will bid the price higher. If they think growth is slowing down, they will discount the P/E. As a result, growth stocks can plummet after management reports quarterly profits below what shareholders expect.

■ Stocks go up when interest rates fall and go down when interest rates rise. Reason: When rates rise, a stock's future earnings and dividends are simply worth less today. Conversely, share prices rise when rates fall, as long as investors are convinced that earnings will continue to grow on schedule. When rates fall during a recession, though, stock prices can weaken because the earnings outlook is deteriorating.

■ Rising inflation will hurt most stocks since their earnings growth probably won't increase enough to offset higher inflation. Stocks that can easily and promptly pass through inflation to customers will be neither hurt nor helped. A few types of companies—such as mining firms, forest products businesses, oil producers, and real estate trusts—actually may profit from inflation because their future profits outpace overall price increases.

■ Anything that increases the risks for a company's future profits will hurt its share price; developments that reduce those risks will boost the stock price.

■ Bond prices are automatically hurt when interest rates rise and benefit when rates fall.

■ Since bond interest payments are fixed, bond prices suffer when inflation speeds up and advance when inflation slows down.

■ Prices improve when a bond's quality rating is raised and are hurt when rating agencies downgrade an issue. Low-quality junk bonds generally sink during a recession and rebound in a recovery, reflecting changes in the likelihood that the company might default.

That concludes the abstract theory—the rest of this book will be about you and your financial needs. But before we get to how the stock market works, we need to address a few financial-planning issues. For starters, how do you balance profit against risk?

CHOOSING SENSIBLE INVESTING GOALS

Like the labor movement, investors can describe their essential goal in a single word: "more." However, since all profits carry a measure of risk, you need to start out with some notion of what you can realistically expect.

As a baseline, there's something that economists call the **risk-less rate of return,** which is the annual interest rate paid by totally safe investments that can be cashed in at full face value on short notice. For practical purposes, this baseline return is the yield on 30-day Treasury bills. Over time, this T-bill yield turns out to be only slightly higher than the rate of inflation. In other words, if you stick with totally safe choices, you will make virtually no real profits—and after taxes you will actually fail to keep up with inflation. To make money, you have to take risks.

Of course, you don't want to take foolhardy gambles, and you certainly don't want to take any risks that you don't get paid for. So what can you really expect to earn, and how dangerous will it be?

The most widely recognized benchmark for stock and bond returns are the historical data put together by Ibbotson Associates, a Chicago consulting firm. Those data show that from 1926 to 1994, Treasury bills earned an average of 3.7% a year. Since inflation averaged 3.1% during that 69-year period, the real return on T-bills has been just over half a percentage point a year. That's hardly a rich payoff.

You can earn more money, of course, if you're willing to accept bigger short-term price fluctuations. Here's a rundown on the returns you can expect, in order of increasing risk. Intermediate-term government bonds—those that mature in about five years—earned an average of 5.1% (2% after inflation) from 1926 to 1994. Top-notch long-term bonds with maturities of 20 years have also returned more than 5% (2.3% after inflation). Roughly speaking, intermediates are 1.7 times as volatile as T-bills, and long-term issues are 2.5 times as volatile.

Stocks offer far greater returns than fixed-income investments

15

HOW DIFFERENT ASSETS HAVE PAID OFF

	Average Annual Return	Average Annual Return after Inflation	Relative Volatility
Large-company stocks	10.2%	7.1%	6.2
Small-company stocks	12.2	9.1	10.5
Long-term corporate bonds	5.4	2.3	2.5
Intermediate-term government bonds	5.1	2.0	1.7
U.S. Treasury bills	3.7	0.6	1.0

Since 1926, stocks have provided much higher average returns than income investments have. After inflation is taken into account, the edge that stocks have looks even bigger. That superior performance, however, comes at the price of greater short-term risk. In fact, annual stock returns vary more than six times as much as the returns of safe Treasury bills. The figures shown here are based on data compiled by Ibbotson Associates, a Chicago consulting firm that tracks returns on financial assets. Returns include dividend and interest payments as well as price changes.

Source: © *Stocks, Bonds, Bills, and Inflation 1995 Yearbook™*, Ibbotson Associates, Chicago (annually updates work by Roger G. Ibbotson and Rex A. Sinquefield). Used with permission. All rights reseved.

do but are a lot more erratic in the short run. For instance, shares of large, blue-chip companies such as those that make up the S&P 500 stock index have returned a whopping 10.2% a year, on average, from 1926 to 1994. That works out to an impressive 7.1% after inflation. Small-company shares do even better, with a 12.2% average annual return. The catch: Over time periods as short as a year or two, big stocks are 6.2 times as volatile as T-bills and small stocks are more than 10 times as flighty.

Don't let those short-term risk numbers scare you. As I mentioned earlier in the chapter, stocks actually turn out to be less risky than most other investments if you can afford to hold them for 20 years or longer. And the difference in return between stocks and fixed-income investments is phenomenal: with typical stock returns, your money will double every six or seven years; with low-risk, fixed-income returns, your money could take three times as long to double—and all the while you'd be losing ground to inflation.

As you progress, you'll want to construct a portfolio of several different investments with varying risk levels and potential returns. The best strategy for doing that is known as asset allocation and offers you the highest return with the lowest risk, even on a short-term basis. In the next chapter I'll discuss in detail how to create and manage such a portfolio.

MONEY magazine follows one such portfolio for the **MONEY** Small Investor Index. That model portfolio, which reflects individuals' investment patterns, is generally invested about 35% in stocks, 25% in bonds, and 40% in short-term income investments such as money-market funds and certificates of deposit. Over the past 20 years the **MONEY** model portfolio would have returned an average of 9% to 10% annually. And you should expect to do at least that well in the years to come.

GAUGING YOUR TRUE APPETITE FOR RISK

So far, I've been talking as though the most important kind of risk that investors face is the danger of a short-term drop in prices. This kind of risk—known as **volatility**—is the easiest to measure and the basis of most sophisticated investing models. For example, when you see numbers for the risk-adjusted return of a mutual fund, the risk that the fund's return has been adjusted for consists of short-term price swings. Such volatility is usually rated with measures known as **beta** or **standard deviation.**

TRUE FACT

Investors in their forties and fifties are willing to take bigger risks than young investors. Reason: They tend to be wealthier and can afford some losses.

Source: William B. Riley Jr. and K. Victor Chow, *Financial Analysts Journal,* November–December 1992

Those calculations are fine as far as they go, but the fact is that there are lots of other kinds of risk that matter for small investors. Though these other varieties of risk are much harder to measure and use in mathematical equations than volatility is, they turn out to be far more important for long-term investors. After all, over the next 20 years you won't care how much your stocks or bonds have bounced around from day to day, you'll be far more concerned about issues like these:

■ **Have your investments suffered any major setbacks?** Though price volatility is the usual measure of investment risk, it is important to remember that it is only sudden *downward* price moves that people worry about. Financial advisers are rarely fired because their stock picks go up unexpectedly. In addition, when losses exceed a certain size, their seriousness changes radically. If a stock falls a bit one day—or one week—and rebounds the next, that volatility is of no importance at all. If the dip is unusually large, you may get a queasy feeling in the pit of your stomach while the share price is down, but your long-term return will not be affected.

It's a completely different story for major losses—even if you eventually get even. For example, if you look at any 25-year period that includes 1932, the year of the final nosedive in the Great Crash, you would find that the average return over those years was less than half the typical return for stocks. The market did rebound, and stocks even returned to the high-flying levels they traded at during the 1920s. But years were wasted while the stock market was making up for its losses in the Crash. That's why a major loss drags down your average return—you lose time while you are waiting to get back to even.

■ **Have you tied up your money so tightly that you are missing out on better investments?** Economists use the term **opportunity cost** to describe the invisible loss that comes from missing out on a great opportunity. Small investors are most likely to encounter this problem when they tie up money in long-term certificates of deposit right before interest rates rise. Because CD holders have to pay a penalty to withdraw their money early, they are unable to take advantage of the higher rates until the CDs mature.

You can be caught in the same bind in more subtle ways, too. For example, say you are fully invested in stocks and the overall market drops sharply. You might then see plenty of bargains you wanted to buy, but you would not be able to unless you were willing to sell and take a loss on some of the stocks you already owned. Passing up great opportunities may not sound like a true cost because you never actually lose any of your money. Nonetheless, its effect on your long-term return can be devastating.

■ **If you had to sell an investment, would you be able to get a fair price for it?** Spotting a great opportunity, you might decide to go ahead and sell some of the investments you already own to raise cash. But that exposes you to another risk—that you will get a lousy price if the investments you have are hard to sell. This danger is known as **liquidity risk** (so-called because your holdings are "illiquid"). Such investments include real estate, limited partnerships, and sometimes even obscure stocks and bonds.

■ **Have you ever got back money from an investment and found you couldn't invest at an equally good return?** You might think you can't lose money by getting a cash distribution from an investment. Think again. Your long-term return will suffer if you are unable to reinvest the money you receive at a rate as attractive as the return on your original investment. This problem arises most often with bonds and other income investments such as mortgage-backed securities.

Say you buy a bond paying 8%, and interest rates subsequently fall to 6%. Obviously you will not be able to reinvest the interest payments you receive at your original 8% rate, but only at 6%. You may think that you have locked in a high return by purchasing 30-year bonds, for example. But reinvestment risk can substantially reduce your return over the lifetime of the bonds. Mortgage-backed securities suffer from an intense version of the problem. Such securities are backed by pools of home mortgages guaranteed by government agencies. Because the biggest guarantor agency is the Government National Mortgage Association (GNMA), these issues are often called "Ginnie Maes."

If interest rates fall, homeowners naturally begin refinancing the mortgages in the pools backing Ginnie Maes. As a result, the Ginnie Mae holders see money come flying back at them that they won't be able to reinvest at an attractive rate (a danger known as **prepayment risk**). If the increase in prepayments is unexpectedly large, the market value of a Ginnie Mae can be penalized. Even if the price of a Ginnie Mae does not actually decline, it may appreciate much less than the prices of competing income investments.

There is a way to avoid prepayment risk—buy a zero-coupon bond. Since zeros pay no interest at all, they compound at a stated rate over their entire lifetime. This fact makes zeros ideal for meeting specific future costs such as paying for college tuition, because when you buy a zero you know to the penny how much you will have when the bond matures.

■ **Have you stayed ahead of inflation?** Realistically the biggest risk most investors face is keeping up with inflation. It is natural to think of risk in terms of preserving the dollar value of your investments, but what you really want to protect is the purchasing power of those dollars. If you doubt that, ask yourself if you would be particularly happy to wake up tomorrow and find you were a millionaire—in Russian rubles. Yet few investors think much about inflation risk. This error is most common among retirees, who consistently underestimate how long they are likely to live and therefore take inadequate steps to protect themselves against inflation. For example, someone retiring at 65 today can expect to live at least another 18 years. Yet if such a retiree invests his or her money entirely in government bonds to protect its principal value in dollars and inflation averages 5%, the purchasing power of the principal will have dropped in half after only 14 years. For this reason high-yield stocks that can increase their dividends over time are a wiser choice than bonds, at least for a portion of your retirement portfolio. Even for younger investors, it is crucial to analyze investments for their capacity to keep up with inflation as well as for their current returns.

■ **Have any of your investments ever defaulted?** The nightmare for any investor is an outright default. Whereas most risks are hypothetical in the sense that you always have the chance to make your money back, an outright default may be permanent. For this reason a small growth stock may be far riskier compared with a large, well-established growth company than its volatility suggests. If the small company's hot product goes out of favor or it runs into serious financial difficulties and goes bankrupt, your investment may be largely lost—forever. Similarly, junk bonds are more dangerous than they may appear. The possibility of bankruptcy adds a toxic element to the junk.

■ **Have you achieved your financial goals?** Putting all of these risks together, here's the ultimate danger you will face over a lifetime of investing: You may fail to achieve your financial goals and be forced to make compromises in your standard of living that you could have avoided. Essentially, the rest of this book will tell you how to make certain that doesn't happen.

PSYCHOLOGY AND THE STOCK MARKET

I've talked about the ways in which psychology affects your overall investing strategy, but it is particularly important in the stock market. Since stocks are likely to be the most important building blocks for your investment portfolio, the ways in which psychological factors influence stock prices are worth a separate discussion.

The heart of the matter is that stocks are hard to value. Whereas bonds can be evaluated mathematically based on easily measured variables such as interest rates and inflation, stock values reflect many factors that are hard to quantify. As a result, no formula, not even the dividend-discount model, can begin to set a value on a stock that you can trust confidently. Historical benchmarks help some, but investors would be wise to consider the price of a stock only slightly more solid than the price of a painting.

Wall Street pundits are fond of describing the ups and downs in the stock market as a battle between fear and greed. Perhaps the best way to view the often baffling swings in share prices is to see them as alternating panics in which waves of greed sweep over investors and prices rise too high, only to be followed by waves of fear in which prices fall too low. For this reason market historians often recommend the book *Extraordinary Popular Delusions & the Madness of Crowds* (Random House), which chronicles some of the weird euphoric binges and panics that have taken place in the past 500 years or so. The best-known example is tulipmania, the unbelievable runup in tulip prices that occurred in Holland in the seventeenth century. By the end, crazed tulip buyers who thought that the boom would never end were willing to sell a house to buy a single flower bulb.

Extraordinary Popular Delusions is fascinating reading but isn't much help to investors aside from reminding you that people are a lot nuttier than you think. What's even more important to remember is that you're a lot nuttier than you think, too. No matter how well you understand the principles of investing, you will feel the same emotional pulls as other investors. You'll grow overconfident at the top and overly timid at the bottom. Time and experience will temper those emotions somewhat but will never eliminate them. None of us is an exception to this rule, but that's okay.

Some of the best work on stock market psychology has been done by David Dreman, a Jersey City, N.J., money manager and author of *The New Contrarian Investment Strategy* (Random House). Dreman has popularized a value-oriented style of investing. That approach favors so-called value stocks; such stocks typically sell at prices that are no more than 14 times yearly earnings and pay dividend yields higher than 3%. With cheap prices and fat yields, value stocks can be attractive even if their earnings are increasing less than 10% a year. Growth stocks, by contrast, generally have to be able to raise their earnings more than 12% annually.

At any rate, though Dreman's system of analysis works most naturally with value stocks, some of it can be applied to growth stocks as well. I won't attempt to summarize all the interesting ideas in his books, but one of them is the crux of stock market psychology: Forecasters consistently underestimate how different the future will be from the present.

TRUE FACT

Stock analysts' profit forecasts are generally too high. They overestimate companies' earnings by anywhere from 10% to 50%.

Source: New Amsterdam Partners

This idea shouldn't come as a surprise, since we see it proven over and over again in history. The world is simply more varied in its possibilities than human imagination can envision. Nonetheless, forecasters never seem to remember this when they are making their predictions. If you want proof, simply consider some of the stupid forecasts made with complete confidence over the past couple of decades (the worst generally come from environmentalists and socialist economists who think the world is running out of everything). Remember during the '70s, when there were only 20 years of oil left and the price per barrel was going to hit $100? Surprise. Adjusted for inflation, oil at $19 is cheaper today than it was in 1974. If you did a little historical research, you'd also find that the same sorts of demographers who are worried about overpopulation today were once wringing their hands over the so-called birth dearth. Similarly, climatologists who warn of global warming were once nervous about the coming of a new ice age.

Of course, some of these dangers might turn out to be real. We just have no way of knowing which ones. The failure of forecasting, however, goes further. While futurologists regularly predict disasters that never occur by extrapolating current trends into the future, they also fail dismally to anticipate new developments. And that's the key point for the stock market. The pros and cons that exist today are already reflected in share prices. It's the unexpected that moves stocks—the bad earnings report or the sudden hit product that no one foresaw. As a result, even when forecasters are right about some new trend, they usually greatly underestimate how big it could turn out to be. Among those economists who saw interest rate increases coming in the late '70s, how many anticipated rates above 14%? Not a lot. And when inflation hit double digits in the late '70s, who would have believed that we would see inflation virtually disappear in the '80s at the same time that the federal government was running record deficits? Yet that's what made the stock market boom over the past 10 years.

This tendency to underestimate just how different the future might be is the basis for a value investing strategy. Here's how the thinking goes: If a company is successful, its shares will be popular and highly priced. Investors will expect continuing good news. The only surprise would be bad news—and that would make the stock price fall. Value stocks, by contrast, are typically the shares of companies that aren't doing especially well. Investors already expect lousy news in the future. Any development that investors didn't anticipate would likely be good news that could make the stock price soar. The bottom line: It's smarter to buy a cheap mediocre stock than an expensive class act. This kind of thinking may seem perverse to you. Why wouldn't you want always to invest in the best companies around? The answer: Investors make their money when a company's prospects get better—if you start off terrific, there's no place to go but down.

TRUE FACT

When the market's P/E is below 12, stocks earn an average of nearly 14% annually over the following decade; when the P/E is above 17, stocks earn less than 8%.

Source: The Leuthold Group

Growth investors disagree with this point of view, of course, and a contrary case can be made for growth stocks (namely that earnings growth is the chief factor that determines stock gains in the long run). In fact, there is a good argument for growth investing, but even with growth issues it's important to try to buy at cheaper-than-usual prices. In future chapters we'll look more closely at how to assess both growth and value issues.

For investors who are just starting out, though, I'd advise leaning toward the value side of the scale. The reason: It's easier to make a horrendous mistake with growth stocks than with value stocks. As evidence, consider these statistics: Cambridge, Mass., investment firm David L. Babson & Co. identified the most popular stock (measured by price/earnings ratios) in each of the 13 years from 1982 through 1995. As of 1995, those stocks had lost an average of 4%, while the S&P 500 had gained 113%.

10 INVESTING MISTAKES TO AVOID

■ **Don't confuse a company with its stock.** When you're considering a job offer, you should look at the quality of the company you would end up working for. But when you're investing, you should pay more attention to the value of the shares. Even a third-rate company can be a buy at a cheap enough price. In fact, one notable study that appeared in the *Financial Analysts Journal* (May–June 1987) makes the point clearly: New York City investment management firm New Amsterdam Partners looked at companies rated *excellent* and those rated *unexcellent* in the early '80s best-seller *In Search of Excellence* by Thomas J. Peters and Robert H. Waterman Jr. Over the five years from 1981 through 1985, the majority of the *excellent* companies underperformed the market; altogether they managed to beat the S&P by only 1% annually. By contrast, the majority of the *unexcellent* companies beat the market, outperforming the S&P by 12% a year on average. When you select a stock, you should be looking for excellence in share price, not simply excellence in corporate management.

■ **Don't pay excessive attention to the overall market.** Sometimes it's obvious that the stock market as a whole is depressed or overpriced (in a coming chapter I'll explain what the signs are). However, a shareholder is investing in a single issue, not the broad market. Though there will be fewer bargain stocks in a high-flying market, you'll always be able to find at least a couple of them that are worth buying. Similarly, when most blue chips are in the dumps, it's still possible to overpay for a particular company's shares. All that you should focus on is the value of—and the outlook for—the issue you are actually buying.

■ **Don't put much faith in forecasts.** I'll explain in this book how analysts make their projections, both for the economy and for individual companies. Those sorts of calculations are essential guides for selecting stocks and putting together a portfolio. But they're only guides—intelligent guesses about what might happen in the future, not solid facts you can rely on. You also should remember that most forecasters are connected in one way or another to the business of selling securities. As a result, both economists and stock analysts tend to be overly optimistic. Projections for the stock market as a whole can be wrong in direction, size, or timing—and forecasts for individual companies aren't much more accurate. Corporate earnings, for example, often come in below the figures that stock pickers project, according to a 1992 study by New Amsterdam Partners. The study found that the estimates analysts make at the start of a year were, on average, 57% too high. And even though earnings projections were revised lower as the year progressed, estimates made late in a year were still 12% too high, on average. So be sure to base your stock-picking decisions on historical data as well as on projections for the future.

■ **Don't buy junk.** It's always tempting for small investors to try to increase their profit potential by buying low-quality securities. In theory this makes sense—marginal issues are more volatile and will profit more than blue chips in a favorable environment.

For example, a small oil company that is barely making ends meet will enjoy a much bigger percentage gain than Exxon if the price of crude oil goes up. Trouble is, a bigger swing can work against you as well as for you. If the outlook for an industry goes sour, it's the marginal firms that will be hurt the most. Junk lovers can always produce historical statistics showing that on balance the upswings for low-quality stocks and bonds more than make up for their downswings. But be careful. Those historical statistics will be skewed because they probably won't include the stocks and bonds of companies that went bankrupt and disappeared. Even if they do, it isn't worth risking a disaster to make a slightly higher average return. It won't matter what the averages are if you happen to be holding the stocks and bonds of one of the companies that goes broke.

■ **Don't reach for yield.** It may look as though you can lock in the highest safe return possible by buying stocks or bonds that offer well above average yields. That's not really true. First, the issues that offer the highest yields, such as junk bonds or troubled electric utilities, are likely to be low in quality and riskier than they may look. Second, the more yield you receive, the less growth you are likely to get. This can be devastating. Though high-yield investments may provide a more predictable return over the space of a year or less, top-quality growth investments are likely to be the best performers over a decade or longer. They're also the ones most likely to outpace inflation, and as we've already discussed, inflation is one of the greatest risks that conservative small investors face.

■ **Don't underestimate dividends.** You shouldn't bet on growth alone, though. Dividends turn out to be a very important part of a stock's long-term return. In fact, yield typically accounts for more than 40% of the total return that blue-chip stocks earn. If you're a conservative small investor, your portfolio should contain a balanced mix of income and growth investments. Since you'll likely be shooting for an average annual return of a little over 10%, the stocks that form the backbone of your portfolio should yield 3% to 4.5%.

■ **Don't trade.** Virtually all the evidence shows that buying and selling stocks frequently is a recipe for lousy performance. At best you'll run up sizable commissions and then lag the overall stock market by that amount. At worst you'll get sucked into short-term market trends, buying high and then selling low. Nonetheless, most investors trade far too much. Why? For the same reason vacationers spend too much on souvenirs—impulse. You'll probably overtrade, too. I do. But the more you hold off, the better your long-term results will likely be. It makes sense to sell if some particularly lucky stock pick shoots up 20% or 30% after only a couple of months, but as a general rule you should buy stocks and bonds that you think are worth holding for at least a year—and preferably for five years.

■ **Don't join a stampede.** When everybody runs for the exits, it's understandable that a small investor would start feeling self-doubt. Resist the urge. It may sometimes be smart to flee at the first signs of trouble and hold your losses to a minimum. But by the time a full-scale stampede is under way, it's usually too late to sell troubled stocks—the damage is already done. More often than not, in fact, a stampede out of a stock or a market sector is a sign of a bottom. When that happens, smart investors make notes on their future buy lists. Even if investments that have crashed lie dormant for six months or so, at some point they'll be great buys again. Of course, you can hold your ground or buy in the face of a stampede only if you have invested conservatively and have cash available for new purchases. So be sure your portfolio is well diversified, and keep a cash reserve.

■ **Don't get impatient.** After panic, boredom is the most dangerous feeling an investor has to control. You shouldn't give up on a stock pick just because it isn't working out as quickly as you would like. It's a lot easier to analyze a company and calculate where its stock should trade than to figure out how long it will take for the share price to get there. Stick with your decisions, unless the outlook for a company changes radically. As long as the business is fundamentally on track, you should just wait patiently until other investors recognize the same strengths you see—and bid up the share price. If you aren't willing to wait, you could easily sit with a stock for six months and then sell, only to see the share price soar a few weeks later.

■ **Don't do anything that makes you fundamentally uncomfortable.** The correct objective for small investors is to create a portfolio of safe stocks and bonds that are likely to outpace the overall market over the next decade or longer. If you do that— by buying high-quality issues, diversifying your holdings, and buying or selling only rarely—you won't spend a lot of time worrying about your investment portfolio. In fact, you'll hardly need to think about it at all. So avoid any kind of investment or any strategy that makes you uncomfortable. If you don't understand a company's business or don't believe some particular investing approach really works, forget about it. There are lots of good stocks and plenty of different ways to make money in the market without getting anxious. And that's your real goal—not just big profits, but peace of mind.

CHAPTER 2

SAVVY MONEY MANAGEMENT:

How to Create the Portfolio That's Right for You and Get a Winning Edge over the Pros

Most small investors worry that the stock market isn't a level playing field and that professionals have an unbeatable advantage. Hard as it may be to believe, the opposite is true. When it comes to earning a market-beating long-term profit, small investors such as you have a winning edge over the pros.

How can that be? How can an individual with only a small amount of money and limited access to information actually have an advantage over institutional investors with their computerized research departments and billions of dollars in assets?

It's easy. The same way a bird can outdistance an elephant. While the pros are lumbering along, small investors can dart in front of them, taking advantage of every opportunity and coasting to maximum long-term gains.

To understand why small investors can have a winning edge, you need to know a little bit about the realities that professional investors face. Generally speaking, the pros handle enormous amounts of money. As a result, they have the same problem an oil tanker captain does. They can sail only where the water is deep and make course corrections only by starting way in advance and turning slowly. In practice this means the typical institutional investor has to put most of his or her money into shares of the 200 or so largest U.S. companies. When smaller stocks—or midsize ones that aren't widely followed by analysts—start to soar, the pros are bound to miss out on the largest available profits.

The pros have a second problem as well—overhead. Wall Street money managers and analysts don't come cheap. And it's not unusual for management fees and other expenses to eat up the better part of a percentage point of a portfolio's return every year. That may not sound like much. But considering that top-quality stocks and bonds may earn only 10% or so a year on average, institutional investors may lose as much as one-tenth of what they earn to overhead.

Then there's another hurdle the pros face, and it may undercut performance worst of all. They aren't investing their own money. Rather, they are managing the assets of corporate pension funds, clients, or mutual fund shareholders. And they get rated on their performance every three months. Turn in a few bad quarters in a row if you're a money manager, and you may start losing clients or find yourself featured in a magazine article about investment stars who have lost their touch.

Don't cry for these guys. They make big bucks when the market is moving their way. But don't sell yourself short, either. If you concentrate on taking advantage of their weaknesses, you can actually do better than they do. And that's true whether you want to invest in growth stocks for long-term price appreciation; in income shares for regular cash dividends that will increase over the years; or in underpriced stocks that could be discovered and turn in big capital gains. Think for a moment about the problems the pros face, and you'll realize that any successful strategy for small investors will be based on the following three ideas:

■ **Minimize your overhead.** Buy stocks and bonds directly when you can, rather than investing in a mutual fund. For example, if you want to put money into Treasury bonds that you plan to hold for seven years, say, buy a seven-year Treasury instead of an intermediate-term bond fund. If you hold such a government-guaranteed bond to maturity, your risk is nil; mutual fund managers probably won't add much to your performance, but their fees will reduce your profits. The same logic holds for a select portfolio of the highest-quality blue chips. Frankly, if you have $25,000 to invest and you diversify intelligently, you can create a safe portfolio of stocks and never have to pay management fees.

■ **Favor investments that the pros are neglecting.** If you're a value investor, look at stock groups and companies that are currently out of favor. If you're a growth investor, consider shares that appear undervalued relative to their likely growth rate. Don't ever feel you need to jump into sectors that are currently fashionable and pay top dollar for high-flying stocks. Just like fashion, investing is a fad-driven business. And the best buys will be among the stocks that are markdowns (in coming chapters I'll explain how to spot these bargains).

■ **Invest for the long term.** On the most obvious level, this will free you from the short-term mindset that requires institutional investors to try to beat the market every quarter. In addition, since your chief cost will be onetime commissions when you buy or sell stocks or bonds, the longer you hold a security, the lower your annual cost will be (because the commissions will be spread over more years). There's another benefit from long-term investing that's easy to overlook—deferred taxes. Since you don't have to pay capital-gains taxes until you sell a security, the longer you hold a winning investment, the more money you'll have working for you. As a general rule, you should invest money only in stocks and bonds that you don't expect you'll need for at least three years. That holding period is also smart because it may take unpopular, bargain-priced stocks several years to come back into favor and pay off with maximum profits.

So far we've been talking about the performance of the pros based on averages. And, of course, not all institutional investors get average results. Some are dunderheads and regularly underperform the market. Others are true stars and do turn in superior profits more often than not. In addition, though most money managers have to put the bulk of their money into the stocks that make up the S&P 500 index, not all do. Some managers specialize in small-company shares, foreign issues, high-technology stocks with rapidly growing earnings, or special situations, the Wall Street name for underpriced stocks with unusual stories. In these cases it may be smart to invest through a mutual fund even though your returns will be reduced by expenses.

TRUE FACT

A growth mutual fund with performance that ranks in the top 10% one year is likely to beat other mutual funds by up to three or four percentage points the following year.

Source: Darryll Hendricks, Jayendu Patel, and Richard Zeckhauser, *The Journal of Finance,* vol. 48, no. 1, March 1993

Let's start with top-performing managers. Does it make sense to pay up for stars? The answer: Yes. Despite the automatic Wall Street caveat that past performance does not guarantee future results, academic research shows that managers who have consistently beaten the market year after year do have a somewhat better than even chance of outpacing the market in the future. This isn't anywhere near an ironclad guarantee that a top manager will continue to be a winner, but it's worth something. What constitutes a meaningful track record? I'd recommend this rule of thumb: Pay up for management only if a fund has ranked in the top third of its category for at least five years.

Similarly, if it's important to your overall investing plan to have some money in racy categories—such as small stocks, foreign issues, technology shares, or junk bonds—think about investing through a mutual fund. Investments such as these, which can substantially outperform blue chips, carry risks that are beyond the expertise of many managers—and most small investors. With such assets it's sensible to invest through a mutual fund.

Though this book is intended principally to help small investors who are ready to move beyond mutual funds and buy individual stocks and bonds, I think funds have an important place in every investor's mix of holdings. You can improve your returns—and lower your expenses—by selecting mainstream stocks and bonds yourself. But for dicier choices, it's wiser to invest through funds. The trick is to figure out what mix of assets you really need to create the portfolio that's best for you and then combine funds and individual issues to get the highest safe returns with the lowest expenses.

SELECTING THE RIGHT PORTFOLIO

One of the great advantages of investing through mutual funds is that you have professional money managers choosing the stocks and bonds you are going to own. That certainly makes life easier for you. However, as we've just discussed, that convenience can cost you quite a lot in management expenses and fees. Even worse, professional management doesn't necessarily contribute much to your own profits.

You might think that it takes years of training and experience to learn how to put together a winning portfolio of stocks and bonds. Nothing could be further from the truth. Money management is nothing more than common sense. In fact, putting together a solid portfolio of safe stocks and bonds boils down to these four rules:

■ **Don't put all your eggs in one basket.** Own at least eight stocks. Make sure they are in eight different industries.

■ **Always go first class.** Buy blue chips, high-quality income stocks, Treasury bonds, or top-rated corporate debt.

■ **Don't overpay.** You should be able to find attractive stocks that are selling at least 30% below prices they have reached within the past three years. If you pay record prices for a stock, make sure it meets other tests for value.

■ **Don't get greedy.** Trying to wring the last few drops of profit out of a stock will lead you into making serious mistakes, such as holding shares too long. When you earn a generous profit, be grateful and sell.

In future chapters I'll explain how you can assess the quality of a stock or bond, how to tell when an investment is a good value, and when to sell. The rest of this chapter will address the first rule—not putting all your eggs in one basket.

This familiar notion is called **diversification** by investment strategists. On the simplest level, diversification means that you should split your money among a variety of investments so that if one goes sour, only a small part of your total wealth will be lost. For example, say you own eight stocks and one of the companies gets into trouble. If its shares collapse to half their value, you'll still have lost only 6.25%. (Each of the eight stocks counts for 12.5% of your total holdings; if one loses half its value, you'll be down 12.5% divided by two, or 6.25%.)

There's a more sophisticated side to diversification, though. And it's probably the single most important principle that small investors need to understand. In fact, optimum diversification is the only way you can maximize your return without taking extra risk.

RULE NO. 2 OF INVESTING: DIVERSIFICATION IS THE ONLY FREE LUNCH.

Here's the idea. Buying a bunch of different stocks isn't enough to ensure adequate diversification. For example, say you bought shares in a dozen different electric utility companies. You'd largely be protected against the failure of any one of the firms, but you'd have no protection at all against developments that were unfavorable to electric utilities in general. If the cost of fuel went up, then almost all electric companies would see their profit margins squeezed. Or if the government passed stringent environmental laws, most utilities would have to dip into profits to pay for reducing air pollution. Further, since most utility stocks offer high yields and therefore behave like bonds, the shares of almost all utilities would suffer if interest rates rose. The bottom line is that buying a variety of stocks protects you only if the stocks are not vulnerable to the same risks.

Let's return to our electric utility example. Say that instead of buying 12 utilities, you bought six utility stocks and six energy stocks (the shares of oil and natural gas producers). Then, if the price of fuel went up, gains on the energy stocks would offset losses on the utilities. If fuel prices went down, gains on the utility stocks would offset losses on the energy issues. This kind of diversification takes risk reduction to a higher plane.

Investment strategists call this **negative correlation.** A portfolio is least risky when some stocks in it react one way to a change in the economy and other stocks behave the opposite way. It's just like being on a sailboat: if everyone leans over the same side, the boat will flip over. Ideally people should be balanced on both sides of the boat. When the wind shifts, the crew moves so that more of them are leaning against the wind. Portfolio management operates the same way. Your job is to buy assets that will balance each other and then adjust those holdings to preserve balance as the economic forecast changes.

It may sound as if this strategy—buying things that move in opposite directions—will reduce your return. If one stock moves up and another moves down, you end up back where you started, right? Not at all. Your objective is to cash in on long-term price increases while neutralizing short-term fluctuations.

TRUE FACT

Owning 12 stocks in different industries provides more than 90% of the diversification you would get if you owned 100.

To see how powerful sophisticated diversification can be, just take a look at what happened during the 1987 stock market crash, the worst stock market disaster in more than two decades. **MONEY** has a unique view of that period, because the magazine maintains an exclusive Small Investor Index. This index is built around a model investment portfolio that reflects what small investors actually own, on average (I'll talk more about the specific makeup of this portfolio in a minute).

The contrast between the overall stock market and the Small Investor Index during the 1987 crash was startling. In the last three months of 1987, Standard & Poor's 500 stock index lost a horrifying 22%. That index—which pretty much represents the bulk of stocks owned by professional money managers—showed no benefit from diversification, even though it comprised 500 different issues. The average small investor, however, lost only 6% in 1987's fourth quarter. The reason: Individual investors had big chunks of their money in bonds, certificates of deposit, and money-market funds, as well as in stocks.

These three basic asset groups—stocks, bonds, and cash—are

the building blocks of the simplest well-diversified portfolio. The reason they work so well together is that each asset group performs at its peak during a different part of the business cycle. These cycles, which I'll discuss at greater length in the next chapter, typically occur between one recession and another.

In the early part of the economic recovery that follows a recession, stocks are usually the best performers. Once the economy is going full blast and interest rates rise sharply, both stocks and bonds are likely to suffer while cash preserves its value. In fact, short-term cash investments such as money-market funds will enjoy higher returns as interest rates move up. Then, once the economy begins to slip into recession, interest rates fall and bonds are likely to turn in the biggest gains. By splitting your money among these three asset classes, you can ensure that at least one of them will show improving performance at any point in the cycle.

The portfolio that the **MONEY** Small Investor Index uses shows that individual investors follow something very close to this three-asset strategy. In fact, the **MONEY** portfolio is based on Federal Reserve statistics and other data that reflect the total assets owned by individuals in the United States. Although some investors may keep all their money in stocks, say, or in bank CDs, as a group small investors divide their money roughly as follows: 40% in stocks and equity mutual funds; 25% in bonds and bond funds; and almost all of the rest in bank accounts, CDs, and money funds. Gold and real estate securities each make up less than 1% of the average small investor's portfolio. (These figures do not include homes or residential real estate.)

Since 1970 the typical small investor's portfolio has earned about 9% a year, on average. Even in 1987 small investors gained 7.8% for the year as a whole, despite losses in the fourth quarter because of the crash. For individual investors, the worst year in the past 25 was 1974, when the stock market suffered its most disastrous decline since the 1940s. Even then, the average portfolio was down only 6.6%. That's a remarkably small loss, considering that blue-chip stock prices can easily drop 20% or more in a full-fledged bear market. The bottom line: Sophisticated diversification can cut your average risk roughly in half and your worst-case losses by three-quarters while allowing you to enjoy a return that greatly outpaces other safe alternatives.

GETTING THE TASTIEST FREE LUNCH

If diversification is the only free lunch in investing, then how do you get a four-star meal? The key to fine dining is called **asset allocation.** That term means nothing more than splitting your total assets among the best mix of investments in ideal proportions. Some theoreticians argue for an updated version of the traditional buy-and-hold strategy that's known as **passive allocation.** This approach consists of figuring out the optimum portfolio based on historical data for the past few decades and then sticking with those allocations no matter what the market does. At most, passive allocators adjust their investments once a year or so to restore the original percentages. For example, if stocks rose considerably during the year while bond prices fell, a passive allocator would shift a little money from stocks to bonds to get back to the optimum mix.

The alternative, known as **active allocation,** allows a money manager to shift money from one asset class to another within prescribed limits. If the optimum strategy called for stocks to be 30% to 40% of the mix and bonds to be 20% to 30%, an active allocator could boost the amount of money in stocks to 40% and cut bonds back to 20% when the outlook was especially promising for equities and later trim stocks to 30% and raise bonds to 30% when the outlook for stocks deteriorated. The other asset classes in the mix could be adjusted in a similar way.

A typical passive asset-allocation plan might consist of dividing money equally among five asset classes—U.S. blue chips, foreign stocks, long-term bonds, short-term Treasury bills, and real estate—and rebalancing the portfolio once a year. Such a portfolio might very well match the return of the S&P 500 index—but with only half the stock market's day-to-day volatility.

While this diversify-and-hold system makes a great deal of sense for giant institutional investors, you may well ask how you can apply it yourself. If you have less than $100,000, you probably can't buy individual stocks and bonds to cover all those categories. And you certainly can't buy an office building for your real estate exposure. Our answer is not to look at this model as something you would follow literally, but to understand the philosophy that underlies it and try to use that basic, sensible thinking in your own investing. For starters, you should make a mental inventory of your total wealth. And be sure to include not just your securities, but other assets such as your home.

Making sure that you don't put a lot of money into stocks in the industry you work in turns out to be a really important point. Why? Because most middle-class Americans have some sort of retirement account, savings plan, or profit-sharing deal at work that allows them to accumulate a lot of money in their own company's shares. This is the worst asset-allocation mistake you can make. If your company gets into trouble, you could see your savings evaporate at the same time your job is in jeopardy.

I remember sitting at a luncheon a few years ago next to a well-dressed woman who was a sales representative for Digital Equipment. That sterling computer company, once number two after IBM, hit the skids in 1987. The stock, which rose from $35 in 1984 to nearly $200 three years later, dropped more than 75% to $46 in the 1990 recession. "We all thought we were going to get rich," I remember her saying, "and now we're all going to get laid off." Sad to say, she wasn't entirely wrong. The company turned around by shedding a big part of its workforce. And the stock fell below $19 a share before recovering. From that low, the shares have tripled; but they still haven't come anywhere near their '87 peak.

Once you've taken inventory of your assets, the next step is to make sure that you are adequately protected against an upsurge in inflation. That may not sound like an important protection nowadays with inflation ticking along at only 3%. But it's precisely when a risk seems far away that it's smartest to buy insurance. Finding protection, though, is tougher than it sounds, because very few assets are true inflation hedges.

If you own your own home, then you have a major insurance policy. Of course, you wouldn't be able to cash it in because you have to live someplace, but at least you know you'd be protected for your retirement when you might want to take your profits and trade down to a smaller, less expensive home. If you also own a vacation home or rental property, then you're probably very well covered on the inflation front.

What do you do, though, if you aren't a homeowner? Make sure that you include inflation hedges in your overall investment portfolio. You can add a little real estate by buying securities known as **real estate investment trusts** (**REITs**), which essentially are shares in a pool of commercial and residential properties. You can also get inflation protection from gold-mining shares. I don't hold with the idea of buying gold coins or other physical metal because it's a clumsy way to invest. But shares in top-quality mines offer excellent inflation protection. Nonetheless, it's generally a mistake to put more than 10% of your assets in gold because it's highly volatile (I'll talk more about gold in Chapter 12).

A more practical approach is to make sure that your stock portfolio contains some of the groups that are inflation beneficiaries. These include oil and gas stocks, which are helped by rising prices for fuel; shares of companies that mine copper and other base metals; forest products companies that own land and forests; and REITs.

Once you're sure you are protected against the risk of inflation, I'd suggest that you follow the basic strategy of splitting your money among stocks, bonds, and cash. At minimum you should keep 10% to 15% in both top-quality long-term bonds and in cash investments such as Treasury bills, money funds, and CDs. At the very least, you'll have assets you could sell during a recession if you wanted to raise cash to go shopping for stock market bargains.

You may well be thinking at this point that diversification sounds swell but isn't practical for you because you don't have the money to buy so many different things. Relax. As long as you are committed to following the diversification principle, there are lots of ways to spread your risk even if you don't have big bucks. For example, you can start buying U.S. savings bonds through your payroll savings plan at work; that will serve as your cash component. For long-term bonds, you can buy issues for as little as $1,000 directly from the Federal Reserve. And there are plenty of excellent mutual funds that will cover some key parts of your diversification plan while you buy individual stocks for other parts.

Once you start thinking diversely, you'll find all sorts of opportunities to hedge your bets. For example, I have a small individual retirement account that now has almost $20,000 in it. I keep it at the Benham fund group and switch it between Benham's excellent gold equity index fund and a short-term income fund. When inflation cools down, I move it into gold stocks and then switch out when gold spikes. The first time I did that, I picked up a 20%-plus profit in less than two years; later I switched back into gold, and I'm up more than 25% since then. I'm not a gold bug, mind you. I just want to hedge against inflation when inflation is low and then stash my profits in a money fund once gold stocks have had a sizable run.

There's also no law that says you have to choose any particular allocation. Say, for example, that you've now got about 40% of your money in bonds, cash, and various inflation hedges. You might want to have more. There's nothing wrong with keeping a big chunk of cash in the bank if that makes you feel comfortable. Or, if you want to buy a fancier house than you really need, thereby boosting your inflation hedge, go ahead. Nobody says you have to own stocks to the max if you'd rather be house-proud. Further, if you're in a high tax bracket, it may be smart to put a lot of money into tax-exempt bonds.

However much you want to invest in stocks—whether it's 30% or 60% of your total wealth—it's smart not to sink it all into

43

U.S. blue chips. Extensive research shows that small-company shares outpace blue chips by a couple of percentage points a year. Much of that excess profit comes in fits and starts, though. Small stocks can go for as long as eight years without outperforming blue chips. So you should put most of your money into S&P 500 companies and add a sprinkling of small growth stocks for extra zip. As a rough guide, studies have shown that on average, individual investors put about three times as much in blue chips as in small stocks.

TRUE FACT

Small-company shares outperform big stocks by about two percentage points a year, on average. However, those gains come in five-to-eight-year spurts, with equally long stretches of mediocre performance in between.

Source: Prudential Securities

Similarly, it's a pretty sure bet that foreign stocks will outrun U.S. shares over the long term. After all, the U.S. economy can grow only about 3% a year, while many foreign countries will manage 5% or more. Don't assume, though, that you should automatically load up on investments in the stocks of developing countries or funds that hold such shares. Newly industrializing nations may have the greatest potential payoff, but their economic performance is erratic. As a result, emerging market investments should account for at most 10% of your equity holdings.

You can safely invest more than 10% overseas, however, if you buy leading European and Japanese stocks. Foreign blue chips, in fact, are crucial to a well-diversified portfolio. The U.S. market accounts for a little over 40% of the world's stocks; Japan is roughly 25%; the United Kingdom, Germany, and France together add up to about 17%. That means that if you buy only U.S. stocks, you are bypassing more than half the attractive stocks in the world. But if you include Japan and the most important European countries, you'll have access to more than 80% of the world's top stocks. Even so, you may want to limit foreign shares to 25% of your equity holdings. Reason: the risk of currency fluctuations. If the value of the dollar rises, investments overseas will be worth less when their prices are converted back into dollars.

TRUE FACT

If you can invest in only one foreign market and want diversification, pick Japan. That country has the lowest correlation with the United States of any major foreign market.

Source: Morgan Stanley Capital International

Putting together all these asset-allocation principles, you get a portfolio that divides up roughly as follows: 35% in U.S. blue chips; 10% in small stocks; 10% in foreign stocks; 15% in long-term bonds; 15% in cash; and 15% in inflation hedges, which may include additional blue-chip stocks.

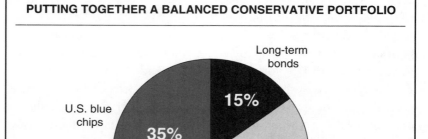

PUTTING TOGETHER A BALANCED CONSERVATIVE PORTFOLIO

Long-term bonds — 15%
Cash — 15%
Inflation hedges — 15%
Foreign stocks — 10%
Small-company shares — 10%
U.S. blue chips — 35%

You should keep at least half your money in stocks, even if you're a conservative investor. This chart shows how you might divide up your money to create a broadly diversified portfolio that could beat the broad stock market while minimizing your risk. The biggest chunk of money is in U.S. blue chips. Small-company shares and foreign issues add a little zip. The income investments and inflation hedges reduce the overall portfolio's volatility.

Of course, this is only a rough guideline, suitable for a moderately conservative investor, such as a 45-year-old professional saving mostly for retirement. If you have other needs or preferences, feel free to alter the mix. But try to put something in each of these basic groups.

ADJUSTING YOUR HOLDINGS

After you've begun an asset-allocation plan, you'll find that the hardest decision is when to adjust your holdings. There's one strategy that isn't too difficult. Just pick a regular time—say, once a year—and rebalance your portfolio to the original allocation percentages you decided on. If your blue chips are up 10% more than everything else, cut them back by that amount and put the money into the lagging groups. Simpler still, make sure that any new money you add goes into the groups that have performed least well.

Does that sound strange, putting money into your worst performers instead of your winners? It isn't. Just remember that asset classes move in cycles and every dog has its day. If you're investing through mutual funds, rebalancing a portfolio is easy because you can shift small amounts of money from one fund to another without penalty. If you're buying individual issues, you'll find that exact rebalancing is impossible. But don't worry about keeping the percentages precisely equal. Take profits from time to time and put that money, along with new investments you make, into the dog that's in the doghouse.

You may, of course, want to take a more active role in directing your investments. As soon as you get comfortable managing your money, odds are you'll find you have lots of opinions about the likely future direction of stocks and bonds. That's great. It's what makes investing fun (and it should be fun). But be aware that it takes a lot of experience to know when you should adjust your holdings and when you should stand pat. As a general rule, far more investors buy and sell too often than too rarely. In fact, newsletter writer Richard C. Young of Newport, R.I., has a maxim that I like a lot: Investing performance is inversely proportional to turnover. That's the term academics use to describe buying and selling stocks in a portfolio. In other words, the less you buy and sell, the better you'll do.

Let's look a little deeper into the turnover question. Essentially, there are four levels of activity:

■ **Passive allocation.** This is the updated version of traditional buy-and-hold investing. Basically, you divide up your money among a complementary mix of asset classes and then rebalance your holdings once a year. Generally you would try to hold on to a stock or mutual fund until there was a compelling reason to sell.

■ **Active asset allocation.** This approach gives you some room to direct your investing but protects you from going too far. Instead of setting fixed percentage goals for your asset allocation, you pick ranges—30% to 40% for blue chips, 10% to 20% for foreign stocks, and so on. Then you can adjust your holdings within those ranges according to your market outlook.

■ **Trading and market timing.** Traders and timers consider the overall market outlook and look for underpriced stocks. They also buy and sell frequently. Their portfolios can end up filled with just about anything; diversification and asset allocation are at most general goals.

■ **Speculating.** This is little more than buying popular stocks on hunches and hoping that they go up. Basically, it's a form of gambling. The only consolation is that you get better odds than you would get at a Las Vegas roulette table.

Of these four methods, which is the best for you? In general, the first two. Choosing between them, however, is a little more subjective. Academics will tell you that passive asset allocation is impossible to beat from a theoretical point of view. It minimizes your trading—and therefore your commissions and fees. In addition, they don't believe that active management adds anything. However, some studies show that conservative management can make a small additional contribution to long-term performance. By contrast, there is little evidence to suggest that investors who time the market and trade can beat the averages with any consistency; and the few pros who do are exceptional and have access to far better information and analysis than any small investor could.

In my view you should adopt a strategy of active asset allocation. To recap, that means you should decide on a mix of stocks, bonds, and other investments you want to own, based on the considerations I've outlined in the previous section. Convert that into a set of percentage ranges—30% to 60% stocks, 10% to 20% in bonds, and so on. Then adjust your holdings based on your assessment of the economic outlook. But be sure to stay within your ranges. That will protect you against a disastrous mistake, such as having all your money in stocks just as a bear market begins.

What if you don't have an economic outlook? Well then, you'll have to acquire one—as soon as possible. I'll tell you what you need to know about economic cycles in Chapter 4, and you'll see a lot more about how to size up individual stocks later in this book. But before we get to all that, I'd like to outline a simple way of thinking about portfolio management.

The performance of each major asset category is determined largely by economic growth and inflation. If you have an opinion about those two factors, you can decide which assets should be emphasized in your overall portfolio mix.

For stocks, the best environment is accelerating growth with falling inflation. Accelerating growth with rising inflation is not too bad, either. Slowing growth with falling inflation is not so good. And slowing growth with rising inflation—stagflation—is catastrophic.

For bonds, rising inflation is always bad, falling inflation is always good.

Cash returns rise and fall in line with inflation. In other words, after inflation is taken into account, the return on cash (that is, short-term income investments) is about the same in all environments.

Inflation hedges such as real estate and gold-mining shares perform best when inflation is rising and worst when inflation is falling. No surprise there.

When you put these simple facts together, you have the basic rules you need to manage a diversified portfolio. When inflation is low and the economy is strong, favor U.S. stocks, keep an average position in bonds, and cut back on cash and inflation hedges. If inflation starts to rise, reduce bonds to a minimum and add to inflation hedges. If the economy starts to slow, increase cash, bump up bonds to a maximum, and cut back on stocks. If stagflation hits, cut back on both stocks and bonds, moderately increase your inflation hedges, and keep as much cash on hand as possible. If these rules seem sketchy, don't worry. We'll go through them again in context and in greater detail. But first we need to make a brief detour and talk a little about putting theory into practice.

CHAPTER 3

BUYING AND SELLING:

When You Need a Broker—
And When You Don't

So far, we've been talking about investing in general terms. We've discussed which assets you should own and how to manage them. But let's get real for a minute. Where do these assets come from? How do you invest in them? And what are your sources of information? To answer those questions, we need to look briefly at how stock and bond markets work and how you have access to securities as well as vital information about them. In short, we need to talk about brokers and the world in which they operate.

For starters, imagine that you've built a successful business. Perhaps you invented a really comfortable office chair, began producing it in your garage, and now have a successful office furniture business. You've done so well that money is rolling in and you want to expand and start making a broad line of modern office furnishings. The only trouble is, you need a lot more capital.

One thing you could do is sell stock or bonds. To do that, you'd go to an investment bank, probably a small one that specializes in young, fast-growing companies. Unlike commercial banks that borrow money and then lend it to businesses, investment banks sell stocks and bonds to institutional investors, such as insurance companies or venture capital firms, and to the general public. Selling such securities is known as **underwriting.**

If the stock market is strong and investors are enthusiastic, an investment bank may be interested in taking your company public, even though your business is still quite small, with sales of, say, $25 million a year. At that size, though, few people will have heard of your company. So who would buy the stock? Perhaps a mutual fund that specializes in so-called emerging growth companies. Or, if your record is really terrific, perhaps a newsletter will write about your firm and some individual investors will purchase shares.

Information about your company can reach potential investors in several other ways as well. The underwriter will probably assign an analyst to follow your company, and a couple of independent analysts who cover small stocks also might track it. In addition to newsletters, financial journalists might think your business is worth a story and write about it in periodicals such as the *Wall Street Journal, Barron's, Forbes,* or *Business Week.* Further, interested investors could obtain copies of the annual and quarterly financial reports that public companies are required to file with the Securities and Exchange Commission or send directly to shareholders.

How would a small investor buy into your company? Well, the most likely way, if your business is small and relatively unknown, is by putting money into an emerging growth mutual fund that owns the shares. But as your company expands and more analysts start to follow it, brokers at the analysts' firms may begin recommending your stock to their customers. In short, individuals who invest in your stock will most likely buy it either through a mutual fund or through a broker. And they will get information about the company either through their brokers, the financial press, or the reports public companies are required to file.

Let's consider the broker's role in a little more detail—and specifically from the small investor's point of view. If you're a beginning investor, you'll probably rely chiefly on mutual funds. If you do, you won't have to do much research or select individual stocks and bonds yourself. But as we explained in the previous chapter, you pay a price for that convenience. If you're reading this book, you're probably ready to invest at least part of your money in individual securities. That means you'll be relying on brokers to buy and sell for you. In fact, for all practical purposes you can't buy or sell securities without a broker.

Brokers come in two types: full-service, which usually means that their firms have analysts and access to other research sources; and discount, which means that they charge low commissions but provide little in the way of research. Among discounters, Charles Schwab and Fidelity Brokerage are generally considered the leaders. Their commissions typically run at least 35% below what a full-service firm would charge for the sorts of trades you would be likely to make. For example, Schwab charges a $55 commission on the purchase of 100 shares of a $30 stock (a $3,000 trade) vs. $86 for full-service Merrill Lynch. That's a saving of 36%. It's worth noting, however, that the savings discounters offer vary tremendously by firm and by the size of the trade. For some very small orders, you may even find that a full-service firm is cheaper.

As far as service is concerned, the chief difference between the two types of brokerages is that a full-service firm can provide information and investment advice based on original research while discounters provide little or no investment advice. (Some discounters offer a limited amount of information on stocks, bonds, and the economy that comes from third parties such as newsletters and on-line services.) That means if you want to save on commissions, you'll have to obtain research and recommendations from other sources such as the financial press, newsletters, and standard reference works. You'll also have to make your own investment decisions without any hand-holding.

Apart from the problem of obtaining investment research, my own experience has been that discounters handle most other brokerage functions as well as full-service firms. For example, the discounter I use has generally been able to execute my trades just as well as—if not better than—the full-service firms I deal with. However, a few other differences are worth noting. At a full-service firm you typically speak to the same two or three brokers whenever you call. That's good if you have a problem you want sorted out—but it can be bad, because they occasionally try to sell you something. Even worse, you know they're smirking when you lose money on a dumb investment. By contrast, at discounters you end up handling a lot of transactions through anonymous 800-number phone networks. That's fast and efficient, and also more private. Once in a while, though, it can cause serious problems.

Let me give you two examples of slipups by discounters from my own experience. I once had a misunderstanding with the Internal Revenue Service, which led to the agency notifying my brokerages to withhold 31% of any dividends and interest I received. I quickly wrote the IRS and got the withholding lifted about a month later. My full-service brokerages were able to halt the withholding immediately. But at the discounter I had to make multiple phone calls and was switched around to several different representatives before I got the problem straightened out; moreover, it took two weeks.

My other disappointment with a discounter involves an obscure type of investment known as a closed-end mutual fund (we'll talk about them more in Chapter 11). Like better-known open-end funds, closed-ends are required by law to pay out to shareholders most of the capital gains they earn on stocks they sell. However, instead of paying you in cash, some closed-ends automatically reinvest capital-gains distributions in more shares, unless you tell them not to. A full-service broker will generally keep track of such distributions and ensure they are paid in cash, if you want. But the discounter I deal with has repeatedly failed to act in time to get my distributions in cash.

It's a minor problem—reinvesting in additional shares complicates my record keeping for taxes, but it doesn't cost me any money. Still, it's annoying. So remember that with a discounter you may get less service. Overall, I think that much lower commissions justify slightly inferior service. You may want to have accounts at both types of brokers. Your decision on which one to use would therefore depend on whether you need research on a specific investment and whether you feel you need hand-holding.

> **RULE NO. 3 OF INVESTING:**
> **USE A DISCOUNT BROKER WHENEVER POSSIBLE.**

In principle, if you have $20,000 or more to invest, there is nothing to prevent you from making all your own decisions, doing all the necessary research yourself, and trading only through a discount broker. In fact, this will require an enormous commitment of time. You'll have to subscribe to stock services such as Morningstar or Value Line, buy newsletters, and read dozens of investing magazines. The cost could easily run to several thousand dollars a year, and you could spend a full day a week doing the necessary research. That's probably more than you want to do.

At the other extreme, you could do all your investing through mutual funds so that you can leave the major decisions to professional money managers. If you're reading this book, though, you probably fall someplace in between. In that case your wisest course of action is to make some types of investments through a mutual fund, others with a full-service broker's advice, and the rest through a discounter. Here's what I would recommend for an intermediate investor who doesn't want to make stock picking into a second career:

■ **Buy U.S. blue chips directly through a discounter.** You probably can get enough information through newsletters and the financial press to make your own investment decisions. Do it yourself and save on commissions.

■ **Buy foreign blue chips as ADRs through a full-service broker.** Many leading foreign stocks trade in the United States as American depository receipts (ADRs). However, you probably won't be able to get the information you need to make well-informed investment decisions yourself even for a company as recognizable as Sony or Benetton. You'll need a large, full-service broker such as Merrill Lynch or Smith Barney that has analysts following foreign stocks.

■ **Buy small-company shares through a mutual fund.** Small stocks are hard to keep up with and require broad diversification (20 different issues or more). Unless you have a total of at least $100,000 to invest, it's really smarter to put the percentage you want to have in small stocks into a mutual fund that holds such issues.

■ **Buy Treasury bonds directly from the Federal Reserve or through a discount broker.** Once you've decided on the maturity you want—five years or 20, for example—all Treasuries are pretty much alike. You might as well buy them wherever the fees are cheapest. (The commission on a $10,000 bond typically runs about $50 at a full-service firm but is less at some discounters.) You also may want to consider buying Treasury bonds directly from the Fed. I'll tell you how to do that in a minute.

■ **Buy tax-exempt municipal bonds through a full-service broker or a firm that specializes in such issues.** You'll get the best buys in tax-exempts if you deal with a firm that is an active participant in the muni market and maintains its own inventory of bonds.

■ **Keep your cash reserves in bank CDs or money-market funds.** CDs carry no commissions, but you have to tie up your money for three months or more, and you may not be able to cash in your CD early without losing interest. Money funds are a good alternative because you can get at your cash any time you want.

If you really want to hold your commissions and expenses to a minimum, it's actually possible to buy stocks, bonds, and cash investments virtually for free. These strategies will limit the variety of your investments. Further, they may make it slow or cumbersome to buy and sell. But if you're interested in building a long-term portfolio at the lowest-possible cost, these approaches are worth knowing about.

Nearly 1,000 companies offer **dividend reinvestment plans** (known as **DRIPs**), which allow you to buy stocks without going through a broker. Some even offer a 2% to 5% discount on shares bought through a DRIP. Here's how the plans work. If you own stock, you can sign up to invest all your cash dividends in additional shares. Further, most plans allow you to purchase shares with other cash at monthly or quarterly intervals. More than half the plans charge no commissions at all, and the rest have minimal fees.

TRUE FACT

More than 100 companies allow you to buy their stock directly—without a broker—including your initial purchase.

Traditionally, you had to own a stock before a company with a DRIP would allow you to buy additional shares through a plan. But increasingly, companies are allowing investors to purchase their initial shares in a DRIP directly, thereby making it possible to bypass brokers completely. Currently more than 100 corporations—from Barnett Banks to Exxon to U.S. West—permit such direct stock purchases, and the number is growing rapidly.

If you're interested in a stock, call the company and ask if a dividend reinvestment plan is available. Even if you have to buy

100 shares through a broker to get started, it may be worthwhile, since you could buy subsequent shares with little or no commissions. Investors interested in dividend reinvestment plans can subscribe to Charles B. Carlson's monthly, the *DRIP Investor* (219-931-6480; $59 a year). The American Association of Individual Investors in Chicago (800-428-2244 or 312-280-0170) also offers an annual guide to such plans for $4 (free for members of the AAII).

When it comes to bonds, you can also invest commission-free if you stick with Treasury issues, which are the most sensible choice for beginning investors. Such bonds are supersafe because they are backed by the full faith and credit of the U.S. government. An added bonus: Interest on Treasury securities is exempt from state and local income taxes. By contrast, corporate bonds pay interest that is fully taxable and are complicated to analyze. Tax-exempt munis also require selectivity; but they may be a smart choice if you are in the 28% tax bracket or higher. If you're buying your first individual bonds, though, it makes sense to start with Treasuries.

Better yet, it's possible to buy such bonds directly from Federal Reserve Banks, with no commission on orders of less than $100,000 (for information, write to the Bureau of the Public Debt at the U.S. Treasury in Washington or call 202-874-4000). There are a couple of catches, though. First, buying Treasury bonds directly is bureaucratic—be prepared to spend a lot of time listening to voice mail and filling out forms. Second, if you need to sell your bonds before they mature, you will have to have them transferred to a brokerage and pay commissions when you sell.

Treasuries that mature in five years or longer are available for minimum investments of $1,000; two- and three-year issues have $5,000 minimums; however, Treasury bills, which mature in one year or less, require an investment of at least $10,000. That's a lot of money. And since Treasury securities are awkward to sell if you purchase them directly, Treasury bills may not be the most convenient place to keep your cash. Of course, you can rely on bank CDs or money-market funds; but there's a third choice that can be quite attractive.

I'm talking about Series EE savings bonds, which are a really easy way to build up cash. If you purchase bonds at work through your payroll savings plan (available at most major companies), the money is deducted automatically from your paycheck. That sort of forced saving provides an enormous psychological benefit. In fact, I'm signed up for the largest monthly savings bond purchase available at my company ($500 a month). Although that's a big bite out of my paycheck, after a year or so I've adjusted my spending expectations downward. Meanwhile I'm piling up savings at the rate of $6,000 a year. And if $500 a month is too much, you can buy savings bonds for as little as $12.50. (For historical reasons, these bonds have face values that are double the price you pay—thus, a $25 bond actually costs $12.50.)

The convenience of savings bonds isn't the only reason they're attractive. If you hold them for five years or longer, the bonds pay interest at a rate equal to 85% of the yield on five-year Treasuries. For example, if five-year notes are yielding 6.4%, savings bonds would earn interest at 85% of that rate, or 5.4%. That formula means that if interest rates rise, the yields on your savings bonds would increase right in step without your having to do anything at all. The bonds also offer tax advantages: not only is the interest exempt from state and local income taxes, but you don't have to pay federal income tax on the interest until you sell the bonds—which you can postpone for as long as 30 years.

CHAPTER 4

BASIC ECONOMICS FOR INVESTORS:

How to Cash in on Business Cycles and Ride Long-Term Trends to Maximum Profits

Have you ever opened the business section of a newspaper and read that the Dow soared fortysomething points the previous day because of news that the economy was slowing? Or that the bond market boomed after higher unemployment was reported? Sometimes the economy and the securities markets seem to move in opposite directions. In fact, there's an old Wall Street joke about a beginning stock trader who was making so much money in a lousy economy that he said: "If this is a recession, give me a depression." Of course, that wouldn't be a very wise prayer. In a really awful economy—like the 1981–82 or the 1990–91 recession—the stock market can fall 15% to 20% or more.

Over the long term, of course, a healthy economy is good for stocks and a feeble economy is bad. For example, the United States suffered four recessions from 1970 through 1982; in seven of those 13 years, the economy was in recession for at least a month or two. Among the reasons: the oil shocks and soaring inflation. The stock market made very little headway during those years. In fact, the Dow spent most of 1982 *below* its 1969 high.

By contrast, the years since 1983 have been golden for both

the economy and the stock market. Since '83, the only meaningful break in the economic expansion has been the 1990–91
recession, which lasted only eight months. Inflation has been
quashed; interest rates have been cut to less than half their early
'80s level; productivity is up; corporate profits have been booming—and the stock market has quintupled since the 1981–82
recession ended.

The bottom line is that the stock market sometimes follows
the economy and sometimes diverges from it. To be a successful
investor you need to understand the connections between the
two. But before I launch into a discussion of the business cycle
and the 60-year Kondratieff cycle and whatnot, let's talk for a
moment about the whole question of market timing (also
known among mutual fund shareholders as fund switching).

As we discussed in Chapter 2, stock trading—buying and selling after six months or less—is a sure way to underperform the
market. Not only do you run up hefty brokerage commissions,
but you are also likely to get caught up in short-term investing
fads. That can result in buying high and selling low. As renowned
investor Warren Buffett says, the stock market transfers money
from the active to the patient.

But it's possible to be too patient. The outlook for industries
and individual companies does change from decade to decade
and even from year to year. You would have lost money by holding on to IBM—the leading maker of big computers—during
the personal computer boom of the late '80s and early '90s. And
you would also have lost money in most major drug stocks if you
had owned them during the recent debate over radical changes
in the U.S. health care system.

In essence, the market-timing discussion consists of three
questions:

1. What is the importance of long-term trends?
2. How should investors respond to changing business conditions?
3. How often should you adjust your holdings?

I'll give you the short answers first: Analyze long-term trends to decide which types of stocks you should focus on. Follow the business cycle to figure out how to fine-tune your portfolio mix. Make changes no more often than once every three months, and aim to turn over no more than one-third of your portfolio within a single year. The rest of this chapter will give you the longer answers.

RIDING THE BUSINESS CYCLE

Let's begin our discussion of the economy with the business cycle, since it provides a crucial context for discussing longer-term trends as well. The business cycle is simply a pattern of economic boom and bust that typically recurs at four-to-six-year intervals. On average, the economy expands for 3½ years and then contracts for a bit over a year. It's rare for contractions to last longer than 18 months. But expansions can sometimes go on for considerably longer than 3½ years. In the 1960s the growth phase of the business cycle continued for almost nine years. Whenever the expansive phase of a cycle goes on for more than three or four years, though, there usually is at least one slowdown that stops short of an official recession (defined as a decline in gross domestic product, after adjustment for inflation, for two quarters in a row). These slowdowns used to be called growth recessions and are now known, more poetically, as soft landings.

This business cycle is particularly important for investors because it drives a similar cycle in stock prices. Since investors generally anticipate the economic trends, the stock market cycle usually leads the business cycle by six months or so. The rising part of the stock cycle is called a **bull market** and the falling part that usually starts right before an economic downturn is called a **bear market.** In bull markets the prices of blue chips often double. In fact, since 1948 there has not been a single business expansion that did not leave stock prices higher than they were when it began. By contrast, in bear markets share prices can fall more than 20%.

TRUE FACT

It takes almost three years, on average, to get even after a bear market.

Source: InvesTech Research

People often use the terms "bull market" and "bear market" sloppily to mean rising and falling stock prices, respectively. But these terms are used properly only for the two big market trends that correspond to the expansion and the contraction of the economy over the course of a business cycle. Together they make up what's called the **primary trend.** That's what I'll be referring to when I use the terms "bull market" and "bear market" in this book.

Of course, the stock market can go up or down over shorter periods of time than a complete business cycle. When share prices drop in the middle of a bull market, that's called a **correction.** And when prices run up during a bear market, that's known as a **rally.** Corrections and rallies of 10% or so over a period of up to six months are **secondary trends.** Any smaller or briefer moves are **tertiary trends.** Journalists often use these terms incorrectly.

The reason I've just gone through all these definitions isn't pedantry. It's that I want to be very clear about what you should be looking at as you make your portfolio decisions. I want you to understand what drives the stock market cycle, how you can gauge the likely size of market moves, and why some market-timing decisions are rational and not merely guesswork or gambling. Essentially, you want to be on the right side of primary trends and keep an eye out for important secondary moves that are headed your way. Anything smaller than that isn't worth bothering about—especially since any move of less than 10% is for all practical purposes completely unpredictable.

So let's walk through a typical business cycle. It begins when a recession has been under way for at least six months and interest rates start to fall. The drop in interest rates powers a bull market in stocks for two reasons. First, lower rates stimulate the economy by making it easier for people to buy big-ticket items that require financing (such as homes and cars). Cheaper money also reduces borrowing costs for corporations, boosting their profit margins. Second, lower interest rates increase the value investors are willing to set on a company's current earnings (for a detailed explanation why, see the discussion of the dividend–discount model in Chapter 1). That means that stock price/earnings ratios expand. The combination of improving business conditions, fatter profit margins, and rising price/earnings ratios creates an ideal environment for stocks. As a result, the initial phase of a bull market—as an economic recovery is just beginning—almost always shows the biggest percentage gains in share prices.

**RULE NO. 4 OF INVESTING:
BUY STOCKS AFTER A RECESSION HAS GONE ON
FOR SIX MONTHS.**

Once the recovery is under way, it begins to feed on itself. As companies earn more, they can expand and add more workers. That, in turn, leads to higher consumer spending that benefits even companies that are not directly helped by falling interest rates.

Six months to a year into the recovery, the decline in interest rates ends, chiefly because the economy has gathered enough speed to cause competition for credit. Businesses want to borrow to invest in more factories and equipment; home buyers want mortgages; and consumers run up their credit card balances. Once interest rates have stabilized, the recovery ends and the economy enters a slower, more drawn-out growth phase that can last anywhere from one to three years or even longer. During this period stock price/earnings ratios are more or less stable and shares move higher in line with earnings growth.

Eventually, energetic business activity forces companies to bring their less efficient facilities into use. They also have to pay employees more overtime or hire additional workers, thereby bidding up labor costs. That starts to pump up inflation. The demand for money continues to grow as corporations borrow more, while the supply dries up as consumers' spending outruns what they earn. The result: Rising inflation and a growing demand for money combine to push up interest rates. Eventually rates reach a point at which they become too much of a burden for business and the economy goes into recession. Declining business activity quashes corporate profits, and share prices tumble. Then, as the recession continues, the groundwork is laid for the next business cycle.

To recap: A classic business cycle consists of four phases: recovery, in which falling interest rates kick-start the economy and stocks boom; expansion, in which inflation and interest rates are in balance and steady growth in corporate profits pushes stocks higher; plateau, in which inflation and interest rates begin to rise rapidly, causing the economy and share prices to level off; and recession, in which persistent high interest rates kill the economy and stocks tank.

Why does this cycle occur? Wouldn't it be simpler if the economy just ran at a comfortable pace all the time so that no one ever had to be laid off? Ideally, yes. But the fact of the matter is that the economy is inherently unstable. Businesses misestimate how much to produce or how much money to borrow. Moreover, when times are good, both businesses and consumers inevitably overextend themselves. Then, when money is tight, they retrench. The economy will inevitably move in fits and starts simply because of human nature.

In addition, the economy isn't operating in a vacuum. The government helps foul things up and make the business cycle even more unbalanced than it would otherwise be.

The Federal Reserve sets the level of short-term interest rates, and it has two jobs. First, the Fed has to protect the value of the dollar by holding inflation to only 2% or 3% a year. Second, the Fed is supposed to reduce unemployment as much as possible. In practice, these two objectives are often contradictory.

If the Fed were to fight inflation militantly, the United States would have a currency as strong as the mighty deutsche mark, but recessions would be longer, expansions would be weaker, and jobs would be fewer—at least until the economy had restructured for a harder currency. Conversely, when the Fed holds interest rates down to stimulate the economy and cut unemployment, inflation pressures start to build. They may not show up for two or three years, but they add to the fits and starts of the business cycle.

Ever since the Great Depression, the government has played an active role in managing the business cycle. In theory, the Fed is supposed to act countercyclically, minimizing the severity of recessions by reducing interest rates and limiting inflation by raising rates once an expansion is well along. In practice, though, the Fed usually makes business cycles worse. One reason is that it is extremely difficult to fine-tune the economy. The other is that political pressures often force the Fed to do the wrong thing.

In particular, the Fed tries to postpone raising interest rates in the year before a presidential election because that might cause a recession and embarrass the incumbent. The result is that inflation is allowed to get out of hand. To fight it, the Fed is eventually forced to raise interest rates repeatedly, until the economy slows almost to a halt or goes into recession. If the Fed has waited too long to suppress inflation, interest rates have to be raised higher than they otherwise would be, and the eventual recession is worse.

> ## RULE NO. 5 OF INVESTING:
> ## SELL STOCKS IF THE FEDERAL RESERVE
> ## RAISES SHORT-TERM INTEREST RATES ABOVE
> ## LONG-TERM RATES.

The combination of the natural business cycle and political considerations means that stocks tend to perform worst in the first two years of a president's term of office and best in the last two years. (This is sometimes called the **presidential cycle.**) And because an incumbent administration does everything it can to pump up growth and hold down interest rates right before a campaign begins, stocks tend to perform best in the year preceding a presidential election year.

Just take a look at the third year of presidential terms over the past three decades. During Johnson's full term, the Dow gained 15% in 1967; during Nixon's first term, 6% in 1971; during the Nixon/Ford term, 38% in 1975; during Carter's term, 4% in 1979; in Reagan's first term, 20% in 1983; 2% in 1987 during his second term; 20% in 1991 during the Bush years; and 26% in 1995, Clinton's third year.

Looking at the entire presidential cycle as a whole, on average blue chips gain 5.2% in the first year of a president's term, 3.6% in the second year, 11.3% in the third year, and 7.8% in election year.

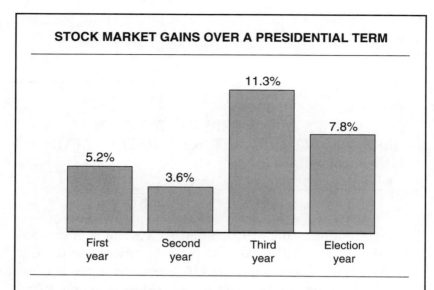

STOCK MARKET GAINS OVER A PRESIDENTIAL TERM

Stocks return the most in the two years leading up to a presidential election. That's because the administration tries to keep the economy humming during the campaign to ensure the incumbent party's reelection. By contrast, in the first two years of a president's term, the stock market's performance is subpar. Smart presidents try to get painful economic policies over and done with early in their terms, so that voters will have forgotten about them by the time the next election rolls around.

FINE-TUNING YOUR PORTFOLIO

Given the business cycle and the presidential cycle, it's obvious that you might want to change your mix of assets as the cycles progress. In theory, the simplest strategy would be to switch back and forth between stocks and cash. To do that, you'd load up on blue chips when the economy had been in recession for six months. Then you'd sell all your stocks once a recovery had been under way for at least three years and the Federal Reserve had hiked interest rates three or four times to bash rising inflation. After selling everything, you'd keep all the proceeds in cash until six months into the next recession.

Even though it's crude, that strategy would probably work.

The advantages are that you would probably never lose money, you would enjoy a big chunk of every bull market, and you would never be in doubt about what to do. I'm going to recommend a more sophisticated approach, but keep the crude version in mind because everything else is just an elaboration of it.

As we discussed in Chapter 2, it's possible to show mathematically that the best balance between risk and return comes from asset allocation with moderate adjustments made according to where we are in the business cycle. At the very least, you should divide your money among stocks, bonds, and cash. And as I've already noted, you may want to hold as many as six or seven different assets, including foreign issues and inflation hedges.

As the business cycle progresses, you would modify your asset mix. If you follow the active asset-allocation scheme explained in Chapter 2, you would establish ranges for each of the assets you hold and then raise or lower your percentages within those ranges. So, for example, if you decided to keep 40% to 60% of your money in stocks, you would start buying stocks after six months of recession until you had boosted your holdings to 60% of your portfolio. Then you would hold on to your stocks through the recovery and expansion phases. Once it looked as though stocks had plateaued, you would start trimming back your stock holdings so that you were down to 40% six months or so before the next recession started.

For bonds you'd follow a similar scheme, increasing and decreasing your holdings according to the phase of the business cycle. However, you would have the maximum in bonds at a different time from stocks. Say, for example, that you decided to keep between 15% and 30% of your money in bonds. Then you would wait to buy bonds until the stock market had plateaued and it looked as though the economy—and long-term interest rates—were weakening. The ideal point to load up on bonds may come after the Federal Reserve cuts interest rates, but it doesn't have to. More often the Fed follows the market, bringing down short-term rates after long-term rates have already started to fall because the economy is getting weaker.

Once you had your maximum bond position, you would hold on to it through the following recession and six months or more into the recovery. Many investors think that interest rates hit bottom in a recession—but that isn't strictly correct. It's true that falling interest rates bring a recession to an end and stimulate a recovery—but rates typically continue to decline through the initial part of an economic rebound. Following the 1990–91 recession, for example, long-term rates kept going down for more than two years.

The end of the recovery phase and the start of the expansion phase is marked by an upward turn in long-term interest rates. Generally that means the end of big profits for bond investors. Once it looks as if long-term rates are creeping up again, you should start trimming back your bond holdings. Also keep an eye on the Fed; if that agency begins raising short-term interest rates, long-term rates could move up sharply in sympathy.

What about cash? Basically, your cash position will reflect whatever decisions you have made about stocks and bonds. But as a rule of thumb, you'll want to build a maximum cash position after the Fed begins raising interest rates and stocks plateau. Then you should hang on to your cash hoard until a recession has been under way for at least six months. As the old saying goes, "In a recession, cash is king."

So far, we've addressed the ways you should change your asset mix over the course of a business cycle. But we've been talking as though all stocks are the same and all bonds are identical. In fact, though, among stocks, different industry groups hit their stride at different times. And bonds also vary somewhat in their performance at various parts of the business cycle.

Altogether there are some 76 industry groups. And obviously, each one has its own story and its own position in the business cycle. But if you oversimplify somewhat, stocks can be divided into five important groups—cyclicals, intermediate products, consumer nondurables, capital goods, and utilities. Utilities are the easiest. Companies that provide electricity, natural gas, water, and local telephone service are relatively slow growing and often government regulated. Since their growth prospects alone are not enough to attract shareholders, utilities generally have to pay fairly high dividend yields of at least 4%. With dividends generally accounting for half or more of the typical utility's long-term return, the shares behave much like long-term bonds. They follow interest rates and score their biggest gains when rates are falling. For that reason you would shift into utilities after most other stocks had plateaued late in an expansion and sell them after the postrecession interest rate decline was over.

At the opposite extreme are cyclicals—especially the shares of automakers, home builders, and other companies that benefit from low interest rates and generally rise and fall in line with overall economic activity. Other industries that behave cyclically include financial services, such as banks and brokerages, and commodities producers, such as forest products and mining firms. Because these companies' earnings track the economy, their shares typically hit bottom in a recession, rebound strongly in a recovery phase, and then show some further gains during the expansion. It is important to remember, though, that some cyclical stocks earn the vast bulk of their capital gains in the first year or two of a recovery—then virtually mark time until the next recession looms.

Intermediate goods producers—companies that make motors, cables, subassemblies, and assorted widgets—follow the same track as cyclicals but trail behind. Reason: Since they provide the parts other manufacturers use, these firms don't see a pickup in business until other manufacturers have had a chance to build up a full head of steam.

Capital goods makers—producers of computers, machine tools, and other equipment used in manufacturing—lag even further behind in the economic cycle. In fact, their shares may not really start moving until cyclicals have posted most of their share-price gains. As long as companies have underused facilities, they don't need to make large purchases of capital goods. Only when a travel agency has more business than it can handle, for instance, will it order extra new computers. As a result, capital goods firms usually enjoy their boom in the last stages of a bull market.

There are also some companies whose business is scarcely affected by the ups and downs of the economy. Among this group are many firms that provide so-called nondurable goods for consumers. Examples: producers of breakfast cereal, soda, beer, cigarettes, and underwear. No matter what the economy is doing, people are going to eat, drink, smoke, and so on. Because nondurable goods stocks are relatively unaffected by the economy, they hold up better than most other industry groups (except for utilities) during a recession.

Of course, there are other stock groups that respond to various cycles and long-term trends. The most important is energy—particularly oil and gas companies. These firms have some of the characteristics of cyclicals, because they depend on economic activity to boost oil prices and also behave a little like utilities since they often have above average yields. Most important, though, energy stocks are inflation hedges. Reason: Ongoing increases in general prices eventually boost the price of oil. In addition, many narrower business sectors fare better or worse at different times.

Because each of these different stock market groups prospers at some point in the business cycle, it would be possible to manage a portfolio solely by replacing stocks of one group with those of another as the business cycle progressed. Money managers and strategists at mutual funds that have to keep most of their money in stocks at all times often follow just this strategy, which is known as **group rotation.**

However, you aren't required to keep all your money in stocks—in fact, you shouldn't. So group rotation will be a smaller part of your overall strategy than adjusting your mix of assets. Even so, you should keep in mind as you add and jettison stocks that different industry groups perform best at one time or another.

CASHING IN ON LONG-TERM TRENDS

So far, our entire discussion of asset allocation and portfolio management has been based on the business cycle. But it's clear that this cycle isn't the only one that's important for making money in the stock market. An investor who decided to replace IBM with Compaq back in the late 1980s would have done so for reasons that had nothing to do with the business cycle. Similarly, an investor who bought mining shares and oil stocks in the mid-'70s and then scored fabulous gains as the inflation rate rocketed into double digits would have been looking beyond short-term trends in business conditions.

What other cycles or trends matter? Well, there is little consensus and few agreed-upon names for economic patterns that exist over periods of more than six years, but in my opinion there are three that are important for investors to be aware of— the inflation cycle, the credit cycle, and the long wave (also known as the Kondratieff cycle).

Whatever the importance and the factual validity of long-term economic cycles, they tend to fascinate the same sort of people who become obsessed with astrology, psychoanalysis, or biblical prophecy. So don't be suckered by some investing letter that promises to forecast all the stock market's twists and turns based on Fibonacci numbers or whatever. Nonetheless, long-term economic cycles do have some basis in reality, and you should factor them into your investment thinking.

Let's start with the most obvious—the **inflation cycle.** Anyone over the age of 30 can remember how inflation soared in the 1970s, only to collapse in the 1980s. In both those decades there were several swings up and down reflecting the turn of the business cycle. But from 1970 through 1980 each peak in the inflation rate was higher than the previous one. By contrast, since '81 each peak has been lower than the one before. So it's clear that there is some sort of inflation trend that can exist for more than a single business cycle.

TRUE FACT

When inflation rises above 5%, the stock market's average price/earnings ratio typically drops from 16 to 12 or less.

Source: The Leuthold Group

In fact, since 1937, when Franklin Roosevelt's transformation of the U.S. economy was entrenched, inflation has topped 6% a year on seven occasions and reached the double digits in five of those cases. In between these peaks, inflation has pulled back at least to the 4% to 6% range. These swings constitute the inflation cycle, which lasts nearly 10 years, or two business cycles, on average. However, the uptrends and downtrends in inflation are highly irregular—in some cases they are only one business cycle apart, while on occasion a single cycle can continue for as long as 20 years.

What gets an inflation wave rolling? Incompetent government policy compounded by bad luck. The classic example: Slipshod Federal Reserve policy in the late '60s—to help finance Lyndon Johnson's Vietnam War escalation at the same time that he was expanding the welfare state—laid the groundwork for serious inflation. The real catastrophe hit with the oil shocks of the early '70s, though. Just at the time the Fed should have been squeezing the economy to kill 6%-plus inflation, the skyrocketing price of oil forced the Fed to hold back. Reason: The Fed feared it might cause an even deeper recession than the brutal downturn that hit in 1973–75.

What stops inflation? Basically, the American people get sick of it. That gives weak-kneed politicians the nerve to take the tough steps needed to stabilize prices (or at least to appoint someone who will, as Fed chairman Paul Volcker did in the early '80s). To oversimplify, then, the inflation cycle exists because when consumer price increases are minimal—typically 3% to 4%—people forget how destructive inflation can be. But by the time it reaches 6% to 7% or more, they are willing to put up with the unpleasant policies needed to stop it.

There are several important lessons you can learn from all of this:

■ **Inflation is never going to disappear permanently.** To prevent a recurrence of the Great Depression, the American economic system was fundamentally changed. Whereas the economy had experienced both inflation and deflation up until 1932, from 1933 on there were virtually no deflations. That helped to limit how bad recessions could be, but it also insured that periodic outbreaks of inflation would be worse. (Most Americans would probably say that trade-off was okay, since it's easier to survive five years of 7% inflation than five years without a job.)

■ **Whenever inflation drops below 4%, the next big move will likely be upward.** There was a stretch from 1959 to 1966 when inflation remained at rock-bottom levels, but generally a 3% to 4% inflation rate like today's is a low point. Moreover, an upswing may not be all that far away. Renowned Columbia University economics professor Geoffrey Moore, who once taught current Fed chairman Alan Greenspan, has predicted a return to 5% inflation within the next couple of years. When a *Forbes* magazine reporter asked him which of the indicators he watches signals such a jump in inflation, Moore replied: "All of them."

■ **Smart long-term investors should buy inflation hedges when everyone is convinced inflation is dead.** If you're inclined at all to buy investments when they are out of favor in order to get a bargain, selecting some inflation hedges after prices have been relatively stable for several years is a no-brainer. I'm not suggesting that you load up on Krugerrands or American Eagle gold pieces; that's a clumsy way to own gold. But be sure that your stock portfolio contains a fair sprinkling—15% or so—of shares in industries such as mining, oil, forest products, and real estate. One thing you can be fairly sure of: If you are under 60 and live to a normal old age, you will have to ride out moderately serious inflation sometime during your retirement years.

There's another cycle you should be aware of, known as the **credit cycle.** It's harder to pin down than the inflation cycle, but since it can have an important effect on your investments, you should at least understand how it works.

When we discussed the business cycle, we talked about money and interest rates as though the Federal Reserve were the only important factor. In fact, though, banks and private corporations play an important secondary role in determining the overall level of business activity.

For all practical purposes, the Fed controls the maximum amount that private banks can lend and effectively sets the minimum interest rates for new loans. Nothing, however, compels banks to lend or corporations to borrow. If bankers and business executives are worried about the future, they can hang back. In that case, far fewer business loans are made than Fed policy would allow for. At other times businesspeople may be confident and enthusiastic. Then they can increase their lending sharply without any significant change in Fed policy—at least until they have used up whatever slack exists in the banking system.

The result of this loose connection in money and credit policy is that the Federal Reserve can rein in the economy but cannot force it to expand (economists call this problem "pushing on a string"). When the Fed raises interest rates and restricts money growth, there may be little effect at first as the slack is taken in, but before long, stringent Fed policy will start to bite. By contrast, the Fed's ability to control the speed of an expansion depends on at least moderate business confidence. When business executives are hiding under their desks, the Fed loses control over the economy.

You might think that the psychology of businesspeople was

always more or less the same—varying perhaps from slightly cautious to mildly overoptimistic. Actually, though, the psychological tone of the business world swings enormously from grudging penny-pinching to openhanded euphoria.

There probably isn't any way to measure credit-cycle swings mathematically, since they are based on psychology, but it's important for investors to have a general feel for where the cycle is. Clearly, when banks are pouring zillions of dollars into third world nations, as they did in the '70s on the theory that a country can't go bankrupt, you might want to think twice about investing in bank stocks. Similarly, if oil drilling is at record levels and wildcatters are sinking wells in the Rocky Mountains that can't be profitable unless oil prices keep rising, you might be wise not to invest all your money in energy issues. In short, when money is flying around, you may be nearing a peak in credit. That can end in one of two ways (or sometimes both): a string of fiascoes, such as bankruptcies by overextended businesses, could puncture confidence; or the Fed could tighten, causing a recession and ending a business cycle. Either way, shares in over-inflated industries are likely to be hit the hardest.

The bottom line for the business cycle, the inflation cycle, and the credit cycle is that you should cultivate a slightly skeptical style as an investor—this is generally known as being **contrarian.** Be reasonably cautious. But don't refuse to invest during bad times. Sooner or later recessions end, inflation abates, and business confidence improves. Even more important, start selling and booking your profits when investors are whooping it up. Business cycles end, inflation revives, and credit standards get sloppy. Even if you can't always tell exactly where you are in the three important cycles, you should have a sense of which extreme is closer. Adjust your investing mix accordingly.

Beyond these three cycles, which are clearly defined if sometimes hard to measure, lies the **long wave.** This megacycle, which lasts about half a century, fascinates a lot of occult and New Age types of investors. So don't take it entirely seriously. Still, it is true that the economy and the stock market tend to

experience lengthy, alternating periods of expansion and stagnation or decline. For example, share prices were in the dumps
from 1929 through 1942 (even though the market hit its
absolute low in 1932, it was weak for the next decade). From
then on, however, stocks scored advance after advance until
1966. After that, stocks made no headway until 1983. And since
then, the stock market has enjoyed an astonishing boom that
looks as if it could run for another decade.

Why does this long wave exist? Well, it's no accident that the
megacycle corresponds roughly to a person's adult life span. Each
generation has to learn the lessons of business all over again from
scratch. To be more specific, the explanations for the long wave
fall into two categories—the social structure theory and the
technology theory.

The **social structure theory** is credited to Nikolai
Kondratieff, a leading Russian economist who formulated a long
wave theory in the 1920s, based on his study of historical com-
modity prices. Not surprisingly, Kondratieff was shipped off to
Siberia in the '30s by Stalin and died there. The crime?
Kondratieff's theories suggested that though capitalism would
suffer from increasingly disastrous crises, it would adapt each
time and rebound. Further, socialism would not be able to eliminate economic downturns through central planning. As if that
weren't enough, Kondratieff's detailed study of centuries of grain
prices led him to have some misgivings about Stalin's agricultur-
al policies. Kondratieff was correct on all three counts—but that
didn't keep him out of the Gulag.

Kondratieff identified the pattern of the long wave—20-
some-odd years of bad times and about 30 years of good times
with key turning points punctuated by major wars. But he never
really explained the cycle, except in the most general terms. The
scheme runs something like this for the United States. A popular
war (the Spanish-American) is followed by a boom whose immi-
nent end is marked by an unpopular war (World War I), even
though momentum carries on through most of the '20s. Then
times are bad until the next popular war (World War II), which is

followed by a boom that starts to fade during the following unpopular war (Vietnam). The current boom was kicked off by the West's slow-motion victory in the cold war and will presumably continue until we do something stupid in a decade or so.

There's a general plausibility to this scheme if you don't press it too far. No one could doubt that events such as the American Revolution, the French Revolution, the Civil War, World Wars I and II, and the Vietnam War caused profound changes in the social structure of the countries involved. Those social shifts can either mobilize enormous productive energy or create long periods of stagnation.

The only trouble with trying to apply Kondratieff's theories in practice is that different people come up with conflicting interpretations. Was the 1987 crash the echo of the Great Crash in 1929? And does that mean we have already entered a period of stagnation and just don't realize it yet? Or, has our victory in the cold war and the collapse of communism begun a 30-year boom that has 10 to 20 years left to run? Stay tuned.

The major alternative to Kondratieff's view—the **technology theory**—is generally credited to Joseph Schumpeter, an Austrian economist active in the 1930s. In brief, he believed that a form of long wave was caused by major technological breakthroughs. Developments such as the automobile spurred periods of entrepreneurship that created long spurts of growth. Equally important, the expansion was caused not by a new invention, but by its widespread practical application. Then stagnation set in once the former breakthrough had been widely accepted and started to become obsolete.

Just as the Kondratieff people try to match up good wars and bad wars against stock market cycles, sometimes coming to opposite conclusions, the Schumpeter people do something similar with steam engines, automobiles, and personal computers—with an equal number of disagreements. Both Kondratieff and Schumpeter were brilliant economists, but that doesn't mean you have to pay attention to every crackpot with a market-timing newsletter who claims to follow them.

My own opinion is that both guys were basically right—the stock market does have long expansions and then stagnates for years. Personally I find it plausible that cheap personal computers will usher in an era in which white-collar workers become more productive than they've ever been before, and that the end of the cold war will allow economic growth to spread around the world. Judging by the progress of the stock market since 1983, I'd say we're only about halfway through the good times. I guess that means we should start worrying round about 2005.

We've now reached the end of Part I: "How to Manage Your Money." In Part II I'll explain how to analyze a stock. Before we move on, though, I'd like to take a moment to recap some of the key principles you should keep in mind once you start selecting specific shares.

- Your biggest risk is failing to keep up with inflation.
- Faster growth, falling interest rates, and lower inflation are good for stocks; slower growth, rising rates, and higher inflation are bad.
- Over 20 years or longer, returns on stocks are likely to average a bit over 10%.
- Forecasters continually underestimate how different the future is likely to be.
- Minimize overhead, always take a look at unpopular stocks, and invest for the long term.
- Own shares in at least eight different industries, don't overpay, and don't get greedy.
- In addition to stocks, keep at least part of your money in bonds and cash.
- Adjust your holdings once a year or so, moving money from choices that look overvalued to those that seem underpriced.
- Don't trade or speculate—you can't outguess the market.
- Use a discount broker whenever possible; for small stocks and foreign issues, consider going through a mutual fund.

- Think about buying stocks through dividend reinvestment plans (DRIPs).
- Share prices anticipate future business conditions by about six months.
- Stocks perform worst in the first two years of a president's term and best in the last two years.
- Think about buying stocks after the economy has been in recession for at least six months.
- Consider selling stocks if the economy has been growing for three years and the Federal Reserve raises short-term interest rates above long-term rates.
- You can't have too much cash in a recession.
- Be sure to have at least 10% of your money in inflation hedges if inflation has been under 4% for three years in a row.
- Think twice about shares in booming industries that are bankers' favorites.
- Remember that neither good times nor bad times last forever.

PART II
_____

THE ESSENTIALS OF STOCK PICKING

CHAPTER 5

INVESTING FOR GROWTH:

The Way to Earn Maximum Capital Gains without Taking a Lot of Crazy Risks

Mention stock investing, and the average person has a simple mental picture of how it ought to work. You buy shares in a rapidly growing company—a drug stock with a hot new product, for instance, or a restaurant chain with a winning concept. As the firm's profits soar over the following two or three years, the stock price doubles. Then you sell your shares and earn a fat profit.

This scenario is a description of growth investing. It leaves out a lot of other potentially successful approaches, including income investing and value investing, just to name the two most important alternatives. Nonetheless, growth is the chief objective of most beginning investors—and the source of most fantasies of stock market profits.

Why does growth investing exercise a strong hold over the minds of most small investors? For starters, it's easy to understand. You don't have to be a rocket scientist to realize that a company with a winning product or a popular new service can make a lot of money and that those booming profits would translate into capital gains for shareholders. If you've ever wondered who got the royalties for inventing the paper clip, then you're a potential growth investor.

Further, many investors believe that going for growth is the best way to earn above average profits over the long term. And they're right—at least up to a point. It's certainly true that companies that post consistent earnings growth of 12% or more a year outperform the broad stock market. In fact, if you think for a minute, it's mathematically necessary that stocks with 12%-plus profit gains would beat the market over the long term. The reason: Over a decade or longer, a stock's price/earnings ratio will generally rise or fall by only a limited amount. Hewlett-Packard's average annual P/E, for example, has ranged from 13.4 to 18.6 since 1988. Earnings, however, can grow enormously over a period of many years. In H-P's case, profits per share have tripled since 1988.

The bottom line is that over a decade or longer, increases in earnings will have a far greater influence on a stock's price than will changes in the P/E ratio. Or as they say on Wall Street: Share prices follow earnings. So it figures that over a long enough stretch of time, any stock with steady annual earnings growth of 12% or more will eventually outpace the overall stock market, which typically returns 10% or 11% a year.

It should be obvious, then, that if you could identify stocks that are able to turn in 12%-plus profit growth, and if you held them for five or 10 or 20 years, you would compile a spectacular performance record. Not surprisingly, the two pros generally considered the best investors in the world—Warren Buffett and Peter Lynch—follow precisely this strategy. Buffett, the 65-year-old chairman of Berkshire Hathaway, basically looks for what he calls wonderful businesses, companies with top-notch management and some fundamental business advantage. The classic example: GEICO, which began by selling auto insurance by mail to government employees. Not only did the company's mail-order approach hold down costs, but government employees are statistically less likely to have an auto accident than the average person. That just about guaranteed that GEICO could undercut its competitors and rack up splendid profits. After identifying such wonderful businesses, Buffett buys them and plans to hold them for many years. Indeed, he sells stocks so rarely that he describes his money-management technique as lethargy bordering on sloth.

Lynch, 51, the former manager of Fidelity's Magellan fund, has long followed a similar discipline. His most notable success was Federal National Mortgage Association (popularly known as Fannie Mae), which he bought in the early 1980s. The stock was then trading for less than $7 a share because interest rates had risen far above the rates that Fannie Mae was earning on its mortgages. Lynch's great insight was that Fannie Mae's problems were temporary and would dissipate over the following 10 years. How did he know? Three reasons. First, he recognized that interest rates could not remain forever at the double-digit levels of the early '80s; as they came down, Fannie Mae's interest rate squeeze would ease. Second, he noted that as new mortgage loans were made, Fannie Mae's old, low-rate mortgages were slowly being replaced with higher-rate loans. Finally, Fannie Mae had begun packaging its loans as mortgage-backed securities and the fees generated by that business were becoming increasingly important relative to what Fannie Mae earned from the mortgages it held. As these trends played out, the stock increased tenfold, topping $70 in 1992.

The fact that the most notable and successful money managers are growth investors may convince you that you should be, too. But before you put all your faith in hot stocks, you should be aware of their pitfalls. In particular, studies show that on average, conservative value-oriented approaches to investing beat the market slightly more often than growth strategies do. The biggest success stories may be growth investors, but they are also rarer.

For one thing, it's really hard to identify a company that can increase its profits faster than 12% every year for the indefinite future. Many stocks can post well above average gains for a year or two, but then they slip back into the middle of the pack. And it takes at least three years—and preferably a five- or six-year business cycle—for the full benefits of rapid earnings growth to kick in.

Furthermore, the results of being wrong about a company's prospects can be disastrous. Consider, for example, a stock trading at a lofty price/earnings ratio of 25 because earnings are rising 25% a year. If the company announces quarterly results that are less than investors' expectations—only a 15% gain, say—the stock's P/E could drop sharply from 25 to 20. In that case, even though profits were still growing relatively quickly, investors would suffer short-term losses of 20% as the P/E multiple contracted.

Even worse cases are imaginable if a popular growth stock actually starts turning in losses. U.S. Surgical, a maker of surgical staplers and other state-of-the-art medical instruments, was one of the highest-flying stocks in 1990 and 1991. Analysts projected that the company's earnings could climb 35% or 40% a year, and investors bid the stock up to phenomenal price/earnings ratios of 50 or more. That was swell for shareholders who had bought their stock before 1990 at P/Es below 20; they saw the share price rocket from less than $16 to $134 within the space of three years. However, investors who bought when the stock was near its peak were destroyed. In the face of potentially tough health care legislation and intense competition from Johnson & Johnson, U.S. Surgical's earnings flattened out in the second half of 1992. Then, in 1993, the company reported a 12¢ loss. Over that period the stock went into a nosedive, plunging to a low of $16 in early 1994. Shareholders who owned the stock for those two years lost as much as 88% of their money.

Trouble is, it's not all that unusual for growth stocks to face setbacks. Even if a company is basically successful, its stock could easily suffer short-term declines of 20% or more. Earnings growth may average 13% or 14% a year, but some individual quarters may be close to 20%, while others may be less than 10%. And when profit increases sink into the single digits, the stock will fall, too, even if everyone still believes that the company's long-term prospects are bright. It's also important to note that this risk increases the higher a stock's earnings growth and price/earnings ratio. For that reason, some market strategists argue that moderate growth stocks—with price/earnings ratios of 15 to 20, say—are likely to outperform the highest-flying shares with multiples above 20.

TRUE FACT

A study of the stock market from 1988 to 1992 found that stocks reporting significantly better than expected earnings went up an extra 9%, on average, in the following year. Those reporting worse than expected results lagged comparable stocks by 6%.

Source: Prudential Securities

Apart from earnings disappointments, growth companies also suffer ups and downs because of the business cycle, just as other companies do. Their share prices, however, typically gain or lose one and a half times as much as the average blue chip. Reasons: Any downturn in overall economic growth will hurt profits, and as I've already noted, growth stocks are extremely sensitive to any slowdown in their earnings. Also, they are especially hard hit by any rise in inflation or interest rates (for the reasons, see the discussion of the dividend-discount model in Chapter 1). As a result, in a bear market, when blue chips fall 20% over the space of a year or so, growth stocks can easily tumble by 30%.

The bottom line: If you want to emulate superstar growth investors like Warren Buffett and Peter Lynch, you must invest for the long term and be sure you buy at reasonable prices. Most important of all, though, you must learn how to identify true growth stocks. These will be the shares of companies that can boost their earnings at a minimum of 12% a year without serious stumbles or the slow erosion of their franchises.

WHAT MAKES A STOCK SIZZLE—OR FIZZLE

By definition, a growth company is able to increase its earnings at a rate considerably higher than that of the average firm. A growth rate of 12% qualifies, and many blue-chip growth stocks post 15% or so. Small-company shares that carry the growth label often manage percentages in the 20s or 30s. As I mentioned earlier, though, the higher the growth rate, the greater the potential risk if earnings disappoint investors.

Trouble is, not all earnings increases are created equal. Many companies can hike their earnings at a double-digit rate for two or three years, either through cost cutting or because the business cycle has moved into a favorable phase. But relatively few firms can be confident of superior results year after year. The essence of being a successful growth investor is learning how to distinguish onetime or short-term profit gains from what stock analysts call sustainable growth.

To understand the sustainable growth concept, it helps to take a tour through an income statement, the accounting table that shows how much of a company's revenues can be counted as profits. With the exception of some banks and insurance companies, which follow a slightly different accounting scheme, almost all companies use an income statement like the one shown here.

On the top line is **sales or revenues** (the latter term is preferred when the company isn't actually selling something, but rather receiving fees or rentals). From that total you subtract the cost of making the items or providing the services being sold. In the case of a vacuum cleaner maker, the **cost of goods sold** would include all the parts and labor that go into producing the vacuum cleaners as well as the wages and benefits of the assembly-line workers who actually make the machines. Subtracting cost of goods sold from revenues gives you the firm's **gross profits.**

READING AN INCOME STATEMENT

Sales or revenues	$100,000,000
Cost of goods sold	55,000,000
Gross profit	45,000,000
Sales, general and administrative (SG&A)	20,000,000
Operating income	25,000,000
Depreciation and amortization	7,000,000
Earnings before interest and taxes (EBIT)	18,000,000
Interest expense	3,000,000
Pretax income	15,000,000
Income taxes	5,000,000
Net income	10,000,000

There are several ways to set up an income statement, which shows how much a company has earned (typically over the course of a year). In this sample income statement for a small, successful industrial company, you start with the year's sales and then subtract the following items, in this order: the cost of making the products; the cost of selling them (including overhead); the noncash cost of wear and tear on plant and equipment; interest on debt; and income taxes. While a company can boost earnings for a year or two by trimming these costs, there's a limit to how much they can be cut. The key point: Only steady increases on the top line (sales or revenues) can boost net income over the long term.

Of course, companies have other expenses—particularly sales costs and what is popularly known as overhead. Securities analysts call these costs **SG&A** (short for **sales, general and administrative**). When you deduct SG&A from gross profit, you get a figure known as **operating income.**

From that you subtract so-called noncash costs such as **depreciation and amortization.** Under U.S. accounting rules, expenses relating to capital equipment and various other long-term costs are not deducted from sales at the time they are incurred. Instead the costs are spread over the anticipated useful life of the equipment. For example, if a company buys a truck, the cost of the vehicle wouldn't all be charged off at the time of the purchase. It could, for instance, be spread over five years. Other expenses, such as the cost of building a new plant or refurbishing an assembly line, could be stretched out as long as 40 years.

These accounting rules mean that a company subtracts depreciation and amortization from its operating profit even though the firm may not actually be laying out any cash corresponding to those accounting costs. Analysts therefore often add these noncash costs to net income to produce a figure known as **cash flow.** This reflects the amount of cash a company generates each year rather than its earnings based on accounting rules. In some situations, ratios comparing a stock's price to the company's cash flow per share are more trustworthy measures of value than price/earnings ratios are. I'll talk more about cash flow and price/cash-flow ratios in Chapter 9.

In any event, once noncash costs are subtracted from gross profit, you get a figure known as **earnings before interest and taxes,** often abbreviated as **EBIT.** Under U.S. tax law, interest is tax-deductible (whereas stock dividends are not). After interest is subtracted—or added, in the rare case that the company earns more on its cash balances than it pays on its bonds—you reach the figure known as **pretax income.** Subtract income taxes from that and you reach the so-called bottom line, also known as **net income.**

I've briefly explained the structure of an income statement

and the meaning of each line for two reasons. First, you should know what the various terms mean. If, for example, you read in a brokerage report that a company's net income rose more than pretax income because of a lower tax rate, you'll understand what the analyst is saying. If you have good mathematical sense, you'll also realize that the pretax gain is a better reflection of the stock's long-term growth rate than the increase in net income is. (Reason: Tax rates could fluctuate up and down from year to year, so the pretax figure is closer to the core growth rate.)

Second, if you carefully analyze an income statement, you'll see the crucial fact of growth investing: Most of the lines can vary only to a certain extent. Lower manufacturing costs, lower interest expenses, or lower taxes could increase corporate profits for a year or two. But over the long term, only revenue growth can continue to boost stock earnings year after year.

RULE NO. 6 OF INVESTING: REVENUE GROWTH IS THE ONLY TRUE GROWTH.

This principle is so important that I'd like to examine it in a little greater detail. Growth investors who get it are the ones who spot winning stocks, while those who don't lose their shirts. So let's go down the income statement again, line by line, and see what doesn't constitute true growth.

■ **Cost cutting doesn't produce long-term growth.** Making factories more efficient and trimming labor costs are worthwhile for their own sake. At the very least, they enable a company to lower its prices and compete better against rivals. Similarly, cuts in SG&A could reduce bureaucracy and make a company more responsive to its customers. But increments to earnings from cost cutting don't mean much. Reason: They aren't repeatable. You might be able to give earnings a big boost for a single year by slashing costs, but you'd have to make even bigger reductions the second year to produce the same percentage gain in net income.

■ **Declining capital spending can't produce long-term growth.** As I explained above, depreciation and amortization aren't cash costs but rather accounting costs created when a company invests in itself. A decline in depreciation and amortization affects a company's actual cash holdings only if the firm is cutting back on capital spending. In other words, if a company stops investing in its products or services and allows these expenses to edge lower, its cash flow will improve—and its earnings are likely to rise as well. However, the long-term implications of slashing capital investing are extremely negative. After three or four years, reduced investment in the business could cause the company to fall irretrievably behind its competitors.

■ **Financial restructuring often doesn't help long-term growth.** Paying off debt and eliminating interest expense can jack up net income. But it's a onetime improvement. The only way in which a company can raise its long-term growth rate by restructuring is if it *shrinks*, selling or spinning off slower-growing operations to reduce debt and concentrating only on the most rapidly expanding business lines.

■ **Lower tax rates won't aid long-term growth.** If changes in tax law lower rates for a particular industry, for example, that may give a company's earnings a onetime shot in the arm. But obviously that gain won't recur year after year. In fact, corporate tax cuts are liable to be reversed in future years when Congress goes looking for loopholes that can be closed to help shrink the deficit.

In short, if you look at every line of an income statement below the revenue line, you find that reduced expenses could pump up earnings for a year or two—or even three. But none of these improvements could possibly power profit growth for five or 10 years. And that's what makes a growth stock. So when you read a brokerage report that predicts a 20% rise in a company's earnings per share because of layoffs or financial restructuring, be skeptical. Such pseudogrowth companies can be the most dangerous investments. The stock runs up on expectations of a pickup in profit growth. Then, when it becomes apparent that rapid earnings gains can't be sustained for more than a couple of years, the share price can give back most of its previous gains.

SUSTAINABLE REVENUE GROWTH

This brings us to the heart of growth investing: What enables a company to post above average sales gains year after year? In a word: innovation. But you have to understand that word in its broadest sense. A biotech stock that develops a successful new treatment will typically experience rapid growth until most of the people who could be treated are using—or at least have considered using—the innovative drug. However, innovation can include more mundane business advances as well. Fast-food restaurants and deep-discount warehouse stores can be just as innovative as high technology, even though they are less glamorous. And just like a biotech stock with a breakthrough drug, they can grow rapidly until they exhaust the potential of their markets (analysts call this point **saturation**).

It stands to reason that all high-flying growth stocks will someday come down to earth. For a company to be able to turn in above average earnings gains, the firm has to earn unusually high profits on its capital. Those exceptional profits will last only until the unique opportunities the company enjoys are exhausted or until so many other competitors emerge that they undercut each other's prices and lower the profitability of the business. To identify a promising growth stock, then, you have to make sure of four things:

95

1. The company must have a business that earns above average profits.

2. Its market must still allow plenty of room for growth.

3. The firm must be able to finance its growth without excessive borrowing.

4. The company must have some sort of advantage over its competitors.

Let's look at these points one by one. The first key—the need for the business to earn above average profits—turns out to be logical if you use a little arithmetic. To measure a company's inherent profitability, analysts use a ratio called **return on equity,** abbreviated **ROE.** This number is calculated by dividing a company's net income by its equity (also known as **book value**). The ratio is very important, and you need to understand what it means. So don't let the following mathematics put you off.

The significance of ROE is best illustrated with a hypothetical example. Say that you and four friends set up a company by putting up $20 apiece for a total investment of $100 (equity, or book value) and borrowing another $100 (debt). Altogether your new firm would have a total of $200 (capital). If you earned $20 (net income) a year after interest on your debt and taxes, you'd have a net return on capital of 10% ($20 divided by $200) and a net return on equity of 20% ($20 divided by $100). Now, say that you paid out $1 to each investor, for a total of $5 (dividends). The company would be left with $15.

What happens to that money? Here's the crucial step. It becomes equity because it is reinvested in the business (retained earnings). In other words, for the second year, the company will start out with $115 in equity, or 15% more than it had the first year. If everything continues in the same proportions—the company borrows 15% more, earns 15% more, pays 15% more in interest and taxes, and so on—dividends will go up by 15% and so will retained earnings. In short, if a company reinvests in itself at a 15% rate and its ROE doesn't decline, all its numbers will increase by 15% annually.

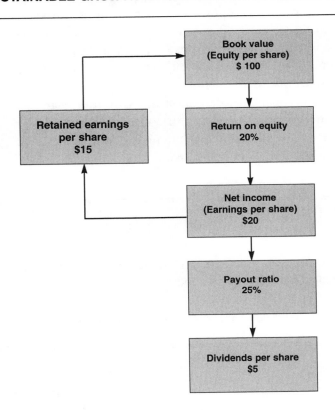

SUSTAINABLE GROWTH REQUIRES HIGH PROFITABILITY

Book value
(Equity per share)
$ 100

Retained earnings
per share
$15

Return on equity
20%

Net income
(Earnings per share)
$20

Payout ratio
25%

Dividends per share
$5

To grow rapidly year after year, a company needs to earn higher than average profits. In this example, a stock with a book value of $100 earns $20 a share. That's a 20% return on equity (ROE). One-quarter of those earnings, or $5 a share, is paid out in dividends. The remaining $15 a share is retained and added to equity. That means the company's new book value will be $115, an increase of 15%. Assuming the ROE and the payout ratio remain the same the following year, earnings and dividends will both be 15% higher as well. In other words, the annual growth rate will be 15%. The bottom line: For a company to sustain fast growth without borrowing, it needs an ROE of 15% or more.

What will the firm's sustainable growth rate be? You got it: 15%.

This model is the most important thing growth investors need to understand. (Read through it again if you need to.) A company can continue to grow rapidly as long as it can earn a high rate of profit on its capital, carry a reasonable debt load, and retain the bulk of its earnings. Most important, the firm has to be able to replicate those conditions year after year. As long as it can, superior profit growth can continue like clockwork. But if one or more of those key elements deteriorates, the growth mechanism can quickly fall apart.

TRUE FACT

The oldest baby boomers are turning 50. Two industries that will benefit: financial services and health care.

Source: Trendline Research and Management Corp.

Let's move on to the second key point: A growth stock's market must be unsaturated. Or, as they say on Wall Street, trees don't grow to the sky. At some point, every business reaches the natural limit of its growth. When that happens, the company's profitability can drop sharply—down to a barely average level. That decline can happen surprisingly quickly. And when it does, a company's share price can go into a nosedive. Why? Because when investors fear that a stock's growth rate is slowing, they stop being willing to buy the shares at a high price/earnings ratio. In fact, it's the P/E collapse, not whatever drop in earnings might occur, that kills a growth stock's price.

Making sure a company's market isn't saturated is straightforward enough. Be sure to check out how much of the firm's potential market is already tapped. For example, if you are look-ing at a restaurant chain, be sure that it hasn't already built out-lets on every attractive street corner. You won't be surprised to learn, for example, that McDonald's fast-food business is grow-ing less than 10% a year in the United States, while its interna-tional business is growing more than 20% annually. Similarly, if you are evaluating a biotechnology company with a hot new drug, make sure there are enough potential patients to fuel its projected growth rate for the next five years. For some special-ized drugs, there may not be.

Occasionally you'll find a company that is able to grow year after year because of its success in constantly launching new products. Classic examples have included 3M, the maker of Scotch tape and Post-it notes, and Rubbermaid, which produces a full line of plastic and rubber kitchen and bath accessories. The ability of management to create new growth is worth some-thing—if the company has a very long record of successful inno-vation. Just remember that even these first-rate innovators hit dead stretches that make their stocks languish, as Rubbermaid did in 1994 and 1995. As a general rule, therefore, you should be able to explain to your own satisfaction exactly where a compa-ny's sales growth will come from over the next five years, at least.

The third key to sustainable growth is that a company must be able to expand without excessive borrowing. This point is less obvious than the first two and often overlooked by growth investors. Sometimes a company increases sales at a substantially faster rate than its profitability can support. In such a case, the company has to finance rapid growth with heavy borrowing. However, when the company has taken on as much debt as it can possibly carry, it will have to slow its expansion. Even in cases where lenders seem willing to provide almost unlimited amounts of money—as they have recently to cellular telephone compa-nies or cable television firms—rising debt can reduce the valua-tions that investors are willing to give the shares.

To see how this would all work out in practice, let's imagine a hot new fast-food chain that serves burgers made from low-cholesterol poultry. We'll call it the Fowl Burger. The menu, which runs from smoked turkey to exotic ostrich meat, has been a hit in California. Now Fowl Burger is ready to go national, building on its existing base of 100 outlets on the West Coast. There's no problem with profitability. The health-conscious yuppies who eat at Fowl Burger will gladly pay premium prices, and poultry is cheaper than beef. Saturation isn't a problem, either. While California is the best market, Fowl Burger has bright prospects in Boston, New York, and other trend-conscious cities.

What rate of growth can the company finance, though? If Fowl Burger opens 10 new stores a year, a modest number, it can easily maintain a 10% unit growth rate. Add to that 3% inflation and 3% annual increases at existing stores from rising store traffic and menu improvements, and the chain should be able to rack up 16% annual sales growth. Sounds fabulous. But there's one vital factor to check before you buy the stock: How long does it take for a new store to pay back the costs of opening? If a new Fowl Burger can reach break-even in six months and pay back its costs within the first year, then the company can sustain its 10% annual rate for new outlets indefinitely. But what if it takes three years for a new restaurant to break even? Then the 10% growth rate is unsustainable. In fact, the natural growth rate might be only 3% or 4% a year. If that's the case, then Fowl Burger can maintain its 10% rate of new store openings only by borrowing. And sooner or later the growth rate will have to decline, falling back toward the 3% to 4% rate that can be financed from earnings. You don't want to be holding the stock when that happens.

The final key that you need to check is the ease with which rival firms can enter the business. Does the company have patents that will protect it from competition that would erode profit margins? Does it have a management style that would be hard to duplicate? McDonald's Hamburger University and Coca-Cola's secret formula may give rise to jokes, but those two companies have been able to retain their dominant positions thanks to those corporate cultures. By contrast, fad-driven success such as the bottled juice and iced-tea craze can be risky because nothing prevents competitors from quickly flooding the market, leading to rapid saturation. Snapple, for example, which traded as high as $32 (more than 46 times earnings) in early 1994, was acquired by Quaker Oats for a measly $14 later that year. The reason: Other beverage companies swiftly introduced fruit and iced-tea drinks that watered down the market, and Snapple's stock slipped as low as $11.50 before the acquisition.

THE GROWTH INVESTOR'S CHECKLIST

Don't worry if you're having trouble getting a grip on the concept of sustainable growth. It's a lot harder to scope out a growth stock than to identify promising income or value stocks (which I'll talk about in coming chapters). That's why there are so few brilliant growth stock pickers and lots of managers who can choose a solid portfolio of cheap stocks with attractive yields. However, while growth investing is the hardest to do well—and the riskiest if you make a mistake—it also offers the biggest payoff by far.

I'm not suggesting that reading a single book, like this one, can make you infallible. But once you know what qualities a company needs if it's going to sizzle, you should be able to improve your odds of spotting winners and avoiding pseudogrowth stocks that can suddenly run out of steam and plummet in price. To make it easier to apply these ideas to practical stock selection, I've tried to summarize the characteristics of a winning growth stock in the following checklist. Next time, before you buy, ask yourself these 10 questions:

■ **Does the company have a unique product or service?** Growth stocks have to earn above average profits. To do that for any length of time, a company must offer an innovative and valuable product or service that is not readily available elsewhere. Be sure not to mistake fads for growth opportunities with long-term potential. Think personal computers, not Hula Hoops.

■ **Does the firm have recurring revenues?** All sustainable growth comes from revenue growth, not from cost cutting, financial restructuring, or lower taxes. The best kinds of revenues are recurring—that is, they come from selling a premium item that has to be replaced frequently, such as twin-blade razor refills. The next best sales are from products that need to be upgraded at regular intervals, such as personal computers. The least desirable revenues come from onetime sales.

■ **Are you early in the story?** Since all growth stocks eventually exhaust their markets, make sure that you are getting in on a company when it is still in the early part of its growth curve. Beware especially if everyone is familiar with the company, knows about its success, and blandly assumes that it will grow forever.

■ **Is the company at the forefront of its industry?** Remember that when an industry is booming, there is no guarantee that all the companies in it will continue to prosper. For example, despite the explosion in sales of computers over the past 10 years, both IBM and Digital Equipment shares collapsed in the early '90s because the companies were heavily dependent on sales of large computers and no longer at the leading edge of the technology.

■ **Is the return on equity higher than 15%?** Even if a company isn't paying any dividends, it generally needs a return on equity of 15% or more to sustain an earnings growth rate of 12% or more. And without average long-term profit increases of at least that much, you aren't dealing with a true growth stock.

■ **Is the company's debt low—or at least stable?** The best growth stocks have no debt. In that case, the company is clearly able to fund its expansion internally. Next best is if the company has debt less than 20% of its long-term capital (which consists of equity plus long-term debt). Companies whose debt is only a fraction of their capital have no immediate barriers to growth since they could increase their borrowing for two or three years and still have debt below 50%. The stocks you have to worry about are those where debt exceeds equity—that is, where debt is more than 50% of capital—and where the debt ratio has been rising steadily. Such firms may be trying to expand faster than their natural growth rates, using borrowing to make up for inadequate profitability.

■ **Does the firm have a valuable franchise, brand name, proprietary technology, or patents?** Companies can continue to earn premium profits as long as they can prevent competitors from undercutting their prices. It's most desirable, therefore, for a company to have some intrinsic advantage—whether it's a widely recognized brand name or proprietary technology—that serves as a barrier against other companies that would like to enter the industry. Otherwise a firm's dominance depends on the quality of its management—and that's an edge that can easily be overcome by hungry competitors.

■ **Is the stock's price/earnings ratio lower than its earnings growth rate?** Growth investors are best advised to choose companies based on their potential for increases in net income rather than their share prices. Still, stock valuation is important. If you overpay for a stock, your future capital gains will be smaller even if earnings go up as expected. And your risk will be bigger, too. Here's one test I recommend to check that a stock is reasonably priced: The price/earnings ratio should be lower than the stock's projected annual earnings growth rate. In other words, if a company's profits are expected to rise 25% a year, on average, you shouldn't buy it if the price is more than 25 times analysts' estimates of earnings per share for the current year.

■ **Is the P/E less than 20?** Studies have shown that stocks with moderate growth prospects (15% to 20% a year) on average out-perform those with the highest projected growth rates (20%-plus). How can that be? The answer is that high-flying stocks are riskier and more likely to disappoint investors than shares with more reasonable objectives. A good way to be sure that you focus on the safer sort of growth stock is to shy away from issues with price/earnings ratios above 20. If you want to include some maximum-growth stocks in your portfolio, you might be smarter buying a broadly diversified mutual fund that holds such issues.

■ **Do you believe the share price can double in five years?** A stock that can meet the sorts of tests we've just described should be able to double in price over five years. To be exact, if a company's earnings per share increase at a 15% rate and the stock's price/earnings ratio remains constant at 15, the share price will gain 101% over five years. If you have questions about whether a firm can turn in the earnings needed for a five-year double, then check your calculations, because something's wrong.

WHEN TO SELL A GROWTH STOCK

I noted early in this book that the less often you trade stocks, the better your performance is likely to be. Nevertheless, from time to time it is necessary to sell. Sometimes your decision may be easy; you may need cash or want a capital gain to offset a loss for tax reasons, or you may have to take profits on some winning stocks because you are rebalancing your portfolio. In other cases, though, you may decide to sell a stock because you think it's no longer worth holding. And that can be a tough call to make. Actually, it's often harder to be sure that a stock is ripe for sell-ing than it is to recognize that a stock is a screaming buy.

Here's my basic rule on when to get rid of a stock: Sell when the reason that made you buy no longer applies. For a high-yielding income stock, that could mean one of several things. The dividend yield could now be lower because the share price has moved up substantially. Or the company's finances could have deteriorated so that the dividend no longer looks safe. Similarly, for a value stock, the share price could have appreciated to reflect whatever unrecognized value you originally spotted. Or the firm's business prospects could have worsened.

For a growth stock, however, the signals that you should sell are trickier to spot. So I think it's worth spending a moment talking about the warning signs.

Of course, you might decide to sell a growth stock for any of the reasons you dump any other kind of stock. The share price might have risen so quickly that the P/E looks excessive, and you might want to take your profits. Or the company's finances might look shaky (remember that growth stocks can lose control of their ballooning debt if they try to expand faster than their natural growth rate).

But the most serious reason to boot a growth stock from your portfolio is that the growth rate is slowing to a point that it will no longer justify the stock's above average price/earnings ratio. And that's harder to gauge. Above all, remember that the company's prospects don't have to be so bad that the business loses money—or even that next year's earnings will be lower than this year's. All it takes to stick a pin in a growth stock is for its earnings increases to be *smaller* than shareholders are expecting. When that occurs, if the shares are pricey, the P/E can drop suddenly and sharply. And that can mean a big price decline.

I can't stress this point enough. If you want to avoid potentially serious losses on growth stocks, you have to be sure that earnings will meet—or exceed—other investors' expectations. That means you are worrying not only about what a company's profit numbers will be, but also about what other investors' expectations are. And it's more difficult to know what is in other people's minds than what is on an income statement.

To minimize the chances that you fail to jettison a growth stock in time, be sure to do these three things:

■ **Be value conscious when you buy.** The rules I mentioned earlier on picking stocks with P/Es below their growth rates and also below 20 will steer you away from the shares most vulnerable to a large P/E collapse if profit gains disappoint.

■ **Look for companies whose projected growth rates are in line with their historical results.** Though any company can stumble, those that have consistently turned in profit gains for five or six straight years (the length of a typical business cycle) are more likely to continue to meet shareholders' expectations than are companies on a recent hot streak.

■ **Consider selling when a company fails to post expected revenue gains.** As I explained earlier in this chapter, increasing revenues are the basis of all sustainable growth. As long as sales come through on track, investors may be willing to forgive a bad quarter's earnings due to an uptick in interest expenses or higher taxes, for instance. But if revenues falter, a company's fundamental qualification for carrying a lofty P/E is immediately called into question. And you might be wise to sell.

CHAPTER 6

GROWTH STOCK ROUNDUP:

Here Are 37 Stocks Worth Taking a Look at for Your Growth Portfolio

Obviously, no book can responsibly recommend individual stocks for you to buy. The market changes from day to day, and I'm writing this chapter months before you'll have a chance to read it. Nonetheless, when you are talking about established, blue-chip companies, there is an elite group of stocks likely to turn up over and over again on analysts' buy lists. Any one of them may be unattractive at one moment—because of a high share price, for instance—but at another time it will be an appealing buy. These are the stocks you should look at first.

Any list such as this one is necessarily arbitrary and impressionistic. For the record, I own a few of the stocks on this list— including AT&T, Time Warner, and WMX Technologies. The stocks are grouped into industries in ways that make it easy for me to talk about them. I don't mean to imply that stocks I leave out are automatically inferior to those I mention. Some of the stocks in this chapter may currently be posting annual earnings growth of less than 12%, although I think that rate will pick up in the future. I've also concentrated on industries and stocks that I've written about in my years as a columnist for **Money** mag-

VITAL STATISTICS ON 37 GROWTH STOCKS

This table shows the projected earnings growth rates of 37 high-quality growth stocks. You can get a rough indication of a stock's likely long-term total return by adding its growth rate to its current yield. In a few cases, I think the projections given here may actually understate a company's growth potential. Further, the data for a few of these stocks do not reflect important corporate developments likely to take place in 1996. For example, AT&T plans to split into three separate companies. Also, Chase Manhattan, Disney, and Time Warner are in the process of completing mergers that would change their numbers. Estimated revenues and earnings growth rates are projections by *The Value Line Investment Survey*.

Company	Ticker Symbol	Est. 1995 Revenues (in millions)	Recent Price	Dividend Yield	Projected Earnings Growth Rate
Amgen	AMGN	$1,935	$59	0.0%	19.5%
AT&T	T	80,000	65	2.0	11.5
Browning-Ferris Industries	BFI	5,779	29	2.3	14.0
Campbell Soup	CPB	7,278	60	2.3	11.5
Caterpillar	CAT	15,800	59	2.4	N.A.
Chase Manhattan	CMB	313,000*	60	3.0	13.0
Chiron	CHIR	1,100	110	0.0	N.A.
Citicorp	CCI	260,000*	67	1.8	N.A.
Coca-Cola	KO	18,250	74	1.2	17.0
Compaq Computer	CPQ	14,100	48	0.0	20.0
Disney	DIS	12,100	59	0.6	17.5
Fluor	FLR	9,250	66	1.0	15.0
General Electric	GE	43,600	72	2.6	13.5
Halliburton	HAL	5,800	50	2.0	23.0
H. J. Heinz	HNZ	9,250	33	3.2	10.5
Hewlett-Packard	HWP	31,000	84	1.0	23.5
Intel	INTC	16,200	57	0.3	20.0
International Flavors & Fragrances	IFF	1,440	48	2.8	11.5
Johnson & Johnson	JNJ	18,750	85	1.5	13.5
Kellogg	K	7,050	77	2.0	11.0
McDonald's	MCD	9,750	45	0.6	16.0
Merck	MRK	16,330	65	2.1	11.5
Merrill Lynch	MER	21,750	51	2.0	8.0
Microsoft	MSFT	5,937	88	0.0	23.0
Minnesota Mining & Manufacturing	MMM	16,400	66	2.8	8.5
Motorola	MOT	27,400	57	0.7	20.0
News Corp.	NWS	9,131	21	0.4	15.5
PepsiCo	PEP	30,850	56	1.4	13.5
Pfizer	PFE	10,240	63	1.7	14.5
Reuters Holdings	RTRSY	4,300	55	1.8	17.0
Rubbermaid	RBD	2,280	25	2.2	13.5
Sara Lee	SLE	17,719	32	2.4	11.0
Schlumberger	SLB	7,500	69	2.2	10.5
Tiffany	TIF	780	50	0.6	18.0
Time Warner	TWX	8,100	38	1.0	N.A.
Viacom	VIA.B	11,300	47	0.0	24.0
WMX Technologies	WMX	11,150	30	2.0	10.5

All data are as of Jan. 1, 1996. *indicates total assets rather than revenues. N.A.—not available.

azine. That means most of the stocks I'm going to talk about are U.S. issues. However, many of them earn a substantial part of their profits overseas. I have also included a few foreign stocks that are easy for U.S. investors to buy. If you want more foreign exposure, add an international mutual fund to your portfolio.

So much of this book is concerned with theory and rules and checklists that I wanted to have a chance to get some real companies into it. My reason: To get a feel for what makes a promising growth stock, it's helpful to look at a number of specific cases. Even if you don't buy these particular firms, they'll give you some benchmarks you can use to size up other industries and companies you're interested in. There's a similar rundown on likely stock picks after the next chapter, which is about income investing. Chapter 9, on value investing, isn't followed by a survey of stocks, because value situations usually need to be evaluated individually.

So whip through this chapter as though you were a pianist sight-reading the complete Scarlatti sonatas. Those pieces may not be profound, but they'll make you feel more confident at the keyboard. In that spirit, here's an allegretto look at 10 industries:

COMPUTERS AND SEMICONDUCTORS
(Compaq, Hewlett-Packard, Intel, Microsoft)

I still don't know how to get on the Internet, but I realize that qualifies me as a member of an endangered species. The fact is, it's hard to see any limits over the next five years to the spread of personal computers, which already number more than 200 million worldwide. What are the best ways to play the growth of the industry? My first choice would be Compaq, which has consistently been the most successful PC maker and actually passed IBM as the world's number one PC vendor in 1994. Despite its well-known track record, the stock has periodically traded at cheap prices. Whenever Compaq's P/E has fallen to 10 or thereabouts, the stock has been a great buy.

The other stock I'd look at among PC manufacturers is Hewlett-Packard. The company has long been highly regarded for its upscale calculators and precision electronic equipment (although some buyers always groused that you got a lot of machine for a lot of money). Then H-P built a hugely successful franchise in computer printers, where it was able to compete on price as well as quality. Indeed, some of its inkjet printers sell for as little as $275. Most recently, the company has been using the popularity of its printers as a jumping-off point for entering the PC business. To date, H-P's computers have been quite well received—they're both well designed and aggressively priced. I paid $700 for one of the company's subnotebooks, and I think it's terrific. If H-P is able to do as well with computers as it has done with printers, it could carve out a big chunk of the PC market.

You can't like the personal computer industry and not like Intel. Quite simply, with more than 80% of the $20 billion microprocessor market, Intel so dominates the production of the most essential chips for PCs that it seems almost to have a monopoly. No other company has been able to shake Intel's hold—though several have tried. As a result, the company has been able to shrug off fiascoes—flaws in early versions of its Pentium chip, for instance—and rebound to record profits once the next generation of chips came out.

Microsoft's position in computer software is comparable to Intel's with chips. Microsoft dominates the market for PC software, and none of its competitors seems able to make permanent inroads into the firm's 60% share of that $10 billion market. If you doubt the strength of Microsoft's position, consider this: The Justice Department went after Microsoft in 1995, ultimately intimidating the company into calling off its proposed $1.5 billion acquisition of Intuit, a leading maker of personal finance software. When the Justice Department is worried that you're too powerful, you've got an imposing franchise.

CONSUMER PRODUCTS
(3M, Rubbermaid)

Three M and Rubbermaid are remarkable for their ability to grind out steady growth from fairly mundane product lines. Minnesota Mining & Manufacturing is actually a specialty chemical company, producing coatings, adhesives, and sealants. But you probably know it best for Scotch tape and those little yellow Post-it notes. The company takes great pride in its ability to find new uses for its tape and adhesive technology. In fact, 3M notes, more than one-third of its sales come from products introduced in the past four years. Recently, however, the company's earnings growth has slowed, largely because of sluggishness in the overall economy. That growth rate may soon improve, thanks to 3M's recent decision to spin off some of its less profitable businesses.

Rubbermaid has been versatile dreaming up new things to do with plastic and rubber. At times the company has introduced new products as rapidly as one a day. Though you're probably most familiar with Rubbermaid's garbage cans and laundry baskets, the firm makes everything from toys to ready-to-assemble furniture. In the past year or two the company's profits have been hurt by rising costs for its raw materials, resin, and polypropylene. That, in turn, has led to other difficulties. For example, Rubbermaid antagonized some of its customers by trying to raise prices too quickly to offset its higher raw materials costs. The company has also failed to trim expenses as effectively as it might have.

Though both companies' earnings growth has been disappointing recently, their problems are temporary. Both 3M and Rubbermaid regularly win accolades for the quality of their management teams, and neither company has much debt. They will undoubtedly come back into favor, and if you're a long-term investor, you should take advantage of any price declines to buy their shares.

DRUGS AND BIOTECH
(Amgen, Chiron, Johnson & Johnson, Merck, Pfizer)

Drug stocks have been hammered since 1992, largely because it has become abundantly clear that if the United States doesn't clamp down on the growth of health care spending, the country's finances will be a disaster. Investors' confidence in the stocks' outlook wasn't bolstered either by President and Mrs. Clinton's clumsy attempts to reengineer the U.S. health care system. The pressure to control costs has made shareholders question whether drug companies will ever again post the 15%-plus profit gains they earned prior to 1992.

My view is that drug stocks are cheap and that they are due for a big comeback over the next five years. The case for the industry is pretty simple: The populations of the industrialized countries are aging and will require more health care. In cases where drugs are effective treatments, they are much cheaper than hospitalization or surgery. That means that drugs are part of the solution to runaway health care costs, not part of the problem. Moreover, the rapid advance of the biological sciences means that drug companies will have a higher success rate in finding effective drugs. In short, the companies will have more products that are cheaper than the alternatives at a time when demand is growing.

Merck is the number one U.S. drug company, with more than 4% of the $230 billion worldwide market. Not only does the firm have a strong lineup of new and recently introduced products, but it has also moved boldly to position its business for a more cost-conscious health care environment. In particular, Merck spent some $6.6 billion in 1993 to acquire Medco, the leading low-cost drug distributor. Once Medco is fully integrated into Merck's sales system, the drug company will have a way to offer a wide variety of its products at competitive prices.

Many analysts also think highly of Pfizer, which has an especially promising lineup of new and recently introduced drugs that could power the company's bottom line over the next decade.

Of course, with the rise of biotechnology, many of the most interesting breakthroughs are being made by independent companies a fraction the size of the billion-dollar pharmaceutical giants. Trouble is, many of these biotech firms are more impressive for their scientific resources than their profits. In fact, most of them lose money, at least on paper, and count on occasional stock offerings to bring in the cash they need to keep going. Such shares might pay off big in the long run, but they are much too risky for the average investor. If you want to own them, you should consider a specialized mutual fund such as Fidelity Select Biotechnology instead of buying individual issues. Also attractive as a way to invest in biotech are two closed-end funds that trade on the New York Stock Exchange—H&Q Healthcare and H&Q Life Sciences.

There are, however, two biotech stocks that are big and stable enough for the individual investor to consider. Amgen, with sales of more than $1.9 billion, made its fortune with only two drugs—Epogen, which stimulates the production of red blood cells, and Neupogen, which does something similar for white blood cells. Both businesses are well established and growing, since these drugs have proved valuable in treating kidney failure and the side effects of cancer chemotherapy. The stock has always traded more or less in line with the value of these two products, which account for more than 90% of revenues. However, Amgen has been plowing a big chunk of its profits into the development of other drugs. At some point in the next five years some of these new products will take off, giving Amgen the stability of a big drug stock and the glitz of a biotech stock.

With over $1 billion in sales, Chiron also works as a combined big health care stock and biotech play. The firm is well diversified in leading-edge technologies from ophthalmics to diagnostic tests—so much so that some analysts have described it as a mini-mutual fund.

113

Aside from drug stocks per se, Johnson & Johnson is an interesting diversified health care products company. J&J has some drugs, but a lot of its business consists of products like Tylenol and Neutrogena soap. Nonetheless, the company has been enormously good at marketing its products. For example, in the past few years J&J's surgical instrument division has knocked the stuffing out of U.S. Surgical, the chief developer of state-of-the-art instruments and the hottest stock in the United States in 1991 and 1992.

ENTERTAINMENT
(Disney, News Corp., Time Warner, Viacom)

When the working day is done, girls just want to have fun. The same is true of boys, even though Cyndi Lauper failed to include them. When it comes to entertainment, it's not too hard to spot the companies with the inside track. The big winners are going to be the companies that create programming and also have the means to deliver it on a large scale.

Who are they? Time Warner and Disney are clearly the two top firms. (For the record, Time Warner owns the magazine I work for and the publisher of this book.) Time Warner is a leading film producer with Warner Bros.; a major music company with Warner music; the biggest U.S. magazine publisher with Time Inc.; and owner of the most successful cable television networks, including HBO and CNN (which would be acquired in Time Warner's planned merger with Turner Broadcasting). In addition, Time Warner is the second largest operator of cable TV systems in the United States. Similarly, Disney unites a successful studio with a broadcast television network, thanks to its recent acquisition of Capital Cities/ABC.

Among the other important entertainment companies, Rupert Murdoch's News Corp. owns the 20th Century–Fox movie studio and the Fox television network and also has big stakes in satellite broadcasting systems in Europe and Asia that one day might be phenomenally profitable. Viacom owns the Paramount movie studio, cable TV channels such as Showtime, Nickelodeon, and MTV, and the Blockbuster chain of video rental stores.

FINANCIAL SERVICES
(Chase Manhattan, Citicorp, Merrill Lynch)

The key trend in financial services over the next decade will be corralling the trillions of dollars that small investors are saving for retirement. And it looks like the clear beneficiaries will be America's biggest banks and brokerages. Merrill Lynch, the largest brokerage and the leading underwriter in the United States, stands out as an awesome asset accumulation machine. Between money held in private client accounts and assets under Merrill Lynch's management, the brokerage has its fingers on more than three-quarters of a trillion dollars.

Neck and neck with brokerages, the largest banks will be racing to snare consumers' savings. In August 1995 Chemical Banking announced an agreement to merge with Chase Manhattan. The new institution, which would take the Chase Manhattan name, would become the biggest U.S. bank, with total assets of nearly $300 billion. Moreover, the bank would rank number one or number two in most of its major businesses. Even more important for shareholders, the combination would offer plenty of opportunities for cost cutting. The new bank would eliminate some 12,000 jobs worldwide and close about 100 branches in New York City alone. The likely result would be annual profit growth of 12% or more at a time when many banks are managing only single-digit gains.

Though the Chemical-Chase merger would push Citicorp into the number two spot among U.S. banks, the company will still be a behemoth, with more than a quarter of a trillion dollars in assets. Citicorp has long been a leader in consumer banking, as anyone who uses its automated teller machines and telephone banking services can attest. Equally important, though, the bank has been aggressively expanding overseas. Those international branches focus on retail banking, but the firm has a sizable international corporate business as well.

FOOD, BEVERAGE, AND RESTAURANTS
(Campbell Soup, Coca-Cola, H. J. Heinz, IFF, Kellogg, McDonald's, PepsiCo, Sara Lee)

Let's face it, American popular culture is rapidly taking over the world. So what could be a better way to play the spread of American tastes than with top brand-name food and beverage companies? Among the U.S. food companies with world-class brand names and franchises are Campbell Soup, Heinz, Kellogg, and Sara Lee. The time will come when the French start the day with cornflakes, have a bowl of tomato rice soup for lunch, and chow down to a steak with ketchup on it for dinner—with cheesecake for dessert.

In the fast-food category, Coca-Cola, PepsiCo, and McDonald's are bent on plastering their logos across eastern Europe, Latin America, and Asia. They don't call it Coca-colonization for nothing. All three are profiting enormously from the fact that their foreign revenues can grow at nearly twice the rate of domestic sales. That means that as faster-growing international business becomes a larger percentage of the total, the companies' earnings growth rates could actually accelerate.

There's one other company I'll throw into this group, although it isn't strictly speaking a food company. I'm referring to International Flavors & Fragrances, the leading maker of secret ingredients. IFF produces the substances that give scents to soaps and savor to baked goods and candy. The company is also expanding in Latin America and Asia on the theory that as household incomes rise, people will pay for piquancy.

MACHINERY AND CONSTRUCTION
(Caterpillar, Fluor, General Electric, Halliburton, Schlumberger)

It may be a commonplace that the United States has lost its edge in manufacturing, but don't you believe it. We may not be the most competitive when it comes to making television sets or cameras, but we still do really big stuff better than anybody else. Take Caterpillar, for example, the world's largest manufacturer of earth-moving equipment. Cat makes tractors, graders, compacters, and just about everything you need to roll out a major highway system. That may not sound like such a great business, if you count only the United States, but think about China and Brazil and you get a very different picture. That's the reason foreign sales account for nearly half the company's business.

The same kind of thinking applies to General Electric, which makes a widely diversified assortment of products, including aircraft engines and turbines for power generation. GE has long been considered one of the best-managed U.S. corporations and has tried to make sure that each of its major businesses is first or second in its field.

Thinking big isn't a strong point of U.S. manufacturers alone. When you want to build an industrial facility or a power plant, you need a general contractor who can handle a giant project without fouling it up. Fluor is the largest U.S. engineering and construction firm, with offices around the globe.

Among all the businesses that call for giant-size services, oil and gas stand out. The number of drilling rigs in use in the United States today is only one-third what it was 15 years ago. But since demand for oil is outstripping new supply, drilling is expected to rebound over the next five to 10 years. Two oil services companies that could become dynamic growth stocks are Schlumberger, which specializes in drilling and oilfield testing services, and Halliburton, whose business is split between oilfield services and engineering and construction.

117

POLLUTION CONTROL
(Browning-Ferris, WMX Technologies)

Collecting and disposing of garbage, trash, and potentially hazardous waste is a guaranteed growth business for the twenty-first century. And contrary to environmentalist propaganda you hear all the time, corporations are the good guys. Of course, waste-disposal firms occasionally get fined for violations, but by and large they run efficient, modern landfills, incinerators, and hazardous waste facilities that do relatively little damage to the environment. The real scandals in the waste-disposal industry are small-town and municipal dumps; not only are they inefficient, but they also aren't big enough to compete with modern landfill facilities.

Environmental laws have been closing down a lot of leaky local facilities, leaving the big corporations with the bulk of the business. The two biggest firms in the industry are Browning-Ferris and WMX Technologies; together they account for more than half of private-sector business. WMX is the biggest firm and the best integrated, with a broad array of waste businesses. Recently, though, Browning-Ferris, which is less than half as large as WMX, has been doing better, and some analysts say it is more focused than its larger rival. It's also worth noting that the waste-disposal business is one in which the United States is way ahead of most other countries in the world—at least when you're talking about operating on a large scale. So these two companies should have great opportunities internationally as well as domestically.

RETAILING
(Tiffany)

When one of my former girlfriends gets married, I always buy my wedding gift at Tiffany. It doesn't really matter what the gift is. Put it in a robin's egg–blue box, tie a white ribbon around it, and you're okay. To put it another way, when a retailer has both Audrey Hepburn and the American Wing of the Metropolitan Museum behind it, that's a franchise. I've also always believed that Tiffany has great opportunities for international expansion. So far, the company's only big outpost is in Japan, where gift giving is a national pastime. But I think the Tiffany box can work its magic anywhere.

TELECOMMUNICATIONS
(AT&T, Motorola, Reuters Holdings)

Have you ever wondered why industrializing countries from Latin America to eastern Europe all seem obsessed with their telephone companies? If they're not privatizing them, they're trying to get cellular telephones as fast as they can—even if it means bringing in foreign firms to mastermind the process. The reason is that if a country doesn't have state-of-the-art phone service, for both voice and data transmission, none of its other businesses can compete in the global marketplace.

So which companies are best positioned to cash in on the communications boom? For starters, you have to pick AT&T. Not only is it the dominant U.S. phone company for long distance (a better business than local service), but AT&T's $12 billion acquisition of McCaw Cellular in 1994 gave it a strong position in cellular telephony. Those advantages are likely to be further enhanced by AT&T's bold plan to split itself up into three separate companies. Once the breakup is complete, the core telephone businesses will be leaner; the telephone equipment business will be more competitive; and the troubled computer business will no longer be a drag on either of the other two.

As cellular phones and pagers that can receive and transmit text become an increasingly important part of the international gabfest, Motorola should thrive. The company is a leading maker of the hardware used for high-tech chatter. In addition, Motorola is a premier maker of computer chips used mostly in products other than personal computers.

Of course, sometimes you need facts as well as gossip. Reuters Holdings, the world's largest electronic publisher, zips financial and other types of news and data around the globe. It's sure hard to see how the stock and bond markets can do well over the next decade without the enormous expansion of demand for price quotes, trading information, and news stories on the markets' latest winners and losers.

Looking back over these companies, I note one fact in particular: Not only do the stocks in this chapter generally meet the tests I outlined in Chapter 5, most of them also have global franchises. Almost all of the 37 stocks mentioned in this chapter figure to achieve their double-digit growth because of their international opportunities. Once you get to the multibillion-dollar level, the United States just isn't big enough by itself.

What this means for you as an investor is that you can meet the international investing requirement in your portfolio simply by buying a properly chosen assortment of giant blue chips. Remember, sometimes the best international opportunities are here at home.

CHAPTER 7

INVESTING FOR INCOME:

How to Get High Income Safely and Still Stay Ahead of Inflation

I'd like to start this chapter by shattering a stereotype. Most people think the term "income investor" is simply code for retiree. That's flat-out wrong. While most retired people need some income from their savings, they would be making a huge mistake to invest all their money for maximum yield. Hard as it may be to believe, some retirees shouldn't put any of their savings into so-called income investments. By contrast, sometimes middle-aged or even young investors may be wise to include such income investments in their portfolios.

This may seem paradoxical. But the fact is that you should buy investments that pay high income because you want predictability, not because you need spending money. On the other hand, if you can afford to take greater risks, you should buy growth stocks, whether you need current income or not (I'll explain how to meet your immediate cash needs later in this chapter). It's a truism that the return you get reflects the risks you're willing to take, and the payoff for extremely conservative income investing just isn't all that good.

To understand why the split between growth investing and

income investing is about predictability rather than ready cash, you need to know something about the historical pattern of stock and bond returns. Over long stretches of time, top-quality stocks have earned an average of 10% to 11% annually. That return includes the value of dividends, which runs around 4.2% a year for blue chips. The 4.2% figure is just an average, though. The yield for any particular stock could range from less than 1% for a highflier to more than 7% for some slow-growing utilities.

The upshot is that investors who own an assortment of blue-chip stocks over several decades can expect to get a little less than 40% of their total return from yield, which is fairly predictable, and more than 60% from capital gains, which aren't predictable at all. Stocks and mutual funds that more or less match those numbers are known as **growth-and-income investments;** those that have lower yields (and higher growth rates) are called **growth investments;** and those that pay higher than average yields are, of course, **income investments.**

The key point here is that the choice between growth stocks and income stocks doesn't necessarily have to do with how much income you need—it has to do with how predictable you want your return to be. Since the dividends or interest you earn from a stock or bond are stated in advance (even if they aren't absolutely guaranteed), the bigger the part that comes from income, the more predictable the return will be. By the same token, the lower the income, the less certain your return will be. For example, the return from a growth stock that pays no yield at all will depend entirely on how the share price moves. You could double your money or lose 30% in the space of a year.

To bring this theoretical argument down to the most practical terms, let's consider three types of investors (the cases overlap but aren't exactly the same):

■ **Very conservative investors.** Shareholders who want to minimize their risk—especially short-term volatility in the value of their holdings—should favor income. That is, given the choice between buying a stock with no yield and an 11% projected annual earnings growth rate and one with a 4% yield and a 7% growth rate, a conservative investor should opt for the yield and slower growth. Reason: The larger the amount of your return that is known in advance (like the yield, for instance), the less variable the overall return will be. In this particular example, the two potential total returns are the same. In many cases a conservative investor will have to give up a little return to get lower volatility. For example, a utility with a 6% yield might have only a 4% growth rate, providing a projected return of 10% (6% plus 4%).

Be careful, however, that in your quest for safety you don't inadvertently increase your risks by concentrating too much money in bonds or utilities. If you do, your portfolio will be inadequately diversified—and therefore overly sensitive to risks, such as rising interest rates, that target high-yield investments.

■ **People who aren't retired but who need cash.** It's always tempting for people who need a steady flow of cash to invest in stocks and bonds that pay the highest income. But there are two problems with this strategy. In some cases, reaching for yield may lead you into the trap of buying low-quality investments. The highest yields are usually offered by junk bonds, troubled stocks, and other risky securities, which have to pay more to attract wary investors. Such choices may have a worthwhile place in a broadly diversified portfolio, but they are too dangerous to be your chief holdings.

The other problem with reaching for yield is that you might give up more potential return than you need to. Since stocks with high yields generally offer lower total returns, you may lose out on profits by leaning too heavily on income stocks. Instead you should put together the overall portfolio that makes the most sense for you, in terms of the risk level you're willing to take and the return you need to earn. What if that doesn't provide enough cash to meet your needs? No problem. You should feel free to spend small amounts of principal.

■ **Individuals who are already retired.** Most retirees consider themselves to be conservative investors, and most need income to supplement their pension and Social Security income. So income stocks, such as electric utilities, would appear to be the ideal investment for those who are no longer working. To some extent this is true, but retirees often make a potentially disastrous mistake. They lean so heavily in the direction of income that they don't build enough growth into their portfolios to keep up with inflation. The result: Over time their purchasing power erodes and they find that their standard of living is falling.

To get a clearer idea of the role that income investments should play in a properly balanced long-term portfolio, it's helpful to look at retirement saving in more detail. After all, most of us have to save for retirement while we are working and then draw on that money after we've retired. And managing savings over a long period of time raises all the questions of risk, return, and cash flow that we need to discuss.

Let's begin with the facts: To continue to enjoy a high five-figure income (in today's dollars) after you retire, you're going to need over a million bucks in savings. Social Security and pension will help some—but not a lot. As everyone knows, the Social Security system is in trouble; and though it's unlikely to collapse, Social Security payments are likely to decline as a percentage of the income that you will need in retirement.

The outlook for pensions isn't any better. Retirees covered by pensions will likely receive only 40% of their previous income; if you've changed jobs several times in your career, the value of your pensions could add up to much less. And that's if you get any pension at all. Only 40% of today's workers are covered by traditional pension plans—and the number is shrinking. The old-fashioned defined-benefits pension plan that guaranteed a certain level of income is being replaced by tax-advantaged savings plans such as 401(k)s that require you to put aside part of your salary or wages to fund your retirement savings.

TRUE FACT

More twenty-year-olds save regularly for retirement than thirty-
and forty-year-olds do.

Source: Kemper Financial-Roper Starch Worldwide

The bottom line is that you have to save for your own retirement yourself—whether you do it in a 401(k), through some
other tax-deferred plan, or simply by buying your own stocks,
bonds, and mutual funds. The sad fact is, however, that only four
out of 10 baby boomers are saving substantial amounts toward
their retirement. (Surprisingly, the so-called slacker generation,
those under 30, are doing somewhat better—about 60% of them
have already started saving for retirement.) These dismaying statistics mean that people who are still working need to step up
their savings rate. And they need to earn the highest return possible on their money before they retire.

Given the need to maximize the growth of your savings—and
the long stretch of time you may have before you actually
retire—it makes sense to pack as much growth into your portfolio as you possibly can. Over a 10- or 20-year-period, temporary price fluctuations will even out and your stocks' core
growth rates will shine through. So it's foolish to give up even a
percentage point of return. You should manage the volatility of
your portfolio with savvy asset allocation, not by dumping all
your money into income investments. And this mistake is more
common than you might think. For example, nearly half of all
401(k) assets are invested in short- and intermediate-term
income investments that can't come anywhere near the 10% to
11% average returns earned by stocks.

You might say to yourself, Okay, it makes sense to invest for
growth when I'm saving for retirement, but once I've stopped

125

working I need to conserve all my principal by buying bonds and high-yield stocks and living off the interest and dividends they pay. Though such reasoning sounds as though it makes sense, it's faulty, too. Reason: People greatly underestimate how long they are likely to live after they've retired and how much damage inflation will do.

The devastating effect of inflation over long periods of time was brought home to me when I went to see Cherry Jones in the 1995 revival of *The Heiress.* The play, which is based on the classic Henry James novella *Washington Square,* is about a doctor's daughter who stands to inherit a small fortune. Although Catherine is plain and has little charm, she attracts the attentions of a gorgeous but totally useless young man, who in the end turns out to be more interested in her future inheritance than in her. Catherine's ultimate discovery that no one has ever really loved her in her entire life is heartrending.

Given that plot, the characters talk continuously about money. But because the original story was set in 1850, it's impossible to make any sense out of the amounts involved. So the *Playbill* for the show provides the following information:

Blue-collar wages for a 60-hour work week = $2 a day
College tuition = $200 a year
Visit to the doctor = $5
New piano = $300
New York City town house = $21,000
First-class fare to London (one way) = $132

None of the 1850 prices is even remotely related to today's costs, except for the fare to London—and that, of course, is because of the invention of the airplane. On average, prices have risen 18-fold in the past 145 years. That's cumulative inflation of 1,700%.

Even over shorter periods of time, the effects of inflation are scary. A man who retires at 65 is likely to live 18 more years, and a woman is likely to live another 21. At 5% inflation, a level many people would describe as not so bad, the purchasing power of a man's retirement savings would eventually fall by 58%. Even with 4% inflation, his living standard would drop in half. For a longer-lived woman, the outcome is worse: the value of her savings would drop almost 56% at 4% inflation and more than 64% at 5%.

**RULE NO. 7 OF INVESTING:
STAYING AHEAD OF INFLATION IS MORE
IMPORTANT THAN EARNING THE HIGHEST
POSSIBLE YIELD.**

The conclusion: Whatever your age, you need to emphasize growth, using shrewd asset allocation to manage your risk. For the portion of your money that you do need to put into income investments, you should make sure that you are not giving up much potential return. In the rest of this chapter I'll quickly review the portfolio strategy you need to know, show you how bonds stack up against high-yield stocks, and then tell you all the basics for analyzing income shares.

CREATING A HIGH-INCOME PORTFOLIO

Throughout the first part of this chapter I've emphasized the idea that you should assemble a portfolio that gives you the highest return possible considering your tolerance for risk. And that raises one natural question: What if such a portfolio doesn't provide enough current income? There's a simple solution: Spend principal. This may sound like heresy to beginning investors who, before they learn anything else, learn that they should spend only interest and never principal. Remember to forget that adage.

The fact is, the distinction between interest and principal is completely misleading in today's economy. Because of inflation, a fixed amount of principal becomes worth less and less as time goes by. Your real objective is to preserve your purchasing power and spend whatever you earn beyond that. In other words, if inflation is 5%, you can afford to spend only what you earn in excess of that amount. In fact, the task is really a little bit tougher, because you will also have to pay taxes on your income and capital gains. That means you actually have to earn enough to offset both inflation *and* taxes. Obviously this means you have to get to a 10% return before you start to have a significant amount of spendable income.

Now here's the crucial point: It doesn't matter where your return comes from—capital gains or interest and dividends. All that matters is that you earn as much as possible. Some years your capital gains will be more than enough to cover your cash needs. Other years they may not be. If that means you spend a little bit of principal, it's not the end of the world.

What you must do, however, is set a fixed percentage of your total assets that you can afford to spend each year. Realistically you will need 4% or 5% to keep up with inflation and another couple of percentage points for taxes. So even if you're a very, very good investor, you can afford to spend only 5% or 6% of your portfolio a year. Generally speaking, it doesn't matter in which form you earn that money—all that matters is that you set up your portfolio to return as much as possible. (In fact, growth investments get more favorable tax treatment than income investments since income taxes may be lower on capital gains than on dividends and interest.)

What does such a portfolio consist of? Look back to Chapter 2. You'll see that a typical well-diversified investment portfolio divides up roughly this way: 35% in U.S. blue chips; 10% in small stocks; 10% in foreign stocks; 15% in long-term bonds; 15% in cash; and 15% in inflation hedges, which may include additional blue-chip stocks. Say, however, that you've decided you want to minimize your risks by emphasizing income. What should you do? These four rules will help you achieve the optimum mix of low risk and high return:

■ **Keep a sizable chunk of your assets in stocks at all times.** The broadly diversified portfolio I described above could have as much as 70% in stocks (including inflation hedges). Retirees and very conservative investors can trim that percentage a bit but should still rely heavily on equities. Some experts suggest this formula: Subtract your age from 100 to find the minimum percentage you should have in stocks. In other words, at age 40 you should have at least 60% in equities; at 50, 50%; at 65, 35%; and at 75, 25%. Others say you should never go below 50%, no matter how old you are.

I tend to favor the maximum stock point of view, but to some extent it depends on how much money you have. If you retire with only a couple of hundred thousand dollars in your 401(k) and taxable brokerage accounts, you may decide to spend it all and not leave anything to your heirs. Further, since your means are limited, you may not want to take any risks with it. In that case it makes sense to shift money steadily out of stocks and into bonds as you age so that you are sure of meeting your financial plan.

By contrast, imagine that you retired with a million dollars. You might want to leave as much money as possible for your estate. And you might be able to live very comfortably with a $50,000 annual return from your investments. After all, you would probably have some pension and Social Security income; also, you would know that you could always dip into your principal in an emergency. To earn your $50,000 annual income, all you would need would be a 5% yield on your portfolio. That means you could keep 75% of your money in stocks, no matter how old you were, and still meet that 5% target, as long as the rest of your money was invested in higher-yielding assets. This strategy could also be tremendously advantageous from the point of view of estate taxes. If you could meet your income needs by investing largely in stocks and living off the dividends, you might never have to sell and pay capital-gains taxes on the price appreciation of your portfolio. Reason: Stocks in your estate are subject only to estate taxes, not to income taxes on unrealized capital gains.

■ **Include some high-growth issues in even the most conservative portfolio.** You may agree that it makes sense to keep as much of your money as possible in stocks, but your instinct may be to shy away from growth stocks, small-company shares, and foreign issues. That would be a big mistake. You balance your portfolio principally by adjusting the asset mix, not by purchasing only stodgy investments. With proper selection, you can keep, say, 10% in big growth stocks, 10% in small companies, and 10% in foreign blue chips, no matter what your overall portfolio objectives are.

Think about it. Even if you follow the formula of subtracting your age from 100 to decide how much to keep in equities, you'd still want to have 30% of your money in stocks at age 70. In fact, you're likely to hold at least some stocks for the foreseeable future, no matter what your age. Since the time horizon for the part of your portfolio that is in equities is longer than 10 years, you should put that money in stocks with the highest growth rates. They're the ones likely to offer the best long-term returns even if they are volatile in the short run.

■ **Wherever possible, replace your current stock holdings with similar but higher-yielding issues.** If you do keep a big chunk of your money in stocks, but feel uncomfortable putting all of it in volatile high-growth issues, here's a simple way to bring down the risk of your portfolio. Stick with the asset-allocation percentages you want to have, but replace high-flying stocks with similar but more conservative issues. For example, sell Pfizer, a dynamic drug stock with a yield of only 1.7%, and replace it with Bristol-Myers Squibb, a more defensive drug, health, and beauty-aids stock that carries a 3.5% yield. Similarly, swap Apache, a leading oil-exploration play that pays only a 0.9%

yield but would profit tremendously from an upturn in the price of crude oil, for Exxon, the largest U.S. oil company, whose shares pay 3.7%. The crucial thing in any such swap is to make sure that you maintain a broadly diversified mix of industries in your portfolio, even if you decide to switch to less volatile stocks.

■ **Be sure to choose securities from groups that balance each other.** The most serious mistake you can make is to load up your portfolio with high-yielding issues that would all be affected in the same way by changes in interest rates, inflation, or economic growth. For example, if you own only bonds and electric utilities, such shares will all be hurt by rising inflation and interest rates. To balance them, you'd be smart to put a good-size chunk of your money into stocks that would benefit from an uptick in inflation—for example, mining, oil, and forest products shares or real estate investment trusts. It also would be a mistake to put all your money in highly cyclical stocks (in other words, those whose prices rise and fall sharply with changes in economic growth). To reduce the volatility of cyclical stocks, you should combine them with shares of companies whose businesses will do well in any economy. Example: Sara Lee, which in addition to baked goods sells consumer products such as Hanes hosiery. Don't worry that the stock yields only 2.4%. In a well-balanced income portfolio, not every stock has to be a high yielder.

WHAT YOU REALLY NEED TO KNOW ABOUT BONDS

Frankly, I don't think you need to know an enormous amount about bonds. In fact, I don't think bonds are terribly good investments. Nonetheless, you can't ignore them completely. They play an important role in a well-balanced portfolio. So here's a fast rundown on how they work.

The basic problem with bonds is that they aren't dynamic

investments. When you buy stock in a company you're buying a piece of a business. You're playing the part of an entrepreneur— making bold judgments about the likely success of the corporation. And then you're putting your money at risk. It's an Errol Flynn kind of thing. By contrast, when you buy a bond, you're lending money. It doesn't really matter to you what the company does or how well they do it. All you care about is that they pay their debts. In short, you're a banker, like Mr. Mooney in *The Lucy Show.*

The return potential for stocks and bonds reflects this difference. Several times in this book I've cited the statistics that stocks provide an average total return (including dividends) of 10% to 11% a year. By comparison, top-quality bonds have historically returned only 5% to 8%. As a general rule, long-term Treasury issues return 2% to 3% more than inflation. Currently, for example, inflation is running between 3% and 4%, while bonds are yielding around 6%.

It may seem strange at first glance that bonds return so much less over time than stocks, expecially since their yields look so much higher. The explanation for bonds' unimpressive relative performance is that they don't grow; as a result, they can't keep up with inflation.

TRUE FACT

The bond with the longest maturity is a tax-exempt New York City issue that comes due in the year 2147. By the time it matures, 4% inflation would erode the value of a dollar of principal to less than a penny.

Source: Grant's Municipal Bond Observer

Say, for example, you buy a 20-year bond that yields 6% and a stock that pays 3% but has earnings that are growing 9% a year.

Assuming that the stock's dividends rise roughly in line with earnings increases, after 10 years its yield will be 7.1% of the price you originally paid, while the bond will still be paying out 6%. That means that for the second 10 years of the bond's life, the stock will actually be paying more. And that's not even counting any capital gains you might earn from the stock's price appreciation. This dismal lack of growth is the reason bonds are dangerous investments for retirees.

I realize I'm making bonds sound so bad that you may be asking yourself why it ever makes sense to buy them. Well, actually there are several reasons. The most important is that a chunk of high-quality, long-term bonds adds ballast to a portfolio. Over the course of a business cycle stocks and bonds rise and fall at different times, so mixing them together will reduce the volatility of a portfolio no matter what the economy does. Further, in certain circumstances bonds can be attractive for other reasons:

■ **Adding bonds to a portfolio will pull up your average yield.** Say you want your portfolio to have an average yield of at least 4%. Then you spot some fantastic growth stocks. The catch is that their yields are only around 2%. What do you do? Do you pass them by because they will pull your average yield down too much? Well, one solution would be to buy some high-quality corporate bonds or bond funds paying 8%. For every $1 you put in such bonds, you could spend $2 on growth stocks and still maintain an average yield of 4%.

■ **Long-term bonds and zero-coupon issues are attractive at certain points in the economic cycle.** Whatever their problems over long stretches of time, bonds are compelling buys at certain points in an economic cycle. The basic principle here is that bond prices rise when interest rates fall (and vice versa); and the longer the term until the bond matures, the more the price will swing. Rates typically peak late in an economic expansion and can then decline sharply after a recession finally begins.

Investors who buy long-term bonds at a rate peak can earn

25% to 35% (counting both interest and price gains) over the following two or three years. There's also a special type of bond—known as a zero-coupon issue because it pays no cash interest—that can be an even bigger bonanza when rates fall. Just like the more familiar U.S. savings bond, zero-coupons are sold at a discount to face value. Their terms make these issues especially sensitive to rate changes. For example, if long-term interest rates fall by one percentage point over the next three years, 30-year Treasury zeros would gain a stunning 50%.

■ **Junk bonds are good buys in recessions.** Normally, when investors consider bonds, they think about supersafe Treasuries and high-quality corporate issues. But junk bonds—which are at the other end of the quality scale—are sometimes appealing for very different reasons. The theory behind junk bonds is that companies of less than investment-grade quality can raise money in the bond market more cheaply than they can borrow from banks. By cutting out the corporate bankers, these companies can afford to pay relatively generous yields on their bonds, so in theory everyone comes out ahead. For example, when Treasury bonds are yielding 6%, a junk-rated borrower might be able to sell bonds with a 9% yield. Investors who bought an assortment of these bonds would recognize that a few issuers might default, but even after subtracting two points or so to cover defaults, an index of junk bonds would return 7%—still a point more than Treasuries.

This theory is great—and it's well supported by academic studies. There are just two catches. First, it's true only if you own a wide variety of bonds, so that you are playing the averages. If you own only five bonds, for instance, and one of them gets into trouble, you could take a big loss. Second, the prices of junk bonds move up and down with the economy. Investors bid the prices up when business is good and dump bonds when a weak economy increases the likelihood of a default. In this sense, junk bonds are more like stocks than bonds—their prices rally when corporate profits improve.

Investors who want to add some high-yielding junk bonds to their portfolio should be sure to follow these three rules:

1. Never put more than 10% of your money in junk.

2. Buy through a mutual fund to assure that you own a large enough assortment of bonds that have been checked out by analysts.

3. Buy in a recession, when junk bond prices are likely to be depressed, and plan to hold for two or three years into the recovery.

■ **Take a look at tax-exempt bonds if you are in a top tax bracket.** Interest on state and municipal bonds is generally exempt from federal income tax—and also from state and local taxes if you live in the state where the bond was issued. That means if you are in a high tax bracket, the yield on munis may be more attractive than what you would keep after taxes from the interest on a regular bond. For instance, if Treasury bonds are yielding 6% and munis are paying 5.4%, an investor in the 31% tax bracket would come out ahead with the munis. Reason: After federal income tax, the 6% Treasury yield would be worth only 4.1%, more than a percentage point below the muni yield. To top a 5.4% tax-exempt yield for a bondholder in the 31% bracket, a taxable bond would have to pay 7.8% (this figure is known as the **taxable equivalent yield**).

Munis have a few drawbacks: most of them don't trade actively, so you can't always get a good price when you buy or sell; some of them aren't of good credit quality, so you need expert advice on selecting bonds; and issues with maturities of less than 10 years are often sparse, so you may have to tie up your money for 20 years or more. That, in turn, means that you run head-on into the fundamental problem of all long-term bonds—you face more than a decade of inflation with no corresponding increase in the payout you receive. Still, conservative investors in high tax brackets may be better off buying munis than taxables for the portion of their portfolio that they need to put in long-term bonds.

WHAT MAKES AN INCOME STOCK ATTRACTIVE

As you've probably gathered, I think that you should rely chiefly on stocks for income once you've put the minimum amount of money that your asset-allocation strategy calls for into bonds, CDs, and money funds. How do you go about choosing an income stock, and what are the signs that a particular issue is attractive? Obviously, a big dividend counts for something, and you also want to be sure that the company is strong financially. But there's more than that to making the right choice. Before we get to the specifics of company analysis, let's first consider three different ways of looking at income stocks. One is to choose shares with high, safe yields. Another is to favor stocks that offer the fastest-growing dividends. The third is to select stocks with prices that are cheap relative to the dividends they pay.

The simplest approach is to pick shares with yields of 5% or more that are financially strong. These stocks may not have a big potential for price gains, but even if their earnings move up at only a 5% or 6% annual rate, you'll do well. Over time, the company will likely increase its dividend in line with profits, so the payout you receive will stay ahead of inflation. Further, the share price will roughly track earnings growth over stretches of five years or more. So you'll enjoy some capital gains as well as dividend income.

Let's see how the numbers work out in a specific case. Say a company's shares sell for $18 and pay a $1 dividend. That would give you a yield of nearly 5.6% ($1 divided by $18). If the company's profits ratchet up 5% to 6% a year and the firm raises dividends as earnings grow, then after five years the dividend would be about $1.30. That means your yield based on the price you originally paid for the stock would be 7.2% (analysts call this the **yield on cost,** as opposed to the stock's current yield based on the current share price). Further, if the stock price had risen in line with profits (in other words, if the P/E ratio had remained constant), you would also have a 30% capital gain on your shares. The rising yield on cost and the possibility of handsome capital gains more than make up for the slight reduction in yield you get from buying an income stock instead of a bond.

This line of thinking quickly leads to the second income stock strategy. If dividend increases make stocks better than bonds, then wouldn't stocks with the fastest-growing dividends be the best choices? Some analysts would say yes. After all, which would you rather own, a stock with a 5% dividend growing 6% a year or a stock paying 3% but growing 10% annually? Actually, it's a close call. Because of faster earnings and dividend growth, the payout on today's 3% yielder will have caught up with the 5% stock after 13 years.

To gauge such situations, in which there's a trade-off between yield today and growth that will produce a better yield in the future, analysts have devised the concept of **total return** (we've already used this measure earlier in the chapter). The idea is to find a simple way to combine the attraction of a stock's current dividend with the likely advantages resulting from its future growth. Fortunately there's a simple way to estimate a stock's projected total return.

Since a stock's price is likely to follow its earnings growth, you can quickly estimate a stock's total return by adding its current yield to its projected earnings growth rate. For example, an electric utility with a 6% yield and projected earnings growth of 3.5% a year would have a 9.5% projected annual total return. And a soft drink company with a 2% yield and a 12% growth rate would have a 14% annual total return.

Of course, a stock's return in any particular year will depend almost entirely on short-term fluctuations in its share price; if the overall market drops 20%, almost all stocks will fall, overwhelming whatever yield or earnings growth they may have. Projected total return, therefore, is only a guide to what a company's shares might return over five or 10 or 20 years. Nonetheless, the number does give you a handy way to compare stocks with different growth rates.

The most sophisticated way of evaluating income stocks is known as **relative dividend yield.** This method not only allows you to find shares with attractive current yields and the best growth rates, but also helps you pick out stocks that are underpriced. The mathematics of relative dividend yield get a little difficult to follow, so let me give you the basic idea in words first. A stock is a buy when its dividend yield is higher than it normally would be—and that's doubly true if the yield premium for that particular stock is higher than the premium for the market as a whole.

Let's take a concrete example. Say that over the past 20 years, one of the major oil stocks has yielded between 3.9% and 5.4%. If it yields only 4.1% today (just a little above its 3.9% low), maybe it's not such a great bargain; but if it pays 5.2% (close to the top of its range), then maybe it is.

That's the basic idea, anyway. For each stock (usually a well-established blue chip), you figure out the range of yields it has had over the past 10 or 20 years. Then you compare today's yield to that range. By definition, when a stock's yield is lower than usual, its share price is expensive; and when the yield is high, its price is cheap.

This is a terrifically shrewd way to size up stocks and is used by a lot of analysts. It has also been popularized by Geraldine Weiss; for a sample of her newsletter, *Investment Quality Trends,* call 619-459-3818. However, there are two possible weaknesses to this approach. First, there's always a danger that a stock's dividend yield is high because the company's business prospects have deteriorated and investors are not willing to pay as much for the shares as they used to. In short, the stock could be cheap for a reason.

The second problem is that the overall market might be very cheap or very expensive, making any individual stock's yield a bit misleading. At the moment, for example, the average blue chip is yielding less than 2.5%, the lowest this figure normally goes. That's a sign that the market as a whole is extremely expensive. In this market, a stock with a yield a bit below the middle of its historical range would actually be quite cheap relative to the overall market. So always remember to take the general level of dividend yields into account.

HOW TO SIZE UP AN INCOME STOCK

As the previous section explains, the basic goal of an income investor is to find a stock with four characteristics: an above average yield; an attractive, predictable growth rate; solid financials; and a cheap share price. That combination gets you the best of all possible investments—you enjoy safe income that rises faster than inflation and also have a strong chance for capital gains.

Of course, analyzing any stock can be complicated, but the essentials of income stock analysis are actually remarkably simple. In fact, income stocks are a lot less tricky to assess than the growth stocks we talked about in Chapter 5. Even more important, if you understand the basics of sizing up an income stock, you'll be far better prepared to understand brokerage reports, newsletters, and other research sources that advise you on how to invest for income. So here's a quick rundown on each of the four essential characteristics for an income stock:

■ **An above average yield.** Over the past 70 years the average blue-chip stock has paid a 4.2% yield. So on the most simplistic level, that's the number a stock's yield has to top for it to qualify as an income investment. Below that benchmark, you're buying growth and income shares, and when you get down to a 2.5% yield or less—a level that implies almost all of a stock's future returns will come from capital gains—you're in growth stock territory.

That's sure an easy formula, but it does have one weakness. It assumes that the overall stock market is close to a normal valuation. That assumption is especially problematic right now, since share prices are high enough to induce nosebleeds, which means that stock yields are unusually low. In fact, since World War II, average blue-chip yields have ranged from a high of more than 6% in extremely depressed markets to less than 2.5%—which is where they are now.

It's not surprising that the number of attractive income stocks would dwindle when the overall market is exceptionally pricey.

One of the hallmarks of an overvalued market is that there are few things left you'd want to buy. Nonetheless, if you want to stay fully invested according to your asset-allocation plans in all markets, you have to shade your yield cutoff a little bit when average market yields are down. In today's high-flying market, you could reasonably consider any issue paying 3.5% or more to qualify as an income investment.

■ **An attractive, predictable growth rate.** The signs of reliable growth prospects are not that different for an income stock than for a growth stock. Clearly, an income investor can't expect as high a rate of earnings gains as a growth investor would, but any shares you buy for income should meet tests for sustainable growth similar to those I outlined in Chapter 5. Since I don't want to repeat that whole section here, I'll just summarize it in a couple of paragraphs.

For starters, while you don't need way above average profitability to fund an income stock's growth, you certainly need a double-digit return on equity. At a minimum, you want your income shares to deliver a 10% total return—combining a 5% yield and 5% annual earnings growth. To finance that, the company needs an ROE higher than 10%. Next, the business must have room for more revenue increases than just those resulting from price hikes and inflation. In particular, you don't want to be in an industry that is about to go through a shakeout because of earlier overexpansion. Third, the company must be on a sound financial footing, which I'll discuss at greater length in a minute. Finally, the firm should have some sort of advantage over its rivals—at least to the extent that it is not likely to face price-cutting competition that would undercut its slow but steady expansion.

There's one other wrinkle to consider. As an income investor, you're more interested in dividend growth than profit growth. The more a company earns, of course, the more it can afford to pay out in dividends. But if current dividends already eat up a big part of a company's annual profits, the firm won't be able to raise its payout very easily. And if earnings drop even temporarily, the company might feel obligated to cut its dividend to conserve cash. To gauge these risks, analysts use a measure called the **payout ratio**, calculated by dividing dividends by earnings. For example, a firm that earned $4 a share and paid a $1 dividend would have a 25% payout ratio, while a company that paid the same $1 dividend but earned only $2 a share would have a 50% payout ratio.

As a general rule, the lower the payout ratio the better. But that figure is meaningful only if you are comparing it to payout ratios for other companies in the same industry with similar current yields. As you may remember from Chapter 5, the profits that aren't paid out as dividends are called retained earnings and are used to finance future expansion. Therefore, the higher a company's yield and the lower its projected growth rate, the higher a payout ratio it can afford. The easiest way to check that a stock you're interested in doesn't have a payout ratio that's disturbingly high is to consult *The Value Line Investment Survey,* which summarizes average statistics for each stock group in a table at the beginning of each section (Value Line calls the payout ratio "% all dividends to net profit"). Just as points of comparison, here are typical payout ratios for half a dozen industries: electric utilities, 75%–80%; major oils 60%–75%; big drug stocks, 45%–60%; brand-name food producers, 40%–50%; major retailers, 30%–40%; leading computer makers, 20% or less. In any group, small, fast-growing companies will likely have lower payout ratios than large, established firms.

■ **Solid financials.** Income investors are typically even more concerned about a company's financial strength than growth investors are. That's easy enough to understand. The whole point of income investing is that you give up some of your potential upside in exchange for a more predictable return. That means, in turn, that you'll be less willing to take any risks on a company with a shaky financial structure.

TRUE FACT

After a firm omits a dividend, its shares can lag the market for as long as three years and underperform by as much as 15 percentage points.

Source: Roni Michaely, Richard Thaler, and Kent Womack, *The Journal of Finance*, June 1995

The first thing to look at is how much debt a company has. Companies whose debt is less than 15% or 20% of their total capital (long-term debt plus equity) are golden. When debt is more than 50% of capital (that is, when debt is greater than equity) you should check out the firm more carefully. Companies supported by extremely high debt levels—say, 75% or more—deserve strict scrutiny.

There are, however, a couple of exceptions you should be aware of. First, the more predictable a company's earnings, the more debt it can safely carry. For example, electric utilities regularly have debt ratios above 50% because they are slow-growing businesses and have always had extremely stable sales. For such firms, high debt isn't necessarily a problem. As with the payout ratio, you can judge a firm's debt ratio only in relation to the range for its industry.

Debt ratios can also be misleading if a firm has undergone some major financial restructuring in the past few years. In particular, repurchases of stock and acquisitions of other firms can produce an extremely distorted debt ratio. For example, imagine that a firm was financed entirely with equity 50 years ago. Since then it has grown in value enormously. Now the management decides to buy back half the stock with borrowed money. Since the stock price is far higher than the amount of equity originally invested, the company will have to take on debt that is much greater than the equity remaining on its books, but it will still be able to pay the interest on the debt without a problem. In this case the company may have only a 50% debt ratio based on the *market value* of its stock, but it will have a far higher debt ratio based on the *historical price* that is carried on its books.

Book figures can also be distorted by mergers and acquisitions. When one company takes over another, it may have to charge off various costs to comply with U.S. accounting rules. Such charges, which may not actually require an outlay of cash, can reduce either the company's equity or its reported earnings. In such cases an analyst must adjust those numbers to make them comparable to those of other companies in the same industry.

Analysts checking a company's financials look at a few other things as well. They note the amount of cash and other current assets the firm has on hand to make sure it can pay its bills on time (the actual measures analysts examine are known as **working capital** and the **current ratio**). They make sure the company's profit margins are not deteriorating because costs are rising faster than earnings, and they determine that the firm isn't building up a bigger and bigger inventory of products, because that may be a sign that sales are lagging. This kind of financial analysis is fairly mundane, and you don't actually need to do it yourself. Instead you can simply check the stock's financial rating in reference sources such as Standard & Poor's *Stock Guide* and *The Value Line Investment Survey.*

■ **A cheap share price.** Everybody loves a bargain, income investors as much as growth investors. But while growth investors generally evaluate a stock based on the relationship between its P/E and its growth rate, income investors have to use other comparisons. Reason: Income stocks rarely have rapid enough profit growth to justify an above average P/E. As a result, buyers of income stocks usually compare the shares' valuations with those for their industries and for the overall market.

The good news is that any stock that has a fairly high yield is probably cheap to begin with. Since yield is a stock's dividend divided by its price, the lower the price goes, the higher the yield will be. A little arithmetic will confirm that income stocks are likely to be cheap. Say a company pays out half of its earnings as dividends and its shares carry a 4.2% dividend yield. That means that its annual earnings per share must be 8.4% of its price (analysts call this the stock's **earnings yield**). To get the P/E, you have to divide the earnings yield into 100%, or 1.00. And 1.00 divided by 8.4%, or .084, equals 11.9.

Does that mean every high-yield stock is automatically a bargain? Of course not. It means that you have to consider the company's financial strength and growth prospects to figure out whether it's worth buying. The best way to do that is to compare the stock's yield and other ratios with what they have been for that stock in the past. Then take into account the current state of the market—if it's very high, for example, you would accept a slightly lower yield on an income stock. Finally, look to see if the company's business outlook is better or worse than it has been in the past.

Let's try to apply this to a specific case. Imagine that a particular company's shares have yielded between 3.5% and 5% over the past 20 years. Currently the stock is paying 4.2%, about the middle of its historical range. That's not so bad, considering that the overall market is high and dividend yields are generally low. The outlook for the company's industry has been depressed over the past few years but is now improving slightly. The firm's particular business prospects are solid, with 8% projected growth, and its balance sheet is strong. Those characteristics sound as though the stock has the makings of a good income investment. In fact, that profile would have applied to any one of several of the slower-growing drug and health care companies before the most recent runup in their share prices.

If you want to reduce income investing to the simplest terms possible, it boils down to this: You want to find a stock with a high yield and a growth rate that will beat inflation. You want to be sure that the yield and the growth rate, added together, give you a total return greater than 10%. Then you want to check the company's business outlook and financials to make sure nothing will go wrong.

Chapter 8

INCOME STOCK ROUNDUP:

Here Are 26 Stocks Worth Taking a Look at for Your Income Portfolio

Let me start with the same caveat I mentioned at the beginning of Chapter 6. No book can responsibly recommend individual stocks for you to buy. The market changes from day to day, and I'm writing this chapter months before you'll have a chance to read it. Nonetheless, certain industry groups tend to include attractive, high-yielding shares, and the same top-quality stocks turn up over and over again on analysts' buy lists.

As I explained in the previous chapter, shares that qualify as income investments pay a large part of their total return in the form of dividends. They therefore have somewhat limited capital-gains potential. Shares with these characteristics often fall into one of three categories: utilities, natural resources, or real estate.

By definition, a **utility** is a business that provides relatively inexpensive but essential goods or services, usually in a specific geographical area. Customers have to buy what these companies sell, and prices aren't high enough to attract a lot of competitors. Such businesses—which include electricity, natural gas, water, and local telephone service—are called natural monopolies by

VITAL STATISTICS ON 26 INCOME STOCKS

This table shows the dividend yield for 26 high-quality income stocks. Those that currently pay less than 4% are likely to top that mark at some point during the stock market cycle. As a general rule, you can get a rough indication of a stock's likely long-term total return by adding its yield and its earnings growth rate. However, the growth rates of a few companies—such as Du Pont, Phelps Dodge, and Weyerhaeuser—may be inflated because their profits have been depressed at some point during the past six years. In any case, it's more important to select a well-diversified assortment of stocks from varied industries than to focus on those with the highest projected numbers. Estimated revenues and growth rates are projections by *The Value Line Investment Survey.*

Company	Ticker Symbol	Est. 1995 Revenues (in millions)	Recent Price	Dividend Yield	Projected Earnings Growth Rate
American Brands	AMB	$11,550	$44	4.5%	3.0%
American Home Products	AHP	13,550	97	3.2	8.5
American Water Works	AWK	800	39	3.3	5.0
BellSouth	BLS	17,775	43	3.3	8.5
Bristol-Myers Squibb	BMY	13,670	86	3.5	8.0
Brooklyn Union Gas	BU	1,216	29	4.9	5.5
Chevron	CHV	32,000	52	3.8	8.0
Cilcorp	CER	610	42	5.8	5.5
Consolidated Natural Gas	CNG	3,580	45	4.3	9.0
Duke Power	DUK	4,450	47	4.3	4.5
Dun & Bradstreet	DNB	5,375	65	4.1	9.0
Du Pont	DD	41,750	70	3.0	17.0
Exxon	XON	111,000	80	3.7	10.5
J. P. Morgan	JPM	167,500*	80	4.0	6.0
New Plan Realty Trust	NPR	765*	22	6.3	N.A.
Nipsco Industries	NI	1,715	38	4.4	9.0
Northern States Power	NSP	2,500	49	5.5	7.5
PacifiCorp	PPW	3,390	21	5.1	7.5
Peoples Energy	PGL	1,033	32	5.7	3.0
Phelps Dodge	PD	4,175	62	2.9	18.0
Philip Morris	MO	66,850	90	4.4	13.5
SBC Communications	SBC	12,500	57	2.9	11.0
Teco Energy	TE	1,425	25	4.1	6.0
UST	UST	1,320	33	4.4	13.5
Washington REIT	WRE	220*	16	6.3	N.A.
Weyerhaeuser	WY	11,970	43	3.7	19.0

All data are as of Jan. 1, 1996. *indicates total assets rather than revenues. N.A.—not available.

146

economists. They are often regulated by the government, and their growth is typically slow but steady.

Shares of **natural resources** companies—including oil, mining, forest products, and chemical firms—are generally slow growing and pay moderately high yields. In addition, these stocks are highly cyclical—that is, they track the ups and downs of the economy. As a result, their prices can be deeply depressed right before or during a recession. At such times the stocks' yields can be high enough to make them appealing as income investments. Further, when their yields are above 4%, financially strong natural resources shares are often good buys for future capital gains as well.

Many **real estate investments** offer the combination of generous yields and long-term capital-gains potential adequate to outpace inflation. Example: A company that buys a suburban shopping center with little mortgage debt can offer investors regular cash payments out of the rents it collects from shops; presumably, over time, the shopping center's value will increase. Most such investments are organized as limited partnerships and are therefore outside the scope of this book. But some are set up as investment trusts, a form that is similar to a stock.

Besides these three groups, various other industries include shares that offer similar combinations of slow to moderate growth and yields that sometimes reach high levels. Among them: business services, financial services, health care products, and tobacco. In the rest of this chapter I briefly profile 11 industries and identify a total of 26 stocks that income investors may want to consider. Most of these stocks yield more than 4%, and all have topped the 4% mark at some point during the last business cycle. I've also favored very large companies with extremely solid balance sheets. One other note: I've confined my picks to U.S. companies because foreign firms often have to withhold taxes on dividends paid to U.S. investors. Although you can take a credit for that withholding on your income tax, it's an awful nuisance. And while you might be willing to ignore the tax on a foreign growth stock that pays low dividends, on an income investment it's a major disadvantage.

As a further disclaimer, I'll add that any list like this is necessarily arbitrary. Don't assume that stocks I haven't mentioned are automatically inferior to those I have. At any given time, many of the stocks I talk about in this chapter will be attractive buys; but some won't be timely. So you'll still have to check out these stocks before you buy. All 26, however, are well worth a look.

BUSINESS SERVICES
(Dun & Bradstreet)

Have you ever applied for a credit card or a mortgage and received a copy of your credit history from TRW, for example? Well, Dun & Bradstreet provides a similar service, except that it compiles credit reports on businesses rather than consumers. The company also sells financial reports through its Moody's division, calculates the Nielsen ratings for television, and publishes Yellow Pages directories for phone companies. All of these businesses have had their ups and downs over the past decade, but the firm is rock solid with virtually no debt.

In January 1996, Dun & Bradstreet announced its intention to break up into three separate companies. One will supply research to broadcasters and health care companies; another will sell company credit information; the third will provide sales data to makers of consumer goods. Some other small businesses would be sold. Analysts generally expect the breakup to boost the share price.

CHEMICALS, FOREST PRODUCTS, AND MINING
(Du Pont, Phelps Dodge, Weyerhaeuser)

Aside from oil and gas, which I'll discuss separately, the important natural resources companies include chemicals, forest products, and mining. As I mentioned earlier, the shares closely track the economy. Reason: These firms all have enormous overhead, and the prices of their products depend largely on the level of economic activity. So when business is sluggish they make relatively little money; but when shortages start to develop, they can jack up prices and make a fortune. Because of this cyclicality, natural resources shares are cheap enough to be attractive as income investments only right before or during a recession. But then they can be terrific buys.

Among chemical companies, Du Pont is the 800-pound gorilla. The best-known forest products companies, such as International Paper, never get up to yields that qualify them as real income investments. However, Weyerhaeuser sometimes noses past our yield cutoff. The most promising mining company for income investors is Phelps Dodge, a leader in copper. When you see the yields on these shares top 4%, you've got to love 'em. They offer the best inflation protection of any stock group with the possible exception of real estate. Remember, in the overall asset-allocation plan you should be following, there's a category for inflation hedges. These are the kinds of stocks you plug into that slot.

ELECTRIC UTILITIES
(Cilcorp, Duke Power, Nipsco, Northern States Power, PacifiCorp, Teco Energy)

At the top of the list of traditional income investments, electric utilities have long combined high yields ranging from 4% to 7% with predictable growth. Recently, however, the industry has begun to change. New legislation is increasingly allowing electric companies to sell power outside of their own local territories. This so-called power wheeling means that an electric company with surplus energy and low generating costs can sell electricity into the power grid of a neighboring utility. For example, Oregon's PacifiCorp could provide power to areas of California where local costs are higher.

Although the new rules for utilities create great opportunities for the most efficient companies, they will make it more difficult for small investors to pick the best stocks. Formerly you couldn't go too far wrong by choosing any company with a high financial rating. In the future, though, utility investors will also have to assess companies' competitiveness to determine which firms will lose ground and which will post above average growth rates.

Further, it's hard for me to suggest specific companies right now, because the rules are still changing. When it comes time for you to buy your stocks, you should try to get investment research from two or three different sources and look for electric companies that are recommended by more than one firm. Stocks that currently appear to be attractive include Cilcorp, which serves Peoria, Springfield, and central Illinois; Duke Power, operating in the Carolinas; Nipsco, supplying electricity in northern Indiana; Northern States Power, chiefly in Minnesota and Wisconsin; PacifiCorp, serving 11 western states; and Teco Energy, the holding company of Tampa Electric.

FINANCIAL SERVICES
(J. P. Morgan)

Many small banks and other financial-services companies are attractive for income investors. But only one meets all my tests for size, financial strength, and yield—and that's J. P. Morgan. The company is the highest-quality U.S. bank focusing chiefly on the needs of corporate customers. Traditionally, Morgan has profited from its top-notch credit rating and its emphasis on so-called relationship banking (developing long-term relationships with top corporate managements).

Two other strategies, however, will help the bank expand over the next 10 years. First, under U.S. law, corporate lending has long been separated from underwriting and other investment banking. Now, though, those legal barriers are being removed, and firms such as Morgan are increasingly able to provide a hybrid service known as merchant banking. Second, the firm has been one of the most energetic banks in expanding overseas. The ultimate result: J. P. Morgan eventually will be able to address all the banking needs of corporate clients anywhere in the world. In addition to its long-term growth prospects, the stock has yielded more than 4% in five of the past eight years.

HEALTH CARE
(American Home Products, Bristol-Myers Squibb)

Until the end of 1991, pharmaceutical and health care stocks were investor favorites, trading at price/earnings as high as 22 and offering relatively low yields. Then the prospect of the Clinton health care plan, which was expected to limit drugmakers' profits, made investors turn sour on the industry. Since then the Clinton plan has collapsed, and companies have begun to reorient themselves for a more cost-conscious environment. The result: It is now possible to find health care stocks that are fairly cheap and offer surprisingly high yields. Most important, their growth prospects look better than they have in almost five years.

One of the highest-yielding stocks in the group is Bristol-Myers Squibb, which manufactures an assortment of health and beauty aids as well as pharmaceuticals. The company's lineup of new drugs is generally considered less impressive than that of many competitors. Nonetheless, for an income stock Bristol-Myers Squibb has fairly good growth prospects. The shares have paid more than 4% during much of the past three years.

American Home Products also sells both pharmaceuticals and more mundane health care products. The company has a higher projected growth rate than Bristol-Myers Squibb, and the shares accordingly offer a slightly lower yield.

NATURAL GAS
(Brooklyn Union Gas, Consolidated Natural Gas, Peoples Energy)

The natural gas industry has never been dominated by large, fully integrated companies to the extent the oil industry is. Frequently, separate firms handle production, transportation, and local distribution. For all practical purposes, investors who want to focus specifically on natural gas have two choices—interstate pipelines, which carry gas cross-country and may also have some production facilities of their own, and local distribution companies, which bring gas into customers' houses.

Most independent gas producers and interstate pipeline companies don't offer yields high enough to meet the cutoff for income investors. The one exception, which combines a fat yield and excellent financials, is Consolidated Natural Gas, a major pipeline company that has sizable gas reserves and also owns several local distributors.

As a rule, though, the big yields in the gas industry are offered by local distributors, which are classic utilities. These distributors are usually government regulated and have fairly modest growth prospects. But they can pay anywhere from 4.5% to more than 6%. Top-quality examples include Brooklyn Union Gas, which provides gas in the New York City boroughs of Brooklyn and Queens, and Peoples Energy, serving Chicago and nearby communities.

OIL
(Exxon, Chevron)

International oil companies are at the top of my list of compelling income investments right now. For starters, the price of oil has remained in the $15-to-$20-a-barrel range so far in the '90s; that's extremely cheap by historical standards. Further, if inflation does start ramping up at some point, the price of crude oil is likely to rise; that makes oil stocks an inflation hedge. Finally, the leading international oil companies are huge, rich, and extremely powerful.

Exxon, the world's largest publicly traded oil, combines exceptional financial strength with a generous dividend yield. It's a hard company not to like—unless you're a seagull. Chevron also provides an attractive combination of high dividends and financial solidity. However, all of the international oils are appealing. Mobil offers lower yields than Exxon and Chevron do but has excellent growth prospects. British Petroleum and Royal Dutch Petroleum can also be good buys. You should remember, however, that such foreign stocks typically withhold taxes on dividend payments for U.S. investors. You can take a credit on your income tax for such withholding, but it means filling out an extra form. So unless you have so many foreign stocks that you're already planning to claim that credit, it's a lot easier to stick with the U.S.-based internationals.

REAL ESTATE INVESTMENT TRUSTS
(New Plan Realty, Washington REIT)

The theory behind real estate investing is hard to beat. Most physical assets wear out within five or 10 years at the most. But a well-built structure can last for a century. On average, therefore, a building's value is likely to hold up well in real terms—in other words, its dollar price will probably rise at least as fast as inflation. There are exceptions, of course. The oil industry bust in the mid-1980s made it difficult to sell Houston houses that were far from the city center. But since the population keeps rising, any well-located properties are likely to become only more valuable.

Besides being an inflation hedge, real estate investments often benefit from favorable tax treatment. That means they may be able to pay you regular cash distributions that are not taxed as dividend income. Here's why: Tax accounting for real estate allows a number of items to be deducted as expenses even though they don't require an immediate outlay of cash. As a result, a real estate investment may be running a loss from a tax point of view while still generating more cash than it needs for operating purposes. If any of that money is paid to shareholders, it is counted as a return of part of investors' original purchase price (also known as a **return of capital**). As such, it is not taxed until you sell the investment, at which point such accumulated payments are included in your capital-gains calculations. Until then, however, part or all of the distributions you receive may be tax-free.

The only trouble is, real estate investments have to be organized either as partnerships or as trusts to preserve these tax benefits. Real estate limited partnerships are outside the scope of this book; they generally require fairly large investments and can't easily be sold. Real estate investment trusts (REITs), however, trade just like stocks and usually pay high yields—6% to 8% or so.

Among well-seasoned REITs, New Plan Realty has long been an investor favorite. The trust owns suburban shopping centers and some apartment buildings, mostly in the eastern half of the United States. Washington REIT owns office buildings, shopping centers, and some apartment buildings in the greater Washington, D. C., area. This REIT posted excellent gains as the area boomed during the glitzy '80s, but the shares have been depressed during the past couple of years. Perhaps investors fear that with talk of balancing the budget in the air, the federal government will stop expanding. Somehow, I doubt it. I expect

Washington to remain a high-growth area no matter what happens to the federal budget.

TELECOMMUNICATIONS
(BellSouth, SBC Communications)

Until the breakup of the old Bell telephone system on January 1, 1984, telephone stocks were classic utilities. Local monopolies such as those making up AT&T, along with a few other firms such as GTE, provided comprehensive telephone service, largely at government-regulated prices. The 1984 breakup, however, blew the industry wide open. Seven regional Bell companies split off from AT&T. These regional Bells began by providing mostly local service but later diversified into cellular telephone and other high-tech businesses. AT&T kept the long-distance operations, but before long, rivals such as MCI and Sprint started cutting deeply into AT&T's market share.

Most important, the creation of many new forms of telecommunication—including paging, digital cellular, computer networking, and even interactive cable television—has made the industry increasingly growth oriented and competitive. As a result, it has become harder to find uncomplicated high-yielding investments. However, a few of the regional Bell operating companies (known as the RBOCs, pronounced AR-box) qualify as solid income choices and offer growth kickers as well.

SBC Communications, the former Southwestern Bell, gets top marks from analysts because it has diversified the most into high-growth telecommunications, such as wireless and cellular telephone services. In addition, the company owns about 10% of Teléfonos de México, the Mexican telephone giant. Despite the peso crisis and Mexico's wavering fortunes, that investment has been profitable for SBC and offers the potential for substantial future gains. BellSouth, the largest of the regional Bells, operates in the Southeast. The company's basic telephone service is expanding faster than that of the other RBOCs, thanks to booming business conditions. In addition, BellSouth has sizable cellular telephone operations with great long-term potential.

TOBACCO
(American Brands, Philip Morris, UST)

The ultimate low-growth industry is tobacco. Personally, I have to admit that if I found out I had only six months to live, I'd run out and buy three cases of Armagnac and 2,000 Dunhill cigarettes. Still, the fact remains that tobacco is being snuffed out restaurant by restaurant in the United States. Usage in this country will doubtlessly decline sharply over the next couple of generations. The industry has responded to this outlook by cutting back investment and advertising expenses and milking its dying brands for as much cash as possible. Overseas the outlook for tobacco is more promising, but it's probably only a matter of time before even the French decide Jean-Paul Belmondo's Gauloises wasn't really all that sexy.

American Brands sold its U.S. tobacco business in 1994 but remains a major presence in the United Kingdom, so that tobacco still accounts for close to half the company's business. The rest comes from liquor and consumer products. Similarly, Philip Morris earns more than half its money from tobacco and gets most of the rest from processed food. Both these companies have sported yields of around 5% over the past three years. However, growth prospects are still hazy because of their substantial involvements in tobacco.

If you're the sort of person who disapproves of investing in tobacco companies, you'll really detest UST Inc. Apart from selling a little pipe tobacco and wine on the side, the company is the leading maker of so-called smokeless tobacco. The product is especially popular with teenagers and has been accused of causing mouth cancer. This raises the big caveat for tobacco companies—they all have an ongoing risk of becoming targets of litigation because of their past sales.

WATER
(American Water Works)

The one product you can be sure will always be in demand is clean water. I daresay people would give up their telephones, gas heat, and even their electricity before they would let go of indoor plumbing. Moreover, water companies are the most old-fashioned utilities. Electric companies are starting to compete in selling power; some local natural gas distributors are losing business because pipelines are selling gas directly; and local telephone companies are invading each other's territories. But water companies still have their local markets to themselves; that means consumers have only two choices—buy or don't buy.

The flip side of this local control is that though there are more than 59,000 water utilities in the United States, fewer than 20 are publicly traded companies of any size. The vast majority are owned by municipalities or are privately held. That creates a great opportunity for the publicly traded firms. As the costs of managing and upgrading water systems rise, small local companies will likely sell out to one of the big guys.

Without question, the standout water company is American Water Works, which owns more than two dozen local water businesses. Not only is it five times the size of most of its competitors, but it is also the fastest-growing water company because it has long been committed to a policy of aggressively acquiring small water firms nationwide. In general, water companies provide total returns of only 10% or so. But for investors who want a top-quality, old-fashioned utility, American Water Works is an unbeatable choice.

CHAPTER 9

VALUE INVESTING:

How You Can Spot Terrific Bargains
That Other Investors Miss

In some sense, all investing is value investing. By definition, stock pickers are always hunting for shares that are selling for less than their true worth. But when securities analysts talk about value investing, they use the term in a much more specific way: the strategy consists of buying a stock (or some other security) at a price far below what it should sell for based on historical benchmarks. The profits the buyer earns come from the higher price other investors are willing to pay as their assessment of the stock becomes more positive.

This last point is the crucial one—and it's why value investing can be harder than approaches based on earnings growth or dividend income. Instead of trying to predict how much a stock's earnings will rise or what future dividends it will pay, value investors hope to anticipate major changes in the way other investors size up a stock's inherent worth. In short, although value analysts may have to make a lot of calculations, they are trying to predict changes in investor psychology as well as objective results.

Some of the oldest maxims about investing, in fact, are about psychology rather than earnings and dividends. These sayings advise buying stocks that are untimely or otherwise out of favor and then holding them until negative investor psychology turns positive. Example: "Buy straw hats in winter." Panama hats are cheap then, and you can turn around and sell them at higher prices when warm weather comes. "Buy when blood is running in the streets." The greatest bargains abound right after a disaster has struck and investors are panicking. "Buy on the cannon, sell on the trumpets." (This sounds better in the original French.) Not only should you buy when times are bad, you should sell when investor psychology has swung over to excessive optimism. Value investors are often known as **contrarians,** meaning that they frequently invest contrary to prevailing opinion.

The fact that value investing is fundamentally about investors' perceptions rather than stocks' attributes was captured well by the great British economist John Maynard Keynes, who once compared investing to betting on a beauty contest. To win, a bettor shouldn't pick the girl he thinks is most beautiful; he should pick the one he thinks *the judges* will think is most beautiful. Anyone who has ever bet on an office pool for the Academy Awards knows about this. The Oscars for best foreign film and best documentary frequently don't go to the films that most moviegoers would select. To win the pool you have to guess how Academy members will vote—not how they should vote.

We can pin down the difference between value investing and other approaches even better by looking at this essential question: Where will a stock's return come from? A growth stock's price/earnings ratio may never change, and it may pay no yield. But as long as its earnings rise as expected, the shares will appreciate. By contrast, an income stock's P/E may stay constant and its earnings may barely keep up with inflation. But as long as it pays a fat, secure dividend you'll get your expected return.

TRUE FACT

To find a fair P/E ratio for the average blue-chip stock, subtract the inflation rate from 20. Example: With 3% inflation, P/Es below 17 are cheap.

Where do your profits come from on a value stock, though? Essentially they come from a change in the valuation of the shares. In most cases this means an increase in the P/E. An undervalued stock may have flat earnings and a meager dividend, but if its P/E goes from 10 to 12, you will make a 20% profit. Of course, sometimes value investors have to look at measures other than price/earnings ratios to determine that a stock is undervalued. But in general, low P/E investing is another name for value investing.

Looking for untimely or out-of-favor issues; investing contrary to general opinion; buying stocks with low P/Es: all of these descriptions suggest a shrewd, skeptical investor who is willing to buy an undervalued issue and hold on until it pays off. But there's an obvious question here. How can you be sure such an investment ever will pay off? That is, how can you know that an out-of-favor stock will one day become popular or that a low P/E stock will eventually command a higher multiple?

Well, you can't be absolutely sure. Some stocks that are cheap stay cheap, and some that burn investors take years to regain a following. You don't have to be a theologian to know that fallen angels don't always make comebacks. The key to value investing, therefore, consists not only of identifying cheap stocks, but also of gauging whether they are likely to recover. It turns out that the odds are on your side in this task thanks to what statisticians call **regression to the mean.**

You might think that if two unusually tall people marry, their children would be likely to grow even taller than they are. In fact, odds are their children will be shorter than they are—that is, closer to average height. This tendency for traits that depart from the norm to come back toward average levels (also known as mean values by statisticians) works out more often than not.

What that means in stock terms is that if you select a large population of stocks with below average price/earnings ratios, for example, you would expect those P/Es to creep back toward average levels over the space of two or three years. And in fact, that is just what happens.

The tendency for undervalued stocks to regress to mean valuations—that is, to rise to fairer prices—is so clear, in fact, that value stocks outperform growth stocks, on average. A recent study by Prudential Securities shows that since 1976 value stocks have outpaced growth stocks by a number of different measures. Value doesn't come out ahead every year, of course. But over a 20-year period value stocks are clear winners by an average of anywhere from one to three percentage points annually (depending on the specific indexes examined). Even more striking, the value stocks are consistently less risky.

TRUE FACT

When top executives own sizable amounts of stock in their own companies, the shares typically outperform the overall market by as much as four percentage points a year.

Source: Watson Wyatt Worldwide

How can this be possible? I've already said in Chapter 5 that growth stocks are the shares capable of the highest returns. And that's still true. If you buy growth stocks at reasonable prices, you'll make more than you could with any other strategy—*provided you make very few mistakes.* If you can meet that last condition, you'll be the next Warren Buffett or Peter Lynch. But don't bet the ranch. The same regression to the mean principle that makes most undervalued stocks return to fairer prices makes high-flying growth stocks accidents waiting to happen. When a growth stock regresses to the mean, its price/earnings ratio goes from, say, 23 to 17. That would represent a loss of more than 25%.

The bottom line here is that while growth stocks pay off better if you're right, your odds of being right are higher with value stocks. If you're wondering where income stocks fit in, they're closer to value stocks than they are to growth stocks. Income stocks generally have below average P/Es, for example. But true value stocks don't just have low P/Es, they have lower P/Es than they deserve. So even though the odds are that cheap stocks will move toward average prices, you still need to analyze such stocks before you buy them. In some cases they may be cheap for a reason; or they may lack the qualities needed to move back toward a fair price.

WHAT MAKES A DEPRESSED STOCK RECOVER

It's all very well to quote statistics showing that cheap stocks tend to rise to fair valuations. But one question remains: Why does a depressed stock recover? The answer is that when a company's prospects are unfavorable, many investors will simply shun its shares. Then, over time, economic conditions change or the company fixes its problems. Suddenly the stock's outlook is a lot brighter, and analysts start recommending it again. When it comes to investing, most people are sunshine soldiers and fair-weather friends.

You can't be complacent, though, when you're considering buying a depressed issue. Sometimes investments don't recover. Buggy-whip makers never did see business turn up, and anybody who bought gold back in January 1980 for more than $800 an ounce is still under water. So it's vital to analyze depressed shares to make sure that they will indeed bounce back. Remember also that the more specific a company's problems are, the greater the danger it won't rebound. Here's what I mean:

■ **A depressed market always comes back and recovers fairly quickly.** Unless you really believe that the U.S. economy could collapse for good, you know that all recessions must come to an end. In fact, since the Great Depression, recessions have never lasted longer than 18 months. So if you are buying a stock in an industry group that is down and out because of the state of the overall economy, you know that its prospects are bound to improve within a couple of years at the outside.

■ **A depressed industry group always comes back, but there's no telling when.** If an entire industry group is cheap, you can be fairly sure it will recover, but you have no way of knowing how long you'll have to wait. The major oil stocks, for example, haven't done much since the 1990–91 recession. Although they have paid good dividends, their price gains have been quite disappointing because inflation has been low and oil prices have remained below $20 a barrel. That doesn't mean oil stocks are bad investments or that there is any risk the industry will disappear. But there's no knowing how long you'll have to hold them before oil shares boom again.

■ **A depressed stock may recover, but then again it may not.** If a company's low share price is caused not by the overall economy or by the industry's troubles, but by the firm's unique problems, then there's no guarantee it will ever recover. When a biotech company's key drug flops or a computer firm loses vital market share, it may be beyond redemption. Even if a corporate turnaround is possible, it could take a decade or more.

The important fact to remember from this entire discussion is that the more general a company's problem is, the more sure you can be that it is reversible. The more specific the problem, the more you have to worry. Since we're concerned here with stock analysis and we've already discussed the overall market and industry group patterns in Chapter 4, let's look next at how the pros size up a specific stock.

HOW DO YOU KNOW THAT A STOCK IS WORTH MORE?

For a troubled stock to recover, it first has to survive. And the higher a company's financial strength, the more likely it is to bounce back in price. After good finances, size is the most important asset for a value stock. If a company is rich enough and big enough, it can afford to solve its problems, no matter how serious they are. In fact, improving financial strength by itself turns out to enable stocks to beat the overall market, on average, according to one recent study.

This shouldn't come as a complete surprise. The originator of modern securities analysis, Benjamin Graham, always devoted as much attention to a company's balance sheet (the record of its financial strength) as he did to its income statement (the record of its current profits and losses). Many of today's top stock pickers, including Warren Buffett, trace their investing theories back to Graham and have updated his methods in various ways. If you want to take a look at his original ideas, you can consult Graham's book *Security Analysis* (McGraw-Hill)—but it's a hard read. For an interesting and accessible overview of Graham's life as well as his investing ideas, I'd also recommend Janet Lowe's book *Benjamin Graham on Value Investing* (Dearborn Financial Publishing). At the risk of oversimplifying greatly, Graham's stock-picking philosophy can be summarized with these five rules:

■ **Don't pay too much attention to the overall market.** It's easier to find good buys when share prices are generally cheap, but you can still spot a few bargains even when the market is out of sight.

■ **Buy a stock as if you were buying the whole company.** Don't try to make a quick buck on a crummy business. Look for firms so good, you would be willing to own their shares forever.

■ **Look for specific signs of value.** The most attractive stocks have below average price/earnings ratios (less than 16); above average yields (over 3%); and earnings that have doubled over the past 10 years with no more than two annual declines greater than 5%.

■ **Focus on quality.** Especially if you're a beginning investor, you should buy only blue-chip stocks with long records of steadily rising earnings.

■ **Above all, be patient.** The biggest rewards come from hanging on to value stocks for at least three to five years.

One fact about these principles ought to stand out sharply: They put as big an emphasis on a stock's quality as on its cheapness. That's key. You shouldn't confuse value investing with speculating in seriously troubled companies. While there are big profits to be made in the shares of companies that rank below investment grade or are even on the verge of bankruptcy, that's a business best left to the pros. Small investors should bet on the strong.

RULE NO. 8 OF INVESTING: A GOOD STOCK AT A SMALL DISCOUNT IS A BETTER BUY THAN A LOUSY STOCK AT A BIG DISCOUNT.

Of course, much of Graham's analysis involved detailed mathematics that I can't go into in this book. Later in this chapter I'll outline some of the simpler techniques value analysts use to spot cheap shares. First, though, I'll explain one of Graham's most important value investing theories. This approach doesn't apply very well to today's stock market because share prices are currently so high, but it's a perfect jumping-off point for any serious discussion of value investing.

ORIGINAL, OLD-TIME VALUE ANALYSIS

Graham's book *Security Analysis* was first published in 1934, when the stock market Crash of 1929 and the Great Depression were still a reality in every investor's mind. Hard as it may be to believe today, back in the 1930s and 1940s it was considered dangerous for small investors to own most kinds of stocks. At that time, conservative investors bought bonds or shares with such low risk that they were known as widows' and orphans' stocks (because they were issues a trustee or guardian could safely recommend). The big boom in individuals' ownership of common stocks came in the 1950s and 1960s. This rush to equities occurred for three reasons. First, by the late 1950s people were confident that another depression and stock market crash were highly unlikely. Second, it had become evident that blue-chip stocks could outperform bonds. Third, by the late '60s some investors were starting to worry that rising inflation could do even more damage to bonds than to common stocks (they were proved right in the long run).

The upshot of all this history is that when Graham first started analyzing stocks, there were plenty of dirt cheap companies around. Investors back then worried mostly about whether the firms whose shares they bought could possibly go bankrupt if there were another depression. As a result, one of the important forms of stock analysis that Graham developed consisted of calculating what a stock would be worth if the company suddenly had to be liquidated.

Graham began by looking at a company's cash and other assets that could easily be converted into cash. Then he figured how much the firm would have left over if it paid off all its debts. If what was left amounted to more than the share price, someone who bought the stock was virtually buying the company with its own money.

Let's go through those calculations again in greater detail. First look at the company's balance sheet to find the firm's **current assets**—these consist of cash, negotiable securities, receipts payable in less than a year, current inventory, and the like. From this figure, which more or less represents the cash a firm could raise on short notice, subtract **current liabilities**—bills to be paid, taxes due, debt that matures within a year, and so on. The result—assets readily convertible into cash minus money that has to be paid out in the near future—is known as a firm's **working capital.** Next, subtract all the company's long-term debt (assuming the company has less debt than working capital). That gives you the firm's **net current assets.** This figure is also sometimes called **net net assets**—the "net net" means that both short- and long-term debt have been subtracted.

Finally, divide those net net assets by the number of shares outstanding. Essentially that gives you the stock's value if the company had to be liquidated suddenly. If that figure is more than the stock's current price, the shares figure to be a buy for three reasons. First, the company isn't likely to have a serious financial problem since it can raise more than enough cash to pay off all its debts. Second, the money the firm would have after settling its debts is more than the stock costs. Third, someone buying the stock would be getting all of the company's business operations for free—and they have to be worth something. Stocks that pass this test are undervalued by definition. And academic research has shown that these stocks outperform the overall market by a healthy margin.

THE ORIGINAL TEST FOR UNDERVALUED STOCKS

Balance Sheet Data for Digital Equipment

Cash and securities	$1,602.1	
Receivables	3,219.1	
Inventory	2,053.6	
Other	397.1	
Current assets		$7,271.9
Accounts payable	1,113.2	
Debt due	14.4	
Other	3,118.7	
Current liabilities		4,246.3
Working capital		3,025.6
Long-term debt		1,012.9
Net net assets		2,012.7
Number of shares	146.8	
Net net assets per share		$13.71

Figures are for the end of the 1995 fiscal year. In millions except for net net assets per share.
Source: *The Value Line Investment Survey*

Benjamin Graham, the originator of modern securities analysis, relied on a measure known as **net net assets** to find undervalued stocks. Using Digital Equipment as an example, here's how the calculations are done. First, you add up the company's short-term assets—including cash and securities, receivables, and inventory. From that figure you subtract current liabilities, such as accounts payable and debt due in less than one year. The result is known as **working capital.** If you then subtract all the company's long-term debt, you get a measure—net net assets—that represents the minimum amount the company would be worth if it paid off all its debts and liquidated. In the 1950s many companies sold for less than net net asset value. But because firms generally have a lot more debt today, relatively few have any net net asset value at all. So when net net assets amount to a substantial part of a stock's price, it may well be undervalued. For that reason, you might have bet on a turnaround at troubled Digital Equipment when its shares fell to $19 in 1994. That would have been a smart move. The stock more than doubled over the following year.

There's just one catch. Nowadays few companies can pass this stringent test. By contrast, Graham figured that in 1932, 40% of all companies sold for less than their net net assets. Today, however, businesses carry a lot more debt than they used to, which makes sense given higher inflation since the 1960s and today's tax laws. Few firms, therefore, have any net net assets at all—their combined short- and long-term debt exceeds whatever near cash assets they have. And of those firms that do have surplus short-term assets, few sell at cheap prices. Only at a stock market bottom—in a bad recession, for example—will you find many shares changing hands below their net net asset values. Even then they may be companies you've never heard of.

Still, even if Graham's original test doesn't turn up much today, the principles it's based on are forever true for value investors. Let's take a quick look at those principles.

■ **Exceptional financial strength is a big plus.** To pass the net net test, a company has to have a lot of cash and securities on hand and not much debt, either short or long term. Rock-solid financial strength remains key to a value investment. As I've already noted, while you can be certain that the overall stock market will rebound if it's depressed, you can't be sure that any individual firm will be able to make a comeback—or how long it might take. So it's critical that a company have the resources to ride out a bad stretch before a turnaround begins.

■ **The company's existing businesses should be valued at relatively little.** You don't have to be as stringent as Graham was and value ongoing operations at zero, but value investors shouldn't assess businesses generously. The very fact that a stock is deeply depressed is a sign that it's in an unrewarding line of work. An oil company may have spent $10 to locate a barrel of crude or a cable television company may have paid $2,000 to acquire each customer, but under current market conditions those investments may be worth only three-quarters of their original value.

■ **The shares should be very cheap.** This may seem like an obvious thing to point out, but value stocks have to be bargains. Ain't no such thing as a premium-priced value stock. There may be lots of different ways to gauge a company's share price—in fact, we'll look at a number of them in a minute. But to be a value stock, a company's shares have to look cheap relative to at least one of these measures. And usually it will score as a bargain on several of them simultaneously.

MEASURING A STOCK'S VALUE

In earlier chapters I've already discussed the two most important gauges of a stock's attractiveness—its price/earnings ratio and its dividend yield. Using these measures is fairly straightforward if you're looking at a growth stock or at income shares. As long as a growth stock's price/earnings ratio is lower than its growth rate and the company appears financially sound, all you really have to watch is whether earnings continue rising at close to their current rate. Similarly, if an income stock offers a high yield—above 4%, say—and has solid financials and projected earnings growth that at least matches current inflation, you don't have much to worry about.

Value stocks, however, are fundamentally different. To be sure a stock is actually underpriced, you may need to look at several different valuation measures. And most of the time, the numbers can't be interpreted in a vacuum. You have to consider where the market is, how other stocks in the same industry are priced, and a variety of other factors.

As an illustration, consider the behavior of defense stocks over the past decade. After Soviet leader Mikhail Gorbachev launched his reform campaign in 1986 and the cold war started to fade away, many investors expected sizable defense budget cuts that would badly hurt the companies that make expensive military hardware such as aircraft. The fall of the Berlin Wall in 1989 seemed to confirm that outlook. In fact, defense spending fell from more than 28% of total federal outlays in 1987 to only 20% in 1993. As a result, many defense stocks declined sharply during that period. In some cases, though, the stocks' prices went down faster than their earnings. Result: Price/earnings ratios got lower and lower.

Why did these P/E multiples drop? Because investors kept expecting that even worse defense spending cuts were still to come. The irony was that most of the required budget chopping occurred during the Bush administration. By the time President Clinton took office in 1993, there weren't many cuts left to make. In addition, defense companies were trying to prepare themselves for the post–cold war world by downsizing and merging. Once investors recognized that military budget cutbacks were almost over, the prices of defense shares began to soar.

The point of this example is that looking at price/earnings ratios alone wouldn't have told you when to buy these defense stocks. From 1987 on, their P/E multiples were below those of the overall market—and the multiples just kept getting lower. Loral, for example, traded for $9 a share in 1986, and you could have bought it at that price or lower every year until 1993. Meanwhile the stock's P/E eroded until it was below 10—or at nearly a 40% discount to the overall stock market.

The same sort of thing is true if you use dividend yield as your measure of valuation. If a stock falls and its dividend stays the same, its yield will get bigger. For example, a $40 stock paying a $1 dividend has a 2.5% yield ($1 divided by $40). But if the share price declines 50% to $20, the yield will be 5% ($1 divided by $20).

Sometimes, though, an unusually large yield doesn't signal that a stock is cheap. Instead it may be a sign that the company is in trouble. Take the case of British Petroleum in the early '90s. In late 1990 the stock traded at $80 and was yielding a generous 5.3%. By 1992 the shares had fallen to $60 and their yield had risen to a staggering 8%. Did that make the stock a compelling buy? Not at all. A couple of months later, British Petroleum slashed its dividend from nearly $5 to about $2 a year. And the stock promptly tumbled to as low as $42 a share.

Of course, if an already cheap stock drops further, that only means it has more upside when it finally rebounds. Within three years, for example, BP more than doubled from the low it hit in late '92. But in investing, as in so many other things, timing is everything. Had you bought BP in 1990, your money would have been dead for five years. By contrast, if you had bought BP at the bottom, you would have doubled your money in three years. That's the difference between a return (including dividends) of less than 5% a year and a return of nearly 30% annually.

The bottom line for value investors is this: It's true that if you bought a random assortment of stocks with price/earnings ratios well below the market average, you would be very likely to outperform the market over time. A study of such stocks over a 20-year period by renowned money manager David Dreman concluded that low P/E stocks beat the market averages nearly two-thirds of the time. And the low P/Es outperformed in both good and bad markets. Most important, in really lousy stock markets they declined much less than the typical blue chip.

Similarly, if you bought a broad cross section of stocks with yields above 4%, you'd be likely to earn a pretty decent return without much risk. That's why retired people have always favored investing in electric utilities and the like.

However, when it comes to choosing any particular issue, you have to look at more than just the crude numbers. Otherwise you'll risk buying a stock that's halfway through a decline or one that's in financial trouble. Sometimes stocks are cheap for a reason, and it can take years to recover your money if you buy into one of those situations. Here's how to evaluate a cheap stock:

■ **Look at the P/E and the yield relative to prevailing market levels.** A 15 multiple today is slightly below the market; in 1974, by contrast, it would have been double the market level. Similarly, a 3.5% yield today is fairly generous compared with the market's 2.5%, but it would have been below average in the last couple of recessions.

■ **Compare a stock to its industry.** Has the entire industry been getting cheaper, like drug stocks during the early part of the Clinton administration, when kooky health care plans were the rage? If so, ask yourself whether you think a stock group's decline is over. What signs would show that the group has finally hit bottom? If in doubt, wait. You'll get a higher annualized return if you're a little late than too early.

■ **Take a hard look at the company's financials.** Especially if a stock is a lot cheaper than its industry, check the company's financial strength carefully. It's entirely possible that the firm will be in trouble. Often a stock will carry a high yield on paper because no one believes the full dividend will be paid.

WHAT THE IMPORTANT VALUE MEASURES MEAN

At this point you may be wondering whether you can analyze value stocks by yourself, what with all the calculations you have to do and the judgments you have to make. And that's a fair question. Many stock analysts would disagree with me, but if your only source of information is the *Wall Street Journal,* I think it's a lot easier to pick a big growth stock or an attractive income stock than to select a solid undervalued company at the right time. After all, you could have made a fortune in technology growth stocks such as Microsoft or Intel just from knowing about computers—who cares if you weren't really sure how to calculate those companies' net asset values per share.

The reality is that when it comes to value investing, you have to have some source of reliable information—whether it's a broker or research services such as *The Value Line Investment Survey* or Standard & Poor's. At a minimum, you need a source that can give you reliable financial strength ratings and a variety of analytical measures and ratios. Though you can learn to calculate all of these figures yourself from the documents public companies are required to file with the Securities and Exchange Commission, that subject requires a book in itself. It's all a lot simpler if someone else does the work. Then you just need to understand what all the measures mean. Here's a quick rundown of the valuation measures you should know:

■ **Price/earnings ratio.** Take the stock price and divide it by earnings per share. If you use the earnings for the past 12 months, the ratio is called a **trailing P/E.** If you use the estimated earnings for the current year, it's called a **current P/E.** If you use projected earnings for the next year, it's a **projected P/E.** If the company's profits are rising, then the projected P/E will be lower than the current P/E, which in turn will be lower than the trailing P/E. Your broker will doubtlessly quote the projected P/E to make the stock sound cheaper. The daily newspapers give the trailing P/E, which sometimes makes stocks look ridiculously expensive.

■ **Earnings yield.** This ratio is simply P/E turned upside down as E/P—that is, earnings divided by price. Analysts use this form because it allows for interesting historical comparisons with dividend yields. The English also use earnings yield sometimes because they're, well, English. It's sort of like spelling harbor and honor with the letter "u."

■ **Dividend yield.** Take the annual dividend rate and divide by the share price. There's a trailing figure based on dividends paid over the past 12 months and a projected figure calculated by taking the most recent announced quarterly payment and converting it to an annual figure (on the theory that in the future the company will continue with any recent dividend increases or cuts). Sometimes analysts will project a dividend rate for the coming year. But since dividend increases are fairly small from year to year, analysts usually do this only with utility stocks, where small differences in total return matter a lot.

■ **Price/dividend ratio.** This is the dividend yield turned upside down (from D/P to P/D). Like earnings yield, it's used mostly for historical market analysis. For example, one might want to compare the market's average P/E ratio to its P/D ratio over the past 60 years to look for significant patterns.

■ **Price/book-value ratio.** This is the third of the essential trio of value measures (after P/E and yield). To figure it, you subtract all of a company's liabilities from its assets to get shareholders' equity, also known as **book value.** Then you divide the share price by this number. Basically this is similar to the net net asset calculation I mentioned earlier when I was talking about Ben Graham. The salient difference is that the net net asset calculation is based only on cash or assets that could be converted to cash relatively easily, while book value is based on all assets—including a company's property, plant, and equipment. Further, since manufacturing assets and the like can't necessarily be converted into cash, they are valued at their actual historical cost, less whatever allowances have been made for depreciation. This may sound like a minor technical point, but it actually makes book value a highly unreliable number.

For starters, there's no guarantee that the amount of money a company spent on an asset has any relationship to what the asset is worth now. *Waterworld* cost an estimated $180 million to make; *Four Weddings and a Funeral,* $6 million. Sadly for Kevin Costner, their box office receipts didn't maintain the same 30-to-1 ratio. Second, because inflation has been so enormous over the past 30 years, the historical cost of assets depends a lot on when they were bought. A factory built last year could be on the books at four times the value of one built in 1969. But that difference would consist almost entirely of inflation; in real terms they would have cost roughly the same amount.

Because of these two basic flaws in historical cost data, the book values of different companies aren't really comparable. Moreover, you can't even fairly compare the book values of the *same* company at two different times. Nonetheless, despite these profound flaws, some analysts like to use book value as a measure for one simple reason: it works. Studies have shown that companies with price/book-value ratios far below the market average (currently around 3.5) outperform the average blue chip by a big margin. In one study, stocks with the lowest price/book-value ratios did twice as well as those with the highest.

■ **Price/cash-flow ratio.** I touched on P/CF ratios in Chapter 5, when I was talking about how to read an income statement. As I explained, standard accounting rules require companies figuring their earnings to subtract certain theoretical costs that don't actually require outlays of cash. Examples include the depreciation of property, plant, and equipment and the amortization of certain costs. In some industries, such as oil exploration, or in cases where a company has made major acquisitions, these accounting adjustments can thoroughly foul up earnings calculations. When this happens, analysts look at cash flow—the amount of cash a company generates each year—instead of earnings. Sometimes they use another variation known as **free cash flow,** which consists of the cash a company generates minus capital expenditures the firm has to make to maintain operations at their current level.

The argument for cash flow is sort of the opposite of that for book value. Cash flow is a more accurate measure than earnings but in practice can be subject to a lot of judgment calls. If you want to figure cash flow the quick, sloppy way, take a company's earnings per share and add back its depreciation and amortization per share. Since cash flow is almost always higher than earnings, P/CF ratios are lower than P/Es. So a P/CF ratio of 13 is highish, while it would be a cheap P/E nowadays.

■ **Price/earning-power ratio.** When it comes to evaluating highly cyclical companies, analysts have a problem. Say that a paper company, for example, earns next to nothing in recessions and then makes buckets of money when the economy is booming. The stock's P/E would be highest during recessions (which is when you'd want to buy the shares) because earnings would be so low. At economic peaks (which is when you'd want to sell) the earnings would be inflated; as a result, the P/E would be low even though the stock might have doubled in price from its recession levels.

Because of this paradox, P/E isn't much of a guide to buying cyclical stocks. Analysts sometimes say that you should buy cyclical stocks when P/Es are high and sell when they're low. That's considered witty in financial analysis circles, but it isn't really very helpful. So how do you get a meaningful number? Well, you could look at how much the company would be earning if it were at the top of its cycle and then calculate a ratio similar to a P/E, based on that peak earning power.

Analysts can figure dozens of methods for projecting earning power, but there are two basic ones. The most common is to take the company's return on equity (net income divided by equity) at the peak of a cycle and multiply it by the current book value (equity). For example, if the company earned $2 on each $100 of equity (2% ROE) in recessions and $25 (25%) when the economy was running full out, you'd get its earning power at any given time by multiplying that year's book value by 25%. Since earning power will be higher than actual earnings most of the time, price/earning-power ratios are usually lower than P/E ratios.

The alternative method of figuring earning power is to take the company's net margin (net income divided by total sales) at the peak of a cycle and multiply by current sales. It's the same idea as with ROE. You take one measure that tracks the economic cycle (ROE or net margin), select its maximum value, and multiply that by a figure that reflects the company's current size (book value or sales). The result tells you how much a company would be earning if it were at the peak of the cycle.

■ **Price/sales ratio.** All the measures I've talked about so far compare a stock's price to some form of the company's profits (cash flow, after all, is an adjustment to net income, while dividends are earnings paid out to shareholders). Sometimes, though, analysts compare share prices to companies' sales per share. For the market as a whole, price/sales ratios above 0.9 indicate that stocks are quite expensive; P/S ratios below 0.65 mean that they are cheap. For individual companies, however, P/S multiples can vary a lot more.

By itself this ratio isn't a very reliable indicator; stocks that fall outside the normal range are either grossly misvalued or are earning far more or far less on their sales than most companies do. Confusingly, this means that exceptional P/S ratios can be either good signs or bad signs. Companies with very high P/S multiples are either extremely overvalued or have wonderful opportunities for growth. Those with very low multiples are either incredibly cheap or on the verge of collapse. You need to look at other figures to know which are which. Still, as a way of turning up unusual bargains, P/S ratios will flag stocks that no other indicator can catch.

SHOULD YOU BE A HIGH-STAKES CONTRARIAN?

So far, we've been talking about value investing and contrarianism as though this approach to stock picking were about number crunching and not much else. But we all know there's another side. Big-name money managers such as Mario Gabelli and Michael Price appear regularly in *Barron's* and other financial journals naming stocks that are so undervalued they look like natural takeover targets. And whenever a stock collapses because of some corporate disaster, there are always experts quoted in the newspapers saying that it's smart to buy distressed shares when everyone else is dumping them.

So what about it? Is it the mark of a nerd to be figuring P/Es, yields, and cash flows? Should you throw away your pocket protector and load up on rumored takeover targets or turnarounds instead? Don't rush. Making money on possible takeovers is a mighty tough game—you can also lose money fast. As far as buying collapsing stocks goes, on Wall Street they say that's like catching a falling knife—depends which way it's pointing.

Let's start with one of the simplest examples of what I'll call high-stakes contrarianism—buying stocks after they slash or omit their dividends. A lot of books on how to be a savvy small investor will tell you that you can't go wrong buying a blue chip after a dividend disaster. A good example is British Petroleum, which I mentioned a little earlier in this chapter. When BP reduced its dividend from nearly $5 to about $2 in 1992, the stock promptly tumbled from the high 50s to as low as $42 a share. Then, over the following three years, the BP shares more than doubled.

The argument for buying at the bottom in such a situation is simple, straightforward—and often true. When a company omits or sharply reduces its dividend, its shares almost always plummet. There are three reasons for this. First, even if most investors have long suspected that such a move is coming, some shareholders are invariably caught by surprise; they panic and sell. Second, some conservative mutual funds have rules that do not permit them to hold stocks with troubled dividends; they have to sell whether they want to or not. Finally, many funds engage in window dressing, which means that they buy and sell before they report their holdings at the end of each quarter; funds are likely to sell any embarrassing losers so that their shareholders won't know they owned them.

All of this selling tends to drive the share price of a dividend disaster stock considerably lower than it would go in a fair market. So if the company is financially sound and has the ability to solve its problems—two big ifs—the stock is very likely to outpace the market over the following two or three years. Only trouble is, academic studies show that those two big ifs are iffier than you might think. One Cornell University study of 887 companies that had missed dividends sometime during a 24-year period found that on average the shares trailed the market by a substantial margin for more than three years after the dividends were skipped. Conclusion: While you can find terrific bargains when stocks collapse after a dividend cut, you still have to do all the analysis you would do for any other value situation to figure out if you should buy the shares.

Broadly speaking, the same turns out to be true in the case of corporate disasters. Say you bought Union Carbide after the stock tumbled because of the 1984 Bhopal disaster, when a gas leak at a plant in India killed thousands of people. You would have doubled your money within two years. Or say you scooped up Exxon in 1989 after the *Exxon Valdez* ran aground and spilled million of gallons of oil into Alaskan coastal waters. You'd have made more than 20% within two years (not to mention a generous dividend yield). Or imagine you bet on Philip Morris in 1993 after the company dropped the price of Marlboro cigarettes to remain competitive. That would have earned you a 50% profit within three years.

Clearly, if you're willing to wait two or three years and you don't feel squeamish about investing in companies that may be politically incorrect at the moment, you can make some serious money. But it ain't necessarily so. Dow Corning, for example, faced a torrent of injury claims by women who had used the company's silicone breast implants and claimed they had suffered from various ailments as a result. Dow Corning repeatedly attempted to settle the case, but each settlement came apart. On several occasions contrarian investors could have bought the stock thinking that it was surely at a bottom. They would have been wrong. In May 1995 Dow Corning declared bankruptcy. Ironically, some experts say there is still no definitive evidence that the implants are health hazards.

In short, when it comes to investing in a troubled stock, remember that such shares are often cheap for a reason. You may be able to snag a company at the bottom and then watch it rally. That makes you feel like a real wiseguy. But it's awfully easy to think a stock has hit bottom—and be wrong. I bought IBM in the low 60s, down from $100, when everybody was sure the mainframe was dead. I knew it wasn't and that IBM would eventually figure out how to make money in whatever mainframe market remained. Then the stock went to $42. By the time IBM had turned around, almost two years had gone by and I was so furious that I sold as soon as I could get out even. Then the stock went to $114. I was absolutely right—and I didn't make a cent. Value investing is harder than it sounds.

THE FOOLPROOF VALUE STRATEGY THAT REALLY WORKS

There is one value investing strategy that works amazingly well. Better yet, it requires almost no work and is so simple that it's virtually impossible to foul up. The strategy consists of buying roughly equal dollar amounts of the 10 highest-yielding Dow stocks on the first trading day of January. Then, each January, replace any stocks that have fallen out of the top 10 with the new Dow top yielders (typically, you have to replace three or four stocks a year). That's the whole strategy. Historically, these top yielders have beaten the Dow in two out of three years. On average they outperform the overall index by more than four percentage points annually.

TRUE FACT

The 10 highest-yielding stocks among the 30 Dow industrials outperform the overall index by an average of four percentage points a year.

The strategy doesn't have any serious drawbacks. You do get a significant chunk of your return in the form of dividends, which may be slightly disadvantageous from a tax perspective. The top yielders do underperform the Dow once in a while, but not by a big margin. Practically speaking, you need at least $25,000 to $50,000 to buy all 10 stocks. However, there is an alternative form of the strategy that requires less money: Buy the five of the 10 top yielders that have the lowest price per share. For some reason, the lower-priced stocks tend to be slightly stronger performers.

Why does this high-yielding Dow stock strategy continue to work—especially considering that it's well known and more than 20 years old? The answer is that the system embodies the most basic style of value investing. Its chief principles:

■ **Diversify among several stocks.** If you buy the Dow's 10 top yielders, you are automatically fairly well diversified.

■ **Buy only financially solid companies.** The majority of the Dow stocks are top-notch financially. Even the weaker Dow issues—such as Bethlehem Steel, Union Carbide, Westinghouse, and Woolworth—are above average relative to the overall market.

■ **Favor large, actively traded issues.** The Dow stocks are all billion-dollar behemoths and market bellwethers.

■ **Look for shares with low P/Es and high yields.** The stocks have above market yields by definition. And as a general rule, they have below average price/earnings multiples.

■ **Hold your stocks for the long term.** At a minimum, the Dow high-yield strategy calls for holding stocks for a year. Since you usually only replace three or four of your 10 holdings each year, your average holding time is two to three years.

PART III

BEYOND THE BASICS

CHAPTER 10

SPECIAL SITUATIONS:

Profiting from Takeovers, Turnarounds, and Other Unique Opportunities

Not too long ago, a friend of a friend of mine—let's call him Ralph—was at a party in New York City's Greenwich Village. It was a large, noisy affair, and the guests included a number of actors and models. Suddenly Ralph looked across the room and saw Uma Thurman. Even more incredible, she was standing by herself. Ralph rushed over to her and said hello. They talked for about 10 minutes, and she couldn't have been more gracious or charming. Then she spotted a friend and said she had to go. As she started to leave, Ralph said, "Tell me, Uma, how can I get in touch with you?"

Turning back for a moment, she flashed a dazzling smile. "Well," she said, "actually you can't."

This story pretty much sums up special situations investing from the average guy's point of view. You may hear all sorts of rumors—companies that are sure to be taken over, near bankrupt firms that are about to make breathtaking turnarounds, undervalued businesses that are going to sell off their assets at an enormous profit. But when it comes to scoring in these dazzling deals, small investors would do well to remember Uma's parting words.

Trouble is, by the time you read about a deal in the newspaper—or even hear about it on cable television—dozens of professionals will long have known what was happening. Odds are that if there's a quick buck around they will already have made it. You'll find out about the opportunity when it's almost over and the insiders are ready to take their profits. And the reason you'll hear about it is that the pros will be trying to get out by selling to you.

The truth of the matter is that small investors get rich by buying sound stocks at fair prices and then holding them for a long time. They don't make money trading, and they certainly don't make money speculating in deal stocks where small investors are at an enormous disadvantage to professionals. Even if the pros don't trade on information that's improper or illegal—which, by the way, they sometimes do—their commissions are far lower than yours, and they will almost always learn about crucial developments before you do.

Having said that, I still want to tell you a little bit about special situations for a couple of reasons. First, a stock you already own may become involved in a deal, and then you'll have to decide what to do with it. Second, special situations are sometimes excellent investments for fundamental reasons. In such cases, though, the analysis required will probably go beyond what I've explained in Chapters 5 through 9. That means you will have to rely on timely outside sources of information—probably reports from your broker or independent newsletters.

Here's a quick rundown of the major types of special situations:

TAKEOVERS

Companies take over other companies for strategic or financial reasons (or both). In the first case, the objective is to gain a business advantage. For example, a large cable television company might buy a small one that controlled three or four urban markets the bigger company wanted to get into. Or a drug company with a mediocre research division might purchase a biotech company to gain access to promising new drugs. In the case of a financially motivated takeover, a big, powerful company could buy an inefficient firm and turn it around. Then, by selling off some operations, the big company might be able to recoup most of the costs of the acquisition, thereby getting the pieces it kept virtually for free.

In simplest terms, the mechanics of such deals can be handled in one of two ways. In a purchase, the acquiring company buys all the outstanding shares of the target firm, usually paying part or all of the price in cash. If the acquirer doesn't have enough cash on hand, it may borrow from banks (promising to repay the loan out of earnings or with the proceeds from asset sales), or it can raise money by selling bonds. The alternative type of acquisition is a merger, in which one company buys another's outstanding stock with its own shares. In that case, shareholders of the target company end up with shares in the combined companies instead of cash.

There are technical differences between purchases and mergers. The most important have to do with accounting. A cash purchase, for example, can force a company to amortize part of the price it pays. That means the firm has to take a charge each year against its earnings even though it isn't actually spending any additional cash. By reducing reported earnings, such amortization can distort the stock's price/earnings ratio by making it appear higher. When that happens, analysts look at cash flow instead of earnings to value the shares (as I explained in Chapter 9).

You don't need to worry about these technicalities. The important thing to remember is that there are very few true mergers in business. No matter what happens from an accounting point of view, one company is the buyer and the other one gets bought. Nine times out of 10, the buyer's stock goes down when an acquisition is announced, while the target company's shares jump in price.

Why do the two companies' share prices usually move in

opposite directions? Shareholders in the company to be acquired won't sell their stock unless they get a premium over its market value. And the management of the acquirer, which generally gains control of the merged firms, is willing to pay that premium either because of the strategic value of the merger or because the managers think they can more than make back the premium by cutting costs or selling assets. Because the acquirer is over-paying in the short run—which dilutes the value of its existing stock—its share price usually declines at least a bit.

If you think about all this for a few minutes, you'll realize that the bottom line for small investors is straightforward. There are basically three possibilities:

■ **If you own stock in an acquirer, you have to decide whether you want to be a shareholder in the new firm.** Few deals boost the acquirer's stock in the short run. Usually the share price falls and may stagnate for months after a deal is announced. The key question you have to answer as a shareholder in the acquiring company is whether the merger will really benefit the combined businesses over the long term. For example, Chemical Banking acquired Manufacturers Hanover in December 1991. Although Chemical's stock declined in the months between the announcement and the completion of the merger, the long-term outlook for the bank was quite good.

Chemical shareholders who rode out the temporary price drop caused by the merger with Manny Hanny profited hand-somely over the following two years. During that time, the Fed was cutting interest rates, which helps banks because it lowers the cost of their chief raw material—money. Further, the bene-fits of combining the two banks was obvious. They would be able to reduce overhead by merging some operations and clos-ing branches in neighborhoods where both banks had formerly maintained offices. As a result, by late 1993 the shares of the new bank had more than doubled from their late 1991 low—and they were up at least 50% from their '91 premerger high. Chemical's strategy worked so well, in fact, that in August 1995 the bank announced a merger agreement with Chase Manhattan in the hope of repeating its success.

■ **If you have stock in the target, you have to figure out at what price you would sell.** After a merger has been announced, shareholders in the target company don't have to worry about what will happen once the deal is completed. They are almost certain to be offered a premium price for their stock. If they are to be paid in cash, they can either sell their shares in the market before the deal closes or hang on until they get their money. Either way they are out of the stock. On the other hand, if shareholders are going to receive stock from the acquiring company, they can sell first or wait and take the shares. You might opt for the shares if you were convinced the prospects for the new company were extremely bright. Reason: If you sold your old stock, you would likely have to pay capital-gains taxes. You could avoid those taxes, however, if you accepted shares in the new company in exchange.

Generally, though, whether you are going to be paid in cash or in stock, it's wisest to take the money and run before the deal closes. Here's why: When one company makes a bid for another, the share price of the target usually rises close to the bid price. Sometimes it can even go higher if investors believe that a second potential acquirer might appear and make a better offer. However, once the initial bidding is over, the stock of the company to be bought normally settles a few dollars below the acquisition price. At that point, professional investors, known as **arbs** (short for **arbitrageurs**), buy the stock and hold it until the deal is finally completed—or until it falls apart.

For arbs, who can diversify among a number of deals and follow all of them minute by minute, earning those last few dollars works out to an enormous percentage return at an annual rate. But small investors would be foolish not to sell out to the arbs a month or so after a firm offer is on the table. It simply isn't worth taking the risk of a deal coming apart to earn the last couple of dollars by holding to the bitter end. Your only chance of a big profit is if there is a higher bid. And generally such bids emerge in the month or so after the first firm offer is made. So don't rush to sell the minute a potential deal is announced—but once the dust has settled, take your profits and leave.

■ **If you are hoping to buy shares in a company that might be taken over in the future, look for a firm that would attract an acquirer.** Not surprisingly, the biggest profits are made in takeovers by investors who owned the shares of the target company before there were even hints of a deal. Unless you want to try being an amateur arb—an idea that I'd advise against—you certainly shouldn't buy stock in a target after the price has jumped on the announcement of a deal.

How could you possibly know to buy shares in a company before a takeover has even been rumored? By looking for the same characteristics that a potential acquirer would search for. To anticipate strategic deals, focus on industries where consolidation is expected. For example, most analysts think that medium-size drug companies will slowly be bought up by competitors (as Upjohn was by Sweden's Pharmacia in August 1995). Similarly, most cable television companies smaller than the five largest will probably be acquired. Ditto high-quality, midsize banks. Obviously there's no way for you to know which firms will go first. However, if you read brokerage reports covering these industries, you'll usually find that two or three stocks in each group are repeatedly cited as likely takeovers.

Similarly, probable targets for financially motivated takeovers are businesses with solid franchises that are selling at deeply depressed share prices. Quite simply, they're the very sorts of firms that you'd be steered toward if you used the value analysis techniques I described in the preceding chapter. In fact, if you select stocks according to the principles I lay out in Chapters 5 through 9, you'll probably gravitate toward the types of stocks that potential acquirers will be looking for. And you can improve your odds of buying a takeover candidate in advance of a deal if you also look at midsize companies in cheap stock groups that are expected to consolidate. Beyond that, be grateful if a stock you own gets an offer, but don't chase shares that have risen in price on takeover rumors. Leave that game to the arbs.

STOCK BUYBACKS

When corporations accumulate extra cash, they can do several things: expand their existing operations; launch new businesses; acquire other firms; raise their dividends; or buy back their stock. Why would a company decide to repurchase its stock? Quite simply because that may be the most advantageous choice for shareholders. If a firm doesn't have compelling opportunities, smart managers will reject the idea of expansion or new businesses. And as we discussed a minute ago, takeovers rarely benefit the share price of the acquirer. That leaves two options: higher dividends and buybacks. Though both return money to shareholders, managers who raise dividends generally feel obligated to continue payouts at the new, higher rate. So if they want to make a onetime distribution of cash, a stock buyback is a more convenient way to do it. In addition, since dividend income is taxed at a higher rate than capital gains, profits from a stock buyback may be more advantageous for investors than higher dividends would be.

TRUE FACT

Companies that buy back their own stock beat the market over three years by more than 12%, on average.

Source: David Ikenberry, Josef Lakonishok, and Theo Vermaelen, *Journal of Financial Economics,* vol. 39, nos. 2 and 3, 1995

In fact, academic research supports the argument for stock buybacks. A 1994 study of more than 1,200 companies that announced stock buybacks during the '80s found that the boost such buybacks give to share prices is much bigger and longer lasting than many experts previously believed. After three years the buyback companies beat portfolios of comparable stocks by more than 12% on average. And stocks that were greatly undervalued scored a lot higher. Companies whose shares were trading at low market prices relative to their book values gained as much as 45% in the four years following their buyback announcements.

Why should repurchasing shares boost a company's stock price? First, buyback announcements show that top executives think their firm's stock is cheap. Of course, the insiders could be overly optimistic, but on balance they're right more often than not. Second, repurchases often increase a company's earnings per share. When a firm reduces the number of outstanding shares, that translates into higher earnings per share (provided the company earns more on its equity than it could by investing its extra cash in bonds). It's like dividing a pie among fewer people—each gets a bigger slice. Further, if the stock has a high current yield, money saved on dividends that no longer have to be paid helps to cover the costs of the buyback.

■ **The bottom line: If a stock looks like an attractive value investment and the company announces a buyback, consider that a very positive sign.** Don't, however, purchase a stock solely because of a buyback announcement. Companies are required to disclose potential share repurchases in advance, but they aren't required to follow through on them. And top executives who want to hype their stock sometimes make a big fuss about their plans for stock repurchases, then actually buy back very few shares. Moreover, the benefits of buybacks are only substantial if shares are somewhat undervalued to begin with.

SPIN-OFFS

Ideally, if a company had a division it wanted to get rid of, the parent firm would sell the subsidiary and reinvest the proceeds in the core businesses it retained. There's just one catch—taxes. If the subsidiary is carried on the books at a price way below its current market value, the sale could generate big capital gains. To avoid a bill for capital-gains taxes, many companies often use another technique to rid themselves of a superfluous division: they spin it off. This means that the parent firm restructures the subsidiary as an independent company with its own stock; then they give those shares to current investors in the parent firm.

This may seem like an awfully convoluted way for a company to shed a business it doesn't want. But spinning off assets can be a winning corporate strategy if it is done shrewdly. For instance, when AT&T announced its plan to break itself up into three separate companies in September 1995, the stock jumped $6, or about 10%, on the news. Here's why investors applauded: The main company—consisting of long-distance and cellular telephone service—would be leaner and more competitive; AT&T's telephone equipment division would be freed to seek business from a wider range of clients; and the troubled computer division would be off on its own, where it would either be turned around or possibly bought by another computer firm.

Apart from the strategic value of splitting up a giant company, there can also be big financial benefits. The parent firm can spin off the subsidiary's liabilities along with its assets. If the subsidiary is heavily indebted, that alone can spiff up the parent company's balance sheet. And if top managers are clever, they can sometimes find excuses for loading some parent-company debt onto the subsidiary before they let it go. Further, a spin-off can qualify for tax-free status if 80% of the subsidiary is distributed to shareholders. That means the parent company can pick up a little extra cash by selling 10% or 15% of the division to the public a year or two before spinning it off.

193

TRUE FACT

When one company spins off another, the new stock often drops in the first month or so but typically goes on to outperform comparable stocks by as much as 20 percentage points over the following 18 months.

Source: Patrick Cusatis, James Miles, and J. Randall Woolridge, *Journal of Financial Economics,* vol. 33, no. 3, 1993

Happily, such spin-offs frequently work to the advantage of shareholders as well. Many academic studies show that shares of newly independent firms can outpace comparable companies by 10 percentage points a year or more. However, spin-offs are an even better deal for investors who buy them a month or so after they begin trading. Why? Because new stocks typically drop in price for the first couple of weeks. So investors who scoop them up when they dip enjoy even bigger percentage gains once the spin-offs begin to outperform the market.

Consider the case of AirTouch Communications, formerly the wireless division of Pacific Telesis, the local telephone operating company for much of California and Nevada. In 1993 PacTel sold 14% of the wireless division to the public. Then, in 1994, the telephone operating company distributed its remaining 86% interest. Each PacTel shareholder received one share in the newly independent AirTouch. In the month after the spin-off, AirTouch stock fell to less than $20. By year-end, though, it had rebounded to $30.

What accounts for a new stock's initial price drop? Many investors who receive the spin-off's shares don't particularly want them and would just as soon have cash instead. Often, spin-offs don't pay any dividends at first, so income-oriented investors and mutual funds also dump them. In addition, index funds are virtually required to sell such stocks. Reason: These funds attempt to match an existing stock index, such as the S&P 500, by holding most of the stocks that make up the index. They can't afford to hang on to odd stockholdings that might throw off their performance numbers. The result: In the month after a spin-off's stock is distributed to investors, there's a wave of selling that temporarily depresses the share price.

Longer term, though, spin-offs can shine. After the initial selling subsides, a new stock usually rebounds. In addition, the company's performance may improve sharply. Subsidiaries are often spun off because they aren't especially successful businesses. But once the managers are on their own, without interference from headquarters, they may be able to make the company more profitable. In brief, investing in spin-offs boils down to two cases:

■ **If you own shares in a company that announces a spin-off, decide whether you'd rather own the new stock or cash out as quickly as possible.** To decide whether to keep the new company, you'll need some brokerage research that specifically analyzes the upcoming spin-off. If you plan to hang on to the shares, be prepared to hold them for at least a year. If you'd rather convert them into cash, try to avoid selling immediately after the shares are distributed. In some cases you can sell on a when-issued basis. That means agreeing in advance to sell the shares at a specified price when they are distributed (you can find out from your broker when when-issued trading will begin). If you don't think the when-issued price is attractive, hold the stock for two or three months to see if it rebounds once initial selling dissipates.

■ **If you don't own the parent company, consider buying the spin-off a couple of weeks after the shares are distributed.** Again, you'll need some up-to-the-minute brokerage research that analyzes the spin-off on what's called a **pro forma basis**. In such research, an analyst looks at the division to be spun off as though it were a free-standing business. You should assess the independent firm as a value investment. Be particularly careful to look at the spin-off's financial strength; the parent company may have loaded a lot of debt onto it. If you are sure you want to buy the shares, wait to see if they drop in the first couple of weeks of trading. That's your best chance for getting a bargain.

ASSET SALES AND LIQUIDATIONS

As I mentioned in the discussion of spin-offs, tax considerations often make it disadvantageous for a firm to sell assets. Sometimes, though, a company decides to do so anyway, either because the taxes will be tolerable or because there is no other practical way to dispose of assets the firm doesn't want. Such situations can benefit existing shareholders but are difficult for a new investor to cash in on.

One study of more than 1,000 firms selling off assets found that the companies generally underperformed the market in the months leading up to the announcement of an asset sale. That makes sense, because sell-offs are frequently motivated either by financial problems that require a company to raise cash or by subpar business performance that leads top management to decide to get rid of the least promising business lines.

Further, the study concluded that sell-offs did give stocks a small boost. But surprisingly, shares showed very little gain after the announcement was made. The study found that almost all of the benefit of the sell-off occurred in the 11 days immediately prior to the announcement. Reason: Undoubtedly, news of what the company was planning to do was leaking and insiders were buying the stock, bidding up the price. So a new investor couldn't profit much by buying after the announcement. You couldn't ask for a better reminder of the disadvantage that a small investor faces relative to the pros in special situations.

Of course, you still might want to purchase such a stock if you thought the money that the firm was raising would improve the company's long-term prospects. Also, one sell-off might indicate that the company was beginning a major restructuring that would include further sell-offs, spin-offs, or other corporate events. In such a case, getting in early might enable you to cash in on future developments.

The extreme sell-off case is when a company begins to liquidate itself. Usually this happens only with fairly small firms, especially those that are family controlled. For example, a family real estate development business may decide to liquidate its land holdings when key family members have to retire. Not surprisingly, the stock may have performed poorly in the months leading up to the liquidation decision, and the share price may well be below the market value of the company's assets.

■ **Conclusion: Sell-offs signal that a company's shares may be undervalued.** By the time you read a sell-off announcement in the newspaper, most of the profits will probably be gone. Nonetheless, a sell-off may signal that the stock is worth looking at as a possible value investment. However, the firm may be small and in crummy shape. Further, you may have trouble finding timely research on the deal. Though these situations can be profit opportunities, they often are not suitable for beginners.

TURNAROUNDS

Investing in potential turnarounds—troubled companies that are attempting to make a comeback—is simply value investing carried to an extreme. Essentially, a turnaround investor looks for companies with attractive basic franchises whose shares are deeply depressed because poor management has led to lousy profitability. If the top managers at such firms are able to solve some of their business problems and get profit margins back to even mediocre levels, the stocks' earnings will come rocketing back and share prices could double or triple.

There are just two problems with turnarounds: not all of them actually do turn around; and the timing of any comeback is hard to predict. It's funny, but investors always seem willing to believe that troubled companies will successfully solve their problems. Rooting for the underdog isn't a particularly smart bet, though. After all, the bozo management and sclerotic bureaucracy that messed up the business in the first place aren't likely to straighten it out. And new managers will barely have time enough to figure out what's going on—much less be able to fix anything.

The less obvious pitfall is timing. Like kitchen renovations, turnarounds always seem to take twice as long and cost twice as much as they were supposed to. As a result, investors who bet that unprofitable businesses will boost their margins can easily buy too early, only to see an already cheap stock get even cheaper. Your analysis of a company may be correct, but if your timing is off, you can sit with dead money for a year or more.

If you want to play the turnaround game, you'll need top-quality brokerage research you can rely on. Pass over any potential comebacks that don't appear to offer at least a 50% gain; otherwise the potential return isn't worth the risk. Also make sure that such stocks score well on basic value measurements. To gauge your potential upside in a turnaround situation, you can use a variation on the price/earning-power ratio that I discussed in the last chapter.

Begin with the company's earnings data back when times were better (don't look at periods of peak performance, but rather at a moderately good level that the business might reasonably attain again). To gauge what the company could earn if it recovered, multiply the former net profit margins by current sales. Then take the firm's former return on equity and multiply that by current book value. Both calculations will give you the stock's potential earning power; average them to get a single number. Then look at the price/earnings ratios the stock has traded at during past good times. Take a slightly below average P/E and multiply that by the earning power you've calculated. That usually will give you a rough idea of where the shares might trade if the company makes a comeback (for a more detailed explanation of these calculations, see Chapter 9).

■ **Remember: To profit substantially, you not only have to correctly anticipate a company's turnaround, but also have to be right on the timing.**

I'm sorry if this chapter seems discouraging. I'd like to tell you that you can easily make spectacular returns in special situations. But the fact is that unless you really make a study of takeovers and other such deals, you're going to risk having some fiascoes. And there's no guarantee that the winners will make up for the losers.

> ## RULE NO. 9 OF INVESTING:
> ## WHEN IT COMES TO TRADING DEAL STOCKS,
> ## SMALL INVESTORS CAN'T BEAT THE PROS.

Nonetheless, you'll be able to profit occasionally from a takeover if you look for the same sort of undervalued stocks that would attract a potential acquirer. After all, a key business franchise and a cheap share price make a stock attractive to everyone. You can also find great value investments by looking at companies that have been buying back shares or firms that have announced they are considering selling assets or spinning them off. And look at spin-offs after they've been trading independently for a couple of weeks; they're one type of deal stock that can pay off handsomely for individual investors.

Above all, remember that you should never buy a stock unless it's attractive as a value investment as well as a special situation. Rumors—or even announced deals—can give an underpriced stock a little extra kick. But the biggest and most reliable gains come from buying bargains with solid fundamentals and then holding the shares for five years or longer.

CHAPTER 11

SPECIALIZED INVESTMENTS:

What You Need to Know about Offbeat Securities and When They Can Beat the Market

Regular stocks and bonds account for more than 90% of the investments that are worth buying. However, there are some lesser-known alternatives—such as convertible securities and closed-end funds, for example—that occasionally offer even better opportunities. Sifting through these investments to find the ones that really pay off can be tricky, though. When companies issue offbeat securities, they have a lot of latitude in the terms they can set. And sometimes escape clauses or other terms in the fine print can blindside investors.

To understand how to evaluate offbeat issues, you first need to know just a bit about how companies are organized. Essentially, one group of investors puts up risk capital known as **equity;** they receive common stock and are the chief owners of the business. Another group lends money to the company and receives **bonds;** these bondholders have only limited ownership rights. In the event the company gets into financial trouble, though, the roles are reversed. Bondholders have higher status than equity holders, and their claims receive priority in a bankruptcy, for example. This reversal makes sense. The stockholders, who direct the company, receive more if the business goes well; the bond-holders, who have little say in the running of the business, are protected the most in the case of failure.

In theory, you could set up a company with only these two classes of investors—or with equity investors alone. But financial engineering has created a number of intermediate types of securities that are sometimes more attractive than either straight equity or debt. Among these hybrids are preferred shares, warrants, options, and convertible issues. In addition, companies can be organized in ways that are variations on the usual corporate structure (often for tax reasons). Examples would include real estate investment trusts, limited partnerships, and closed-end funds.

Limited partnerships are outside the scope of this book. They have many of the tax advantages of a partnership without the chief drawback—that a partner can lose more than his or her original investment. Such vehicles are ideal for certain real estate ventures. Another type of organization, known as a trust, can also be advantageous for real estate (for more on such trusts, see Chapter 8). In addition, there's a similar type of investment company—known as a closed-end mutual fund—that is well worth knowing about. As I'll explain in a minute, under certain circumstances closed-end funds are a low-risk way to beat the market.

When it comes to unusual securities, pretty much anything goes. Corporations can create a range of issues that fall in a gray area between bonds and common stock. **Preferred shares,** for example, pay dividends like stock, but the size of the payouts is fixed, like bond interest. These preferreds get better treatment than common shares in a bankruptcy but still rank below bonds. Companies can also issue warrants and options, which typically give holders the right to buy common stock at a specified price (but don't obligate them to buy if they don't want to). Special features can also be combined: some bonds and preferred shares, for instance, can be converted into common stock if the holder wants to. And as you'll see in a moment, some of these preferred and convertible securities can be quite profitable.

PREFERREDS

In theory, straight preferred shares (without a convertible feature) shouldn't be particularly attractive for small investors. The chief reason that companies issue them is that they offer tax advantages to corporate shareholders; the dividends they pay are partially exempt from corporate income tax. Nonetheless, because preferred shares constitute a small, often overlooked market, they will occasionally trade at generous yields. At a time when Treasury bonds were paying 6%, for example, you might be able to discover some high-quality preferreds that were paying 8% or so. Many preferreds are also easy for small investors to buy because they trade on the New York Stock Exchange in 100-share lots. That means the price for a so-called **round lot** could be $2,500 to $5,000; standard lots for bonds, by contrast, are often $10,000 or more.

Preferreds never have the credit quality of a Treasury issue or a AAA-rated corporate bond. But because they have some of the characteristics of a bond, their financial strength ranks above that of comparable common shares. The bottom line is that if you follow preferreds closely, every once in a while you will find one that is low risk enough to meet your parameters for income investments and offers a higher yield than you could get elsewhere.

Because the number of interesting preferreds is small, it isn't really worthwhile for you to devote a lot of energy to following them yourself. Instead you should rely on research—either from newsletters or a full-service broker. As far as I'm aware, the preferred stock information available in most investment newsletters is kind of spotty; one letter that does cover them from time to time is *Richard C. Young's Intelligence Report* (800-848-2132 or 401-849-2137; $99 a year). In any event, preferred stocks are one type of investment where you will almost certainly want to work through a full-service broker at a large firm who is likely to have access to detailed research on such securities. You would certainly want to know if, for example, there were terms under which a particular preferred stock could be bought back by the issuer for less than you would currently have to pay to buy it.

CONVERTIBLES

As I mentioned earlier, some corporate bonds or preferred shares can be converted into a specified amount of common stock at the holder's option. In some ways, these **convertible issues** behave like fixed-income investments; for example, their prices generally fall when interest rates rise and rise when rates fall. In other respects, however, they act like stocks. Specifically, they tend to move up in line with the value of the common shares they can be converted into.

TRUE FACT

From 1973 through 1992, convertible bonds had higher returns and lower risk than both regular bonds and blue-chip stocks.

Source: Scott L. Lummer and Mark W. Riepe, *Journal of Fixed Income,* vol. 3, no. 2, September 1993

You might think that a hybrid investment like a convertible would be a bad deal, a compromise between a mediocre bond or preferred and a second-rate stock. In fact, though, several academic studies show "converts" frequently offer the best of both worlds. Two recent studies show that from the mid-'70s through the early '90s, convertibles outperformed fixed-income investments and also earned better returns than high-quality stocks, with less risk. How is this possible? Well, convertibles can outperform bonds over 10 years or longer for the simple reason that the stock market is likely to rise substantially over long stretches of time—and since converts rise with stocks, their upside is greater than that of straight bonds.

It's less obvious why convertibles can often beat stocks, but two factors help. First, because converts carry high yields (on average, more than 6% vs. less than 3% for common shares), they have a head start. Second, they generally share more of the upside on common stocks than they share the downside. For example, a convertible might go up $.70 for each $1 the common shares rise but go down only $.50 for each $1 the common falls. The full explanation for this is too complicated for me to discuss here, but one reason converts hold up better is that their higher yields provide some price support when the stock market is going down.

When it comes to analyzing a particular convertible, there's a widely accepted rule of thumb for deciding if it's attractive as an alternative to the common shares. The rule is easier to understand by working through a specific example, but I'll give it in general terms first: Convertibles almost always trade at a premium over the value of the common shares they could be exchanged for. And a convert is a better buy than the common if its extra yield would pay off that premium in four years or less.

If that sounds confusing, let me go through a recent case. With annual revenues of more than $2 billion, Olsten is a leader in personnel services for both temporary office staff and home health workers. In addition to its common shares, Olsten has a convertible bond outstanding that sold for $1,160 in late 1995 and sported a 4.2% yield. That payout is 3.4 percentage points higher than the puny 0.8% the common provides. If you owned the convert, you could have exchanged each bond for 28.736 common shares, which would have been worth $1,114, or $46 less than the price of the bond. In short, the convert was selling for 4.1% more than the value of the common but yielding 3.4 points more. The extra yield would therefore pay for the conversion premium in less than 15 months—far less than the four-year cutoff.

There are a few other things to check with a convertible, besides looking for a four-year payback. Sometimes companies can **call** an issue, or redeem it early; this can occur either at a specific date, known as the **call date,** or sometimes can be triggered by the common rising above a specified price. Being called is bad news. Essentially you are forced to sell your convertible back to the company—at a price that may be below what you paid—or else you have to convert. Either way you will probably lose the conversion premium. In Olsten's case, the convertible bond could be called in May 1996 at a price of $1,034. If the bond were called, your alternative to accepting cash would be to exchange it for common stock. That stock was worth $1,114 in late 1995—or 4% less than the price of the convert. Companies don't always call converts at the earliest opportunity, but you should always be aware of the call date because in some cases you risk a substantial premium loss.

Another important point to check is the financial quality of the bond or preferred stock. Some experts figure that anywhere from half to three-quarters of all convertibles are below investment grade. That's because small growth companies and firms with financial troubles often find issuing convertibles an attractive way to raise money. Reason: If such an issue is exchanged for common stock, the company will never have to redeem the bond or preferred; in other words, the firm won't have to pay back the principal. Further, since the common will almost certainly have a lower yield, eventual conversion would reduce the cost of the interest and dividends the issuer has to pay.

For specific recommendations, you can subscribe to services such as *The Value Line Convertibles Survey* in New York City (800-833-0046 or 212-907-1500, $625 a year). Whatever your sources of information, though, keep in mind one final caution. Never buy a convertible if you dislike the common shares. If the yield on the convertible is fairly high and the terms are otherwise attractive, it may be worth buying an issue that converts into a common stock that's just slightly above average. But it never pays to buy a convertible backed by a stock you wouldn't want to own at all.

CLOSED-ENDS

Of all the unusual securities available to small investors, closed-end funds are the most interesting—but also can be the most dangerous. Because these funds sometimes sell for less than the value of the securities they hold, you have excellent odds of beating the market if you invest in them shrewdly. However, you can lose as much as half your money if you buy them carelessly. The key to being a winner instead of a big loser is knowing how to tell when closed-ends are undervalued and when they are a rip-off.

Let's start by defining our terms: a **closed-end fund** is a stock company that invests in securities—either stock, bonds, or issues such as convertibles. Historically, closed-ends were the forerunners of today's mutual funds (known technically as **open-end funds**). In fact, several big closed-ends go back to the 1920s. These funds are like open-end mutual funds in many ways—they typically hold diversified portfolios of securities and distribute their income and realized capital gains to shareholders each year. One popular type of closed-end holds shares of a single country.

Closed-ends differ from open-end mutual funds, however, in two important respects. First, their size is fairly constant. Unlike regular mutual funds, which are constantly selling new shares or redeeming them, closed-ends generally have a fixed amount of stock outstanding. A closed-end fund makes an initial public offering just as any other corporation would and then occasionally sells or buys back stock through formal offerings. But in between those offerings—which may be years apart—the number of shares in a closed-end doesn't change. You therefore can buy shares only from an investor who owns them or sell shares you own only to someone who wants to purchase them. Most closed-ends trade on the New York Stock Exchange or another exchange more or less the same way any other stock would.

If you have a good head for economics, you may already have guessed the second feature that separates closed-ends from regular mutual funds: their share prices can vary considerably from the value of the securities they hold. Here's why: Since you buy shares in a regular mutual fund from the fund company, the price is based on the daily value of the fund's holdings. But since you buy closed-ends from other shareholders, the price you pay doesn't have any automatic connection to the value of the fund's portfolio. Because the number of shares is fixed, if a growing number of investors want to buy stock in a closed-end, the price will sell at a premium to the fund's net asset value (NAV). And if a lot of investors want to sell, the closed-end's share price will drop to a discount to NAV.

Changes in premiums and discounts are what can make closed-ends so profitable—or so risky. By buying funds when discounts are big, you stand to multiply your potential profit. If the value of the fund's portfolio goes up, the shares are likely to become more popular and attract new investors. That means you will benefit not only from the fund's rising NAV, but also from a reduction in the discount. This probably sounds confusing, so let's look at a specific case. Say you buy a closed-end with a portfolio worth $12 a share at a 17% discount; you'll pay $10 a share. Then say the fund's NAV climbs to $14 and the discount disappears; your shares will sell for $14. Your profit will be $4 ($14 minus $10), or 40%, even though the fund's NAV has gone up only 17% (from $12 to $14). As you can see, the potential leverage from buying a closed-end fund at a deep discount is enormous, turning an ordinary 17% profit into a 40% bonanza.

The only catch is that the same leverage can work against you if you are foolish enough to buy a closed-end fund at a big premium. If you want an example of just how badly you can be burned in a closed-end, take at look at what happened to shareholders in the Korea Fund between 1989 and 1992—they lost 78% in three years. In 1989 Korea Fund shares were selling for

$43, or at a premium of as much as 70%. The reason for this unusually large premium was that the fund was one of the only ways small investors could put money into what was then among the hottest stock markets in the world. By 1992 the premium was down to as little as 6% and the share price had tumbled to less than $10. One reason: The 1990–91 recession in the United States depressed world trade, and the South Korean economy has always been dependent on exports. And though the shares have since rallied as high as $27, the premium has never come anywhere near its 1989 level.

As an example, the Korea Fund is a bit unusual; closed-ends rarely sell at a premium of more than 10%. Large discounts of as much as 20%, by contrast, are more common. Here's why: When a particular type of investment is hot and premiums are large, fund companies can launch as many closed-ends as they like— investors will buy them. However, when those closed-ends become unpopular, their prices fall to discounts. In theory the fund companies ought to offer to buy in shares when that happens, but actually they try to avoid buybacks. Why? Because they earn fees on the money they manage, and shrinking their funds' assets would reduce their income.

There's also another reason that closed-ends trade at discounts more often than at premiums. Funds often have investments in their portfolios that they bought at cheaper prices. When they sell those holdings, they will have to distribute the gains to shareholders, who will then have to pay capital-gains taxes. So investors generally mark down the value of closed-end fund shares to reflect the hidden tax liabilities resulting from the funds' past gains.

For information on closed-ends, you can consult *Morningstar Closed-End Funds* in Chicago (800-876-5005 or 312-696-6000, $195 a year), which follows more than 360 of them, or *The Value Line Investment Survey* in New York City (800-833-0046 or 212-907-1500), which tracks more than 40. There are also several newsletters that specifically cover these funds; one that I like is *The Scott Letter* in Richmond, Va. (800-356-3508 or 804-741-

8707, $150 a year). If you're interested in a further explanation of the ins and outs of closed-ends, I'd suggest calling the Institute for Econometric Research in Deerfield Beach, Fla. (800-442-9000 or 305-563-9000), which publishes a variety of interesting newsletters, including *Market Logic,* and which recently completed an analysis of closed-ends. *Barron's* and the *Wall Street Journal* also publish data on closed-end funds once a week.

All of these sources provide fund profiles as well as specific recommendations. If you want to select closed-ends on your own, though, you should generally follow these three rules:

■ **Don't buy a closed-end on the initial offering.** Not only do most funds eventually fall to a discount to net asset value, the firm that underwrites a fund offering generally skims off fees of more than 5%. That means a new fund's price could easily drift 10% or so below the initial offering price. Obviously it's smarter to let other investors pay for all the costs of bringing a fund public and then come in and buy once the fund price appears to have stabilized.

■ **Don't buy a closed-end trading at a premium of more than 5%.** Except in cases such as the Korea Fund, where a closed-end provides access to a market that is otherwise out of the reach of many investors, these funds are likely to trade at a discount sooner or later. And when a particular fund frequently carries a premium, it is likely to be a small one. My rule of thumb, therefore, is that you should never pay a premium larger than the commissions on an attractive load fund or the cost of buying and selling an equivalent dollar amount of common stock. Generally speaking, investors should try to avoid paying more than 5% for such costs—and 2% or 3% is a lot more like it.

■ **Do buy closed-ends trading at larger than usual discounts.** The excellent study by the Institute for Econometric Research that I mentioned earlier includes three statistics that I will quote here. First, from 1981 to 1994 closed-end stock funds outperformed open-end equity funds by more than three-quarters of a percentage point a year, on average. Second, closed-ends at discounts outpaced those at premiums by more than eight points. Third, funds at 10%-plus discounts beat those at 10%-plus premiums by more than 17 points. See a pattern?

Here are the reasons that closed-ends at bigger than average discounts do so well: They edge out regular mutual funds because open-ends have to cope with money surging in and out as investor sentiment changes. That means open-ends often have to invest new cash when the market is high and pull money out when stocks are depressed. Closed-ends at discounts also have more assets working for you. When a fund earns 5% on its portfolio and is trading at par, you earn a 5% return on each dollar you invest. But if you could buy the same portfolio at 90¢ on the dollar, 5% earned on the portfolio would be the equivalent of 5.6% on the 90¢ you actually invest.

Finally, just as closed-ends selling above NAV are likely to see their discount narrow or disappear altogether, those at larger than average discounts will probably come back to more normal levels. And a narrowing discount will add a couple of percentage points to your return. The only caveat: Don't buy a closed-end solely because the discount is large; that can be the sign that the management is badly regarded or that the prospects for the assets the fund holds is poor. However, if a closed-end's track record is decent and you like the prospects for its portfolio, buying a fund at a discount will give you one of the best shots you'll ever get at beating the market.

CHAPTER 12

SPECULATIONS:

Do You Have What It Takes to Be a High Roller Instead of a Sucker?

When it comes to making money on risky investments, you might think that the most important personality traits would be daring and courage. You'd be wrong. Without question, the most important characteristic for an investor who hopes to make money as a high roller is restraint. Fact is, it's harder to make back a loss than to build on an existing profit. If you lose 50% on a bad investment, you have to earn not 50%, but 100%, to get even. That means risky investments have to offer exceptional potential returns before they are better choices than alternatives that are less profitable but also less likely to lose money. And since few high-risk investments do offer such wonderful opportunities, the chief trait an aggressive investor needs to be successful is the ability to say "no."

Most investments that offer such compelling returns will be stocks—either shares in small growth companies or potential turnarounds at bargain prices. Elsewhere in this book I've explained how to analyze those types of securities. In this chapter I'll touch on a few other kinds of risky investing. As you'll see, there are a few smart ways to come out ahead and lots of ways to end up holding the bag. In general you should try to follow these three principles:

■ **Carefully monitor your risk level, and never raise it unless there is a truly compelling reason to do so.** For example, investors who buy stocks with borrowed money—a practice known as **margin investing**—should avoid borrowing more than 20% of the value of their accounts. Moreover, you shouldn't take a margin loan at all unless there is an exceptional stock you want to buy or you need a small, temporary loan for some personal reason and would have to pay much higher interest rates if you borrowed elsewhere.

■ **Recognize that with high-risk investments, the deck is usually stacked against you.** Look for the rare situations in which you can get favorable odds on a speculative investment. If you want to trade stock options, for instance, consider selling options against stock you own, rather than buying options.

■ **Remember that investments always have to be evaluated in the context of your total portfolio.** Once in a while you'll find that an investment that would be risky if you bought it by itself will actually limit the volatility of your overall portfolio. A perfect example: putting 5% of your money in gold-mining shares.

Often, though, you'll discover that speculative investments are nothing more than bad deals with fantasy appeal. In advertising, people say you should sell the sizzle and not the steak. Well, in investing, you should buy the steak and not the sizzle. Now here's a look at five risky investing techniques that are likely to tempt you.

BUYING ON MARGIN

The most common speculative investing technique is buying on margin. In fact, you may already be using margin without even knowing it. Most brokerage accounts that allow you to write checks or offer some sort of charge card are essentially tur-bocharged margin accounts. Used correctly, such accounts are wonderfully convenient. They can pump up your investing prof-its and may even allow you to borrow money at lower interest rates than you could otherwise get. But all margin accounts carry an enormous hidden risk. If the stock market falls suddenly, you could sustain exceptionally large losses—or even be forced to sell some of your holdings at horribly low prices.

The basic idea behind margin investing is simple: Rather than having to put up all the cash needed to buy a stock or bond, you can pay only part of the price and borrow the rest of the money. (The rules governing margin generally permit you to borrow up to 50% of the value of your stocks and even more on some other assets, such as Treasury bonds.) The interest rate on a margin loan is much lower than what you would pay on a credit card, for example, because the loan is secured by your stocks and bonds. Margin loan rates change constantly, but as a benchmark, I'm currently paying 9¼%.

TRUE FACT

Interest rates on margin loans can vary from broker to broker by as much as 2.5 percentage points.

If you do a little arithmetic, you can easily understand how investing on margin increases both your potential profits and your risks. Say that you buy $10,000 worth of stock, and the shares soar to $20,000. You've earned a $10,000 profit and doubled your money. Now imagine that you had used the same $10,000 to buy $20,000 of stock by borrowing $10,000 on margin. Again the shares double—to $40,000. You then pay off your $10,000 margin loan and have $30,000 left. That's not double your original investment, but triple. By using margin, you've turned a 100% profit into 200%.

Now let's look at the downside. If you bought the same $10,000 of stock and it dropped in value to $7,000, you'd have lost $3,000, or 30% of your money. However, if you had borrowed another $10,000 and bought $20,000 of stock, the same size loss would leave you with shares worth only $14,000. Pay off the $10,000 margin loan, and you would have only $4,000 left. In other words, by using margin, you would have turned a 30% decline into a catastrophic 60% loss.

In fact, your results would be even worse than these examples suggest. Reason: You have to pay interest on your margin loan—and it will almost always be greater than the extra dividends you earn by holding more shares. If your margin money costs you 10% and you earn a 3% yield on your stock, then the loan costs you 7% a year. That may not sound like much when we're talking about stocks doubling, but it can take quite a bite out of profits in the 15% to 20% range. In fact, since the average return on blue chips is only a bit over 10% (including dividends) and the interest on your margin loan will probably be nearly that high, you're not likely to increase your profits much by buying extra shares with borrowed money. That's why brokerages are willing to lend to you; they get most of your profits in interest while you get to eat all your losses.

All in all, using margin is like casino gambling—it's rigged in favor of the house. Nonetheless, you may occasionally decide to borrow against your stocks and bonds either because there's a stock you really want to buy or because you need money for some other reason and can't borrow at a lower interest rate elsewhere. But before you take a margin loan, be sure you're aware of these three drawbacks:

■ **The interest on the loan is tax-deductible only if you invest the money (and buying tax-exempt bonds doesn't count).** If you borrow against stocks to pay for a vacation, you can't deduct your margin interest on your income taxes. You also can't deduct margin interest if you buy tax-exempt municipal bonds. Moreover, it's difficult to deduct margin interest in excess of your investment income. In other words, if you earn $3,000 in bond interest and $2,000 in stock dividends, you probably won't be able to deduct more than $5,000 of margin interest even if you borrowed the money solely to buy additional shares. My advice: Use margin sparingly and preferably only for investment purposes.

■ **Rates on margin loans vary considerably from broker to broker.** A recent **MONEY** magazine survey found that margin loan rates can differ by more than two percentage points from one broker to another. Further, rates will likely be higher on a $10,000 loan than a $75,000 loan. So don't be afraid to shop around—and ask your broker to match the best rate you find elsewhere. If worst comes to worst, you can always threaten to transfer your account to another firm.

■ **Your broker may have to sell your securities.** If your stocks and bonds fall sharply in value, you can get what is known as a **margin call,** requiring you to put up more securities or cash as collateral. If you don't ante up, the broker may be required to sell at least some of your investments to reduce your balance. When this happens, it's a disaster. You are almost certain to be selling near the bottom. To be sure you never get a margin call, follow this rule: Never borrow more than 20% of the value of your account. If you don't go above that mark, it's unlikely that you would be faced with a margin call even during a bear market.

SELLING SHORT

For most small investors, **selling short**—essentially betting that a stock will go down—is an even worse idea than buying on margin. To understand why, you need to know the mechanics of the deal. Basically, a short seller borrows shares from a brokerage and sells them. Eventually the investor has to buy the stock back and return it to the firm. If the share price has declined in the meantime, the short seller will pay less to buy back the borrowed shares than he or she received for selling them. By contrast, if the stock has gone up since the borrowed shares were sold, the investor will lose a bundle. Already you may think short selling isn't so attractive—but actually it's even worse than it sounds. Here's why:

■ **Your gains are limited, but your losses are almost unlimited.** The best case for a short seller is that you buy a stock, the company goes bankrupt, and the shares become virtually worthless. If that happened, you would be able to buy the stock back for next to nothing and thereby earn almost 100% on your investment. Your potential losses have no such limit, though. If you short a stock and it doubles, you lose 100%; if it triples, you're out 200%; and if it quadruples, 300%.

■ **Brokerages rip off small investors who sell short.** When you borrow money to buy stock on margin, you receive dividends on the shares but have to pay interest on the loan. So it stands to reason that when you sell borrowed stock, the reverse should hold true: you would have to pay the dividends due on the borrowed stock but receive interest on the cash proceeds from selling the shares. Forget about it. You do have to pay the dividends, but unless you're a big professional investor, you don't get any of the interest on the cash proceeds from the stock sale.

■ **The stock market goes up more often than it goes down.** Short selling might make sense if it were a fair gamble—that is, if a stock were just as likely to fall as it were to rise. But it isn't. On average the stock market returns 10% or more a year, including a yield of just over 4%. Obviously that means prices must rise at a compound rate of 6% or 7%. As a result, share prices have to go up two or three times as often as they go down. That's why bear markets last only about 18 months, while bull markets often last three or four years.

These three problems add up to a possible nightmare scenario for a short seller. Normally, if you buy a stock and it turns out to be a turkey, you can just let it sit. Perhaps one day it will recover. At worst you can wait to sell it until you need a tax loss. Since you can't lose more than you invest, inaction is always an option. But if you sell a stock short and it starts rising, it may never come back down to where you bought it. Month after month you may see it climb—and your potential loss will keep getting bigger. Eventually your brokerage will force you to buy the shares back to stop the bleeding. There's an old Wall Street saying about selling borrowed shares that pretty well sums up this situation: "He who sells what isn't his'n must buy it back or go to prison."

TRADING STOCK OPTIONS

One of the great feats of financial engineering over the past 20 years has been the rise of modern **stock options.** Although such options have long existed in some form, it was only in the early 1970s that an active public market developed, enabling investors to trade options. Equally important, economic theorists figured out how to value options at about the same time (Fischer Black and Myron Scholes published their classic paper on option pricing in May 1973). The existence of a reliable pricing model was essential for options to gain the enormous popularity they have today. In fact, the whole question of how options should be priced is essential for deciding what role they should play in your own investment strategy.

So let's begin at the beginning: Imagine that a stock is trading at $39 a share and you have an option to buy it for $40 anytime within the next year. Why is that option worth $6 or $7? In fact, why is the option worth anything at all, since all you have is the right to buy the stock for more than it currently costs? The answer is that your option is a lopsided deal; you can buy the stock for $40 anytime within the next year—but you don't have to buy it at all. If the stock goes above $40 and you exercise your option to buy it at that price, you can turn around, sell it at the market price, and keep the difference as your profit. By contrast, if the stock never breaks $40, you never have to exercise and you don't have to share in any losses.

As an analogy, you could compare the way an option works to a gambling game based on a coin toss. If the coin comes up heads, you win $1. If it comes up tails, you lose $1—but you don't have to pay it. If someone offered to play this one-sided coin-toss game with you but wanted to be paid something for each toss, what would be a fair price? That's not too hard to figure out: you have an even chance of winning $1 and an even chance of losing nothing. For a fair wager, you should pay the person who takes the other side of this game 50¢ for each toss.

The value of an option can be calculated exactly the same way, except that there are so many variables and they are so complicated that you need a computer. For one thing, stocks are more likely to rise than fall—so options that give you the right to buy a stock at a specified price (known as **calls**) cost more than options that allow you to sell shares at a certain price (known as **puts**). Further, you aren't gambling for a fixed profit of $1; the shares could trade at a wide variety of prices. I won't even try to explain all the mathematics of option valuation, but there are three important things to remember:

■ **The more volatile the stock, the more an option is worth.** This is just common sense. The higher the stock price can swing, the bigger your profit might be. You don't need to worry how low it might go, of course, because you don't have to buy the stock if it would result in your losing money.

■ **The longer an option runs, the more it is worth.** This also is easy to understand. The longer an option's term, the greater the chance that the stock will rise enough for you to be able to exercise at a profit. Further, it stands to reason that a two-year option would cost more than one lasting a single year. A two-year option is nothing more than a one-year option for the current year plus another one-year option for the following year.

■ **The higher interest rates are, the more an option is worth.** This is less obvious, but let me give you an example that works as a partial explanation. Imagine there were a stock that was almost certain to go up. If you had to choose between buying the shares or buying an option in such a situation, how much would you be willing to pay for the option? Well, if you bought a one-year option, you would have to put up only a fraction of what the stock would cost you, so you could continue to earn interest on most of your money. As an option owner, however, you would miss out on the dividends that stockholders would receive. The value of the option would therefore reflect both the extra interest you would earn and the dividends you would forgo. And the higher interest rates were, the more the option would be worth.

The reason I have gone into so much detail about the valuation of options is that it helps explain why buying stock options is such a bad idea. The fact is that when you have taken into account all the factors that determine pricing, you find that options are extremely expensive for the buyer. If the return you can expect from a blue-chip stock is about 11% a year, then you will find that options on that stock generally trade as though its expected return were 12% or 13%. Just as with margin investing and short selling, these are casino odds—where the house always has an edge of a percentage point or two.

RULE NO. 10 OF INVESTING:
SMALL INVESTORS WHO BUY STOCK OPTIONS
GENERALLY END UP LOSERS.

Stock options differ, however, from the other speculations we have discussed because you can get on the same side as the house. How? By selling options instead of buying them. If you do, then you can easily earn several percentage points more than the return on stocks. There's just one catch: When you sell a call option (the most profitable type) without owning the stock, you essentially become a short seller. The reason is that the investor who buys your option has the right to purchase the stock from you at a specified price. So if you sell an option on a stock at $40 and the shares soar to $60, you will have to buy the stock at $60 and then sell it for $40 to the person you sold the option to. That means losing $20 a share. There's a way around this problem, however. Only sell options on stocks you own (a strategy known as **covered writing**).

There are two ways to profit by writing covered calls. The first is to buy a stock you like and sell a call against it. For example, you could buy IBM at $100 a share and sell a one-year call for $13. Since IBM pays a $1 annual dividend, your annual return would be $14. If the stock is above $100 and is called away from you after a year, you'll earn 14% on your investment. And if the stock is below $100, then you'll keep the stock but also get to keep the option premium, which will reduce your real cost to only $87 a share.

The other way to use calls is as a way to sell. Let's return to the IBM example but assume you bought the stock at $80. With the shares now trading at $100, you have a 25% profit. That's awfully nice, but you think the stock could go higher—and you want at least a 35% profit. By selling a $100 call for $13, you'll have a 41% profit in a year if the stock stays above $100 ($100 plus $13 vs. $80). In fact, you'll reach the 35% profit you want even if the stock declines to $95 because you'll get to keep the $13 option premium ($95 plus $13 vs. $80).

I've actually done quite well by selling options on stock I owned to leverage my profits. Because premiums are bigger on volatile stocks, I've found the strategy particularly helpful with technology and biotechnology shares. For example, I've bought a biotech stock like Amgen when it was depressed. Then a few months later, after it had rebounded to a modest 15% profit, say, I've been able to sell a six-month or one-year option and leverage my gain to more than 30%. The only drawback of this strategy is that you have to be prepared to sell the shares on which you write the option. In some cases you may regret this, because the stock may go on to a much bigger gain. That's never bothered me. When I've made 30% or 40% in less than a year, I don't spend much time worrying about what I could have earned.

INVESTING IN NEW ISSUES

When a company sells stock to the public for the first time, that sale is known as an **initial public offering**—or IPO, for short. And as I explained in Chapter 3, such new stock offerings are a common way for small growth companies to raise money from small investors. Next time you pick up the phone, though, and a pushy broker tries to get you to invest in an IPO, hang up. The deal will probably be a dog.

There's no question that IPOs are potentially profitable; a number of studies show that they return anywhere from 10% to 20% in the first week of trading. Only trouble is, that's an average figure, which includes both good and bad IPOs. And usually you won't be able to buy the good ones. By the time a company goes public, all the brokerages know whether it's likely to be any good. Since most initial offerings are fairly small, there won't be enough stock to go around if a particular IPO looks like a winner. So what do the brokerages do? They allocate hot IPOs to their important mutual fund clients or millionaire customers who do a lot of business with the firm. If you're just an average guy, you won't be able to get any stock. And when you can get stock, it's probably an IPO you don't want to own.

TRUE FACT

Three-quarters of all initial public offerings (IPOs) trade at a discount to their offering prices within a year.

Source: *California Technology Stock Letter*

The result of all this is that new offerings typically shoot up as soon as they begin trading—and they keep those gains for anywhere from a few hours to a few months. Then they fall back. In fact, after their initial gains, such stocks often underperform the market for as long as three years—and frequently even post losses. Three-quarters of all new issues trade below their offering prices within the first year. The bottom line: If an IPO is worth buying, chances are you won't be able to get any stock on the offering. And if you buy once the stock begins trading in the market at a 15%-plus premium over its offering price, the odds are very high that you'll lose money in the following year.

Does this mean that there's no way to make money on IPOs? Not at all. Just follow the popular ones and see if they fall back to a price less than 10% above their offering price. If you like small growth stocks, they might be smart buys at that level.

OWNING GOLD

Without doubt, gold is the most misunderstood investment. If used properly, it protects you against some of the biggest threats to your wealth—and offers you a shot at easy profits. Used improperly, it's a moronic investment that marks you as a fool or a crackpot.

The great thing about gold is that it's one of the few investments that usually moves in the opposite direction from stocks. If you remember our discussion of asset allocation from Chapter 2, that makes gold worth its weight in whatever. Quite simply, by putting, say, 5% of a diversified portfolio in gold or gold-mining shares, you will lower your risk without hurting your return. In fact, there is no argument I know for not having 5% of your total assets in a mutual fund that holds North American gold-mining shares. The reason is that this holding gives you an enormous measure of protection against the biggest economic danger that stocks face—a sudden flareup of inflation.

TRUE FACT

Though gold is a risky investment by itself, adding gold to a portfolio reduces your overall risk and increases your return.

Imagine, just hypothetically, that inflation confounds all the experts and jumps to 7% over the next five years. As a result, the price/earnings ratios of your stocks sink from 16 to 13. Your profits will be 19% below what they would have been had the average P/E remained constant. Your gold mutual fund, however, could easily quadruple under these circumstances. That enormous gain on your gold investments will almost be enough to make up for your entire shortfall in stocks.

Historically, it has usually been a winning strategy to buy gold when inflation was below 3% or so, as it was from 1991 to 1995. For another benchmark, buy when the price of gold is close to the cost of production—say, around $350 an ounce nowadays. The gold price can't go much lower than that, because if it remains below the cost of production for any length of time, mines will start shutting down. And inevitably, if you buy gold cheap, inflation will creep up enough for gold shares to outperform the rest of the market—at least for a stretch. Now here's what not to do with gold:

■ **Don't buy gold when inflation is out of control.** As soon as inflation eases—and it will—the price of gold will collapse. And you'll end up like those poor suckers who bought gold for more than $800 an ounce back in 1980—under water for the next 15 years.

■ **Don't buy gold to make a profit.** Gold doesn't provide any earnings at all. It just sits there like a lump. In fact, over the past 100 years, gold has roughly kept up with inflation—and earned no real profit at all. Gold-mining shares do earn something. After all, mines are businesses that produce profits. But they are not very good businesses. The real virtue of gold is protection against inflation. It's a store of wealth, not a source of profit.

■ **Don't buy gold coins.** Unless you are paranoid, physical gold is a silly investment. Instead of earning a profit, you have to pay money to store it in a safe-deposit box or elsewhere. And unlike a stock, you can't get a replacement copy if you lose it.

CHAPTER 13

TECHNICAL ANALYSIS:

How to Spot a Stock Market Trend and Ride It to Big Profits

Imagine that you are an art dealer and you regularly buy and sell late-nineteenth-century and early-twentieth-century paintings. One day you notice that paintings by so-called California impressionists are bringing remarkably high prices. That surprises you. Obviously, French impressionists—even minor ones— have enduring market value. And you like the work of some of the well-known American artists who studied with the impressionists in France—painters from New York and New England such as Childe Hassam and William Merritt Chase. But you've scarcely heard of these California guys, and frankly you don't much like their work. Too many of the California paintings look as though they belong on wall calendars.

Nonetheless, more and more California impressionist paintings turn up at auctions. And their prices keep rising. Works that might have gone for $5,000 10 years ago are bringing anywhere from $20,000 to $50,000. Finally you decide that you'd be smart to buy some for your gallery. Rising values may be more than a fad, you figure. There are plenty of wealthy people in California who can afford paintings. And a lot of people like to collect works by local artists—especially local landscapes. So you start buying some top examples as they come up at auction. After all, it doesn't matter whether you like the paintings personally or not—all that counts is that they'll be a good addition to your gallery's inventory.

Stock pickers who make their buy and sell decisions about stocks in much the same way are called **technical analysts.** Usually, when investors buy shares in a company, they base their decisions on facts about the business. They may look for firms with leading positions in their markets, exciting new products, or superb management. Buyers who select shares on those grounds are known as **fundamental analysts.** They are like art dealers who buy paintings they themselves would like to own.

Technical analysts, by contrast, buy stocks not because they necessarily like the companies, but because other investors appear to like them. In particular, a technician watches a stock's behavior in the marketplace, focusing on changes in share prices and trading volume. When a particular issue begins attracting broader interest, technicians may buy it in the belief that the stock will become increasingly popular and move even higher. The combination of bigger volume and rising prices constitutes a trend. And as the old Wall Street saying goes, "The trend is your friend."

Both the advantages and the disadvantages of this approach are obvious. On the positive side, the fact that a growing number of investors are willing to pay increasing prices for a stock may well be a tip-off that the company has something going for it. On the negative side, buying a stock just because other people are buying it doesn't make a whole lot of sense. Sometimes this is called the greater fool theory: however dumb you were to buy some dubious stock, there will always be a greater fool you can sell it to. Trouble is, sometimes when you invest on this theory, there isn't a greater fool—you turn out to be the last fool in the chain.

Precisely because technical stock picking can backfire, identifying genuine trends turns out to be tricky. To spot them, technical analysts, who are also known as **chartists,** rely heavily on graphs. These plottings can get so complex and arcane that they become the butt of jokes. Moreover, there is little solid evidence that such charts give reliable signals. But even market analysts who are hostile to charting rely on some technical principles—whether they realize it or not.

Technical analysis itself rests on two basic beliefs. First, major events in the stock market rarely occur out of the blue; they are the product of trends that develop over extended periods of time. Second, history repeats itself; certain patterns recur with identifiable signposts that can tip off an astute investor. Those two beliefs are true, in my opinion. However, their value as a guide to investing decisions is seriously undercut by one great weakness: Most of the key signs and signals that a technical analyst looks at are ambiguous. As a result, the value of any technical assessment of the market is only as good as the analyst doing it.

Nonetheless, it's worthwhile to be aware of some of the basic principles that lie behind technical analysis. The stock market certainly does repeat itself—although it never does exactly the same thing the second time around. Further, for the simple reason that investor psychology doesn't change much, patterns do recur with the same signposts. In addition, you should know what common technical terms mean, since you're likely to run into them when you read brokerage reports or news stories about the stock market. So I'll give you a quick run-through of the essentials. While I don't believe these notions provide secret keys to the stock market, I do think they contain some first-rate common sense about investing. Here are the concepts you need to understand:

■ **Volume.** The most important technical idea is that by following the flow of money, you can tell where stocks are headed. The reasoning is that the so-called smart money has information that most investors don't; so by watching where this smart money goes, you can spot new trends before most other investors do. As a result, it's crucial to be alert for surges in trading **volume** that could signal a change in direction by the smart money (presumably the "dumb money" invests at random).

I don't really believe in this distinction between the smart money and the dumb money. It's true, of course, that some professional investors do have access to inside information and use it illegally to help them in their trading; that's why takeover targets and some of the other special situation stocks discussed in Chapter 10 often rise noticeably in the days leading up to an important announcement. But considering insider trading to be the most important factor in the entire market sounds to me a little too much like a conspiracy theory. There are millions of investors out there, analyzing stocks in dozens of different ways and relying on a variety of information sources.

Nonetheless, rising trading volume is often a signal that something important is happening at a company. Fact is, although the stock market reflects all the public news on a company, information doesn't travel instantaneously. It spreads over time. First a handful of people discover an attractive stock; then knowledgeable investors join in, and finally everyone jumps on the bandwagon. Just as with any other fad, a few set the trend, the fashion-conscious follow, and then the masses catch on. Not long after everyone is on board, the fashion becomes passé. In stock market terms, this means that any move is more significant if it occurs on above average trading volume. By contrast, decreasing volume is often a sign that a trend is running out of steam.

■ **Momentum.** Literally, this term refers to the speed with which a stock price or a market index moves. If a price starts rising quickly, odds are it will continue to go up for a while. In fact, momentum is the first cousin of trading volume. Just as rising volume alerts you to the start of a trend, so does increasing momentum. And just as dwindling volume signals the end, so does weakening momentum. This is all common sense: the more money investors are willing to spend on a stock and the faster they mark up the price, the higher the value is likely to go before

A JUMP IN TRADING VOLUME CONFIRMED THE START OF THE 1982 BULL MARKET

The start of a new bull market is usually marked by two signs: strong momentum and rising volume. For instance, when a major bull market began in August 1982, the Dow rose steeply through the end of the year. Even more important, trading volume soared to as much as twice what it had been in the first half of 1982. That higher volume confirmed that the upturn in the Dow would have staying power. And, in fact, share prices continued to climb for the following five years.

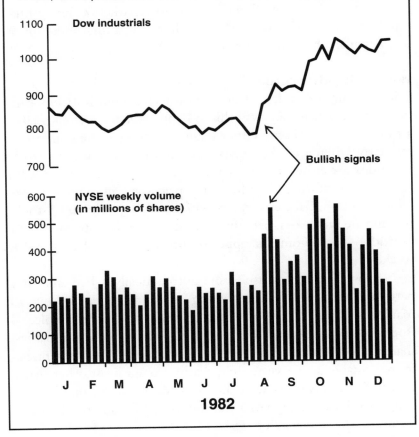

the boom runs its course. Together, volume and momentum define a trend.

While trends generally have the same beginnings, they can end in two very different ways. In the first case, volume and momentum begin to get progressively weaker. If this happens after a rapid price runup, the stock is said to be **topping out;** the same process after a decline is called **bottoming** or **building a base.** Alternatively, trends can end by going to an extreme. After a market rise, this is known as a **blowoff;** prices accelerate until they can't rise any faster. Following a market decline, a final rapid drop is called a **sell-off.** In either case, a final spike up or down signals the end of the trend.

■ **Breadth (advance/decline).** So far, we've talked about a stock price or a market index advancing or declining in isolation. But, of course, that isn't the way things happen. When a stock makes a move, other stocks are either rising or falling at the same time. Similarly, when a market index goes up or down, stocks outside the index are either moving with the index or against it. Breadth is a measure of the extent to which prices are all moving in the same direction. Greater breadth—an increasing number of stocks moving in synch—signals that a trend is getting stronger. Less breadth—stocks going in opposite directions—means a trend is weakening.

Narrow breadth, in itself, isn't automatically a bad sign. If a particular group of stocks is rising at a time when the overall market is falling, the group could be really hot. For example, oil stocks soared between 1979 and 1982, while many companies' shares did poorly. Reason: High inflation made oil potentially more valuable at the same time that it eroded most other firms' profits. Smart investors were able to cash in on the oils for several years. However, when a trend starts off broad and then gets narrower, the end may be near.

To monitor changing breadth, investors often calculate an index called the **advance/decline line.** Typically this consists of taking the number of stocks on the New York Stock Exchange that closed higher for the day and subtracting the number that ended lower (the starting point of the index is arbitrary). If the line rises, it means that stocks are up more often than they are down, and vice versa. Generally, investors consider a broad market trend confirmed if the advance/decline line is moving in the same direction as the stock price index.

■ **Divergence.** When important indexes move in opposite directions, that disparity is known as **divergence** and can be a warning of trouble ahead. For example, from late 1980 through early 1981 the Dow industrials moved higher, while the equally important Standard & Poor's 500 stock index edged lower. Since the S&P reflects a broader range of companies while the Dow tracks only 30 (mostly industrial) firms, the divergence between the two indexes indicated that much of the U.S. economy was failing to rebound from the brief 1980 slump. Sure enough, the economy tipped back into recession in late 1981 and the Dow fell more than 15% from its peak.

Divergence can exist between any pair of indexes or even between individual issues. Big stocks could be rising as small stocks fall. Industrial shares could decline while financial stocks do well. Ford could go up while GM sinks. By itself, divergence doesn't mean anything. However, when all stocks are moving up or down together, you can afford to be a little complacent. Some very powerful, broad force is pushing everything in the same direction. On the other hand, when you see a stock or group you own diverging from the rest of the market, you should be just a bit nervous. Be sure you have a good reason to think that your holdings can buck the overall trend.

■ **Bottom (support).** When a stock goes down for a while and then stabilizes, technical analysts say it has **found support** or **made a bottom.** As I mentioned earlier, this low point can be signaled by a sharp sell-off on heavy volume (sometimes called **capitulation**) or by a succession of lows on diminishing volume. Chartists give various names to the patterns made by vari-

DIVERGENCE SIGNALED THE 1981–82 BEAR MARKET

During a healthy stock market advance, shares of all kinds should be going up at the same time. When they don't, that so-called divergence may be a sign of a weakening market and a coming price decline. For example, from late 1980 through early 1981, the Dow industrials continued to move higher. But Standard & Poor's 500 stock index—which reflects a broader range of companies—edged lower. Sure enough, that was a warning sign of a bear market. As the economy tipped into the 1981–82 recession, share prices fell more than 15% from their highs.

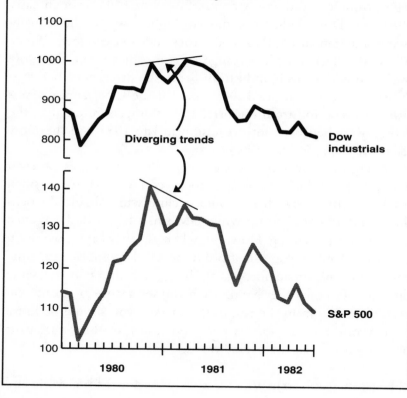

ous types of successive lows. If several lows are all at the same level, they may be called a double or triple bottom; if the lows make a smooth, curving line with very little "bounce," they may be called a saucer bottom. Beyond that, the possible patterns get even fancier—including triangles, wedges, flags, and pennants.

Don't worry about such nonsense. I don't believe that the specific shape of a technical chart tells you anything about what a stock is likely to do. All that matters is that a stock makes a bottom when all the people who badly want to sell have had a chance to get out (which means that future trades will likely be initiated by people who want to buy). Either all the sellers panic and dump their stock simultaneously in a sell-off or they have to exit in waves as a stock bumps up and down. Whichever happens, once most of the likely sellers are out, a stock can lay the groundwork for a new advance—assuming nothing else changes. That last condition is crucial. No matter what chart pattern a stock has made, it can always drop further if there is additional bad news that no one has anticipated. The same general principles apply to the market as a whole. A bear market ends once all the sellers have dumped their shares, assuming that most investors have correctly gauged the extent of the bad economic news.

■ **Top (resistance).** Generally speaking, **tops** are the mirror image of bottoms. In two important respects, however, they differ. First, they are more likely to end in climaxes than bottoms are. That's just simple psychology: people can be more easily persuaded to go on buying sprees than to sell at a loss. As a result, a popular stock can rocket to an unsustainable height powered by little more than investor enthusiasm, while a sharp sell-off requires real panic to convince shareholders to sell when they are down.

Second, it's easier to know that you're at a bottom than that you're at a top (or, as a technician might say, support is more solid than resistance). To understand why, consider the two situations: At a bottom a stock has found support because all the shareholders who want to sell have had a chance to get out and the share price has fallen to an undervalued level. For all practical purposes, the pool of likely sellers is limited to investors who already own the stock; once they are out, they are out. And the price can be shown to be undervalued based upon the prices at which the stock has traded in the past. By contrast, the resistance to further upward movement that stocks run into is inherently weak. First, the pool of potential buyers isn't limited, the way the pool of sellers is; every investor is a potential buyer, so you can't be sure when buying is exhausted. Second, there are fewer benchmarks to show when a stock has gone too high. Whereas a bottom can be defined by where a stock has traded in the past, historical prices provide little guidance if a stock is setting records.

Stock traders summarize these two differences between bottoms and tops by saying that you can pick a bottom, but you can't pick a top. What that means is that you can find stocks that are obviously cheap, buy them, and know that sooner or later they will recover. By contrast, even if share prices are overvalued, you can't be sure that they won't get even more overvalued. That's what makes it hard to decide when to sell a successful stock—and extremely dangerous ever to try selling a stock short (selling borrowed shares in the hope of being able to buy them back later at a loss).

■ **Trend.** Throughout this chapter I've talked about trends without defining the term. In technical analysis, a **trend** refers specifically to the chief underlying direction of a stock or of the overall market. Technicians generally prefer to look only at their charts, deliberately ignoring the business and economic factors that underlie major trends. I think that's a mistake. Personally, I believe that technical analysis is helpful *only* when it enables you to get a clearer picture of the market's fundamentals. For example, say that you like a growth stock that has been turning in 15% annual increases in earnings per share for three or four years. Assuming that the overall market's average price/earnings ratio doesn't change substantially, you'd expect that growth stock's price to rise in tandem with its earnings. In fact, if you graphed the share price, it would roughly follow a straight line corresponding to 15% compound earnings growth. And that trend would continue as long as investors expected those profit gains to come through on time.

When analysts talk about trends, they use a few other terms as well. The chief force driving share prices up or down is known as the **primary trend.** If the primary trend is upward, it is called a bull market; if downward, a bear market. Temporary departures from the primary trend are known as **secondary trends.** A **correction** is a short-lived decline in an upward primary trend (or bull market). A **rally** is a brief advance in a downward primary trend (or bear market). Anything smaller than a secondary trend is called a **tertiary trend** and is regarded as largely meaningless.

■ **Break.** The essential technical view of the stock market is that one primary trend follows another—and you want always to invest in line with the primary trend. Remember: The trend is your friend. But how do you know that one trend is over and a new one has begun? Good question. With typical circular reasoning, technical analysis holds that a primary trend continues until it stops. To determine that a new trend is starting, technicians look for key changes of directions that are known as **breaks.** Sometimes new uptrends are called **breakouts,** while downtrends are known as **breakdowns.**

Like everything in technical analysis, determining that a break has occurred is subjective, and the signals are ambiguous. Generally, technicians believe that a break has occurred when the market deviates from trend by more than 5% (or some other specified amount). To pick the simplest example, if a stock has surpassed $38 a share three times in the past 18 months but never topped $40, a technician would conclude that there is resistance at $40—in other words, $40 is a likely top. However, if on the fourth try the stock passes $38 and then, instead of falling back, continues to rise and tops $42 (5% above $40), the technician would probably decide that the stock had "broken out" and was headed substantially higher.

DOW THEORY

When it comes to assessing the direction of the stock market as a whole, technical concepts fit neatly together into an approach known as Dow theory. This system was conceived by Charles H. Dow of the *Wall Street Journal* around 1900 and developed further over the following 30 years. The basic idea behind Dow theory is that bull and bear markets alternate, depending on whether the economy is expanding or heading into recession. To be a successful investor, you need to know which type of market you're in. And it's more important to be absolutely sure that a shift in the primary trend has occurred than to jump on board right at the beginning.

In a true economic expansion, Dow figured, both industrial companies and transportation firms would prosper. His reasoning: For a strong economy to be sustainable, goods would have to be not only manufactured, but also shipped for sale to consumers. If both manufacturing and transportation were robust, an economic boom could be self-sustaining: higher sales of manufactured goods would boost workers' salaries and enable them to consume more. In turn, higher consumer spending would increase the demand for manufactured goods. Dow therefore devised two stock indexes—the first consisting of the shares of 12 manufacturers and the second of 20 railroads. As you may have guessed, these two indexes later evolved into the Dow Jones Industrial Average and the Dow Jones Transportation Average.

Now here's Dow theory's key test: For a new primary trend to be established, both the industrial average and the transportation average have to change their primary trends. When that occurs, the indexes are said to have confirmed—and a new bull or bear market officially begins. Later on, the Dow system added a third index, a utilities average. Since utilities are hypersensitive to investors' expectations about interest rates, the utilities average often reacts to the economic outlook more quickly than the other two indexes. That makes it a leading indicator for the bull and bear markets tracked by Dow theory.

TRUE FACT

Advances and declines in electric utility stocks often anticipate moves in the overall market. Reason: Utilities are hypersensitive to interest rates and may react faster to changes in investors' expectations for the economy.

These three indicators, used together, work quite well. A rising utilities average tips off investors that a bear market may be about to end. Then, when the Dow industrials break out by setting a record high, they signal a potential new bull market. However, it is only when the transportation average confirms the rise that the bull market is considered to be under way. Similarly, when the utilities start to drop, that's a warning bell that the stock market advance may be over. Investors should wait to sell, however, until both the industrials and the transports have turned down.

Of course, technical analysis has developed enormously since the 1930s, and there are a wide variety of approaches besides Dow theory. Frankly, though, I don't think you need to waste much time learning about fancier technical theories. As I've already said, there is no real evidence that technical analysis can accurately predict the future based on any objective tests. To the extent that the technical approach works, it is subjective—in other words, technical measures can help someone with a good feel for the stock market sharpen his analysis. And in the final analysis, the most reliable technical concepts boil down to simple common sense.

Most important is the idea that the stock market follows some major trend most of the time; such a trend is defined by volume, momentum, and breadth. Further, not every departure from that trend signals the start of a new trend.

RULE NO. 11 OF INVESTING: YOU MAKE MONEY BY PARTICIPATING IN THE STOCK MARKET'S MAJOR MOVES, NOT BY FIGHTING THEM.

That may sound obvious, but you'd be surprised how many investors think they have to be wise guys to earn above average profits in stocks. Fact is, it's more important not to make any errors. Based on Dow theory and other basic technical principles, here are the five common mistakes you should avoid:

■ **Don't overtrade.** Since investors make the biggest profits by riding major trends, it's self-defeating to buy and sell any more often than absolutely necessary. Most moves that appear to be changes in the primary trend are actually secondary trends you can ignore. An investor who bought stocks at the bottom in 1982, for example, could have held them right through the '87 crash and the 1990–91 bear market without any great cost. The Dow has risen more than sixfold over that 14-year period.

■ **Don't jump the gun.** You don't have to buy at the bottom and sell at the top to make money in the stock market. All you need to do is catch the middle part of the important trends. In fact, your biggest danger is buying too soon. Often you can anticipate a rebound in a stock or a recovery in the overall market. But if you invest before there is clear evidence that a comeback has started, you can easily end up sitting with dead money for six months or even a year. That takes a far greater toll on your compound rate of return than you might imagine.

■ **Don't expect the stock you own to be an exception.** Three out of four stocks rise in a bull market and nine out of 10 fall in a bear market. Moreover, divergences are usually a sign that a bull market is breaking down. So if you own a stock that is continuing to rise when the rest of the market has turned down, be careful. While a handful of issues are exceptions that can swim against the current, most of the time stocks eventually get drawn into the trend for their industry groups or for the market as a whole.

■ **Don't worry too much about short-term moves.** Almost everything that happens to a stock in the space of less than a week is insignificant. There are a few obvious exceptions, of course. For example, an extraordinary one-day price jump on heavy trading volume may well be a sign that a major news story is about to break. Nonetheless, if you buy blue-chip stocks for the long term and read the news stories on your companies that appear in financial publications, you actually wouldn't need to check your stocks more than once a week—or even once a month.

■ **Don't fight the tape.** Originality and high spirits are not big pluses when it comes to investing. Success with stocks depends on more homely virtues such as patience and humility. To win with stocks, small investors should wait until a bull market appears to have started, buy high-quality issues, and ideally hold those stocks for the entire move. In fact, the secret to making money in the stock market is longevity. Buy some stocks—preferably when you are young—and hold on to them. Or, to paraphrase Woody Allen: Ninety percent of investing is just showing up.

CHAPTER 14

SOURCES OF INFORMATION:

Where to Get the Information You Need to Make Successful Investing Decisions

By law, corporate insiders are restricted from using their special knowledge to profit unfairly. They also are required to treat all outside investors equally. A chief executive, for example, cannot legally tell friends to buy or sell stock based on inside information. Nor are top executives allowed to favor large professional investors over small shareholders. That's the theory, anyway. In practice, however, the principle that all shareholders should be treated equally is impossible to implement. In fact, even if all the top executives at a company were scrupulously honest, they would not be able to provide shareholders with a level playing field.

The basic problem has to do with the way information flows. Top executives maintain ongoing relationships with large shareholders and with securities analysts. They do this not to cheat small investors, but to be sure that information about their company is disseminated throughout the stock market. As a result, even if everyone always acted impartially, some large investors would have a context that immediately allowed them to grasp the importance of corporate developments—and small investors wouldn't.

Of course, that isn't the end of the pros' advantages. It's the way of the world that the rich and well connected help their friends and are helped in turn. Specifically, stock analysts who talk regularly to the companies they follow often make investment recommendations to their own firms' brokers before they write up reports for small investors. And the brokers, in turn, pass along the info to their best customers first. The bottom line is that even if none of the pros does anything that comes anywhere near being illegal—and sometimes they do, of course—small investors will learn important information after thousands of other well-connected people already know it.

Does that mean that the stock market is rigged and that small investors can't compete? Not at all. But you do have to understand the disadvantages you face so that you can pick your spots and fight where the terrain favors you. In simplest terms, you should try to avoid competing with pros where rapid access to information is crucial. They'll learn everything before you do. That's a good reason, for example, not to buy shares in companies that are involved in takeover struggles.

By contrast, the pros' information advantage is much smaller when it comes to picking depressed, undervalued stocks that could recover over the space of three years. When Merck traded below $30 a share in 1993 and 1994—less than 60% of its price a couple of years earlier—little special knowledge was needed to recognize that the stock would eventually rebound. The reason for the price decline was investor anxiety about the Clinton health care plan, which would have hurt drug companies. And it was fairly clear that Merck would rebound once the turmoil caused by that plan was past. Insiders didn't really have any special insights into how long that would take.

Fact is, in situations where the long-term outlook is the key to profits, small investors actually have an advantage over the pros: they don't have to beat the market on a quarter-by-quarter basis. Talk to mutual fund managers and they will tell you that the competitive pressure to lead the rankings every quarter forces them to make investing decisions that they know are second rate. The pros simply can't afford to lag the market for several quarters in a row even if they know a particular strategy will pay off in the long run.

Here, then, are the key principles to keep in mind when you try to decide how to get the best investing information:

1. Have a buy list of top-quality stocks you would like to own, and develop your own context by following the general business news about those companies.

2. Try never to trade on news reports; odds are that investors more plugged in than you will long have snagged whatever profits were there to be made.

3. Always play for the long term, where small investors have an advantage.

**RULE NO. 12 OF INVESTING:
ANYTHING REPORTED IN THE NEWS IS ALREADY
REFLECTED IN A COMPANY'S SHARE PRICE.**

Wise investors, therefore, resist the urge to make short-term trading decisions based on the morning's headlines. Nonetheless, having good news sources is essential to investing success. Unless you are prepared to spend hours and hours analyzing stocks yourself—which is out of the question for most small investors—you will have to rely on newspapers and magazines for general background and on standard research sources and newsletters for stock analysis. In addition, if you're a high-tech sort of person, you'll find an increasing amount of helpful information available through on-line computer services. In a few pages, I'll tell you how to get the most out of these sources.

First, though, you should be aware of two organizations that are dedicated to helping small investors build long-term stock portfolios based on the sorts of principles I have outlined in this book. The American Association of Individual Investors in Chicago (800-428-2244 or 312-280-0170) publishes an excellent monthly journal as well as books and other reports on topics of interest to small investors (dues: $49 a year; this includes a subscription to the journal). The AAII also sponsors seminars and sells books and computer software at a discount to members.

The National Association of Investors Corporation in Royal Oak, Michigan (810-583-6242), focuses on helping individuals set up investment clubs. In addition to providing instructions on how to set up a club, the NAIC offers guides and worksheets for stock analysis. Clubs pay $35 a year plus $14 per club member to belong to the organization. Even if you are not interested in being part of an investment club, though, you will probably find the NAIC's information well worth the cost of joining. Dues for individuals are $39 a year, which includes a subscription to the organization's monthly journal, *Better Investing*.

Beyond these two organizations, there are an enormous number of places you can turn to get information on stocks. Here's a quick rundown of the sources in four important areas:

NEWSPAPERS AND MAGAZINES

When it comes to using general news sources, there is no substitute for reading the *Wall Street Journal* every day. In addition to a wealth of information about business, the newspaper runs lots of articles about top money managers' investing strategies. Don't feel that you should act quickly, however, when you see a favorable article on a stock. You should read the *WSJ* as a way of keeping up with the market.

Always remember that a company that's attractive today may be just as appealing six months from now—and the price may be cheaper. Reading the *Wall Street Journal* will help you decide which stocks you want to include in your portfolio for the long term. The decision to buy one of them should always be based on your own appraisal of the current price. Compaq didn't become a leading U.S. computer maker overnight. To make money on the stock, though, you had to buy it during one of its periodic pullbacks. Other newspapers may be helpful as well, but none comes close to the *Wall Street Journal,* in my opinion.

When it comes to magazines, though, the variety of worthwhile periodicals is much greater. *Barron's* and *Forbes* are probably the ones most oriented to investors who want to buy individual stocks rather than limit themselves to mutual funds. In particular, *Barron's* runs long—and unfortunately rather dull—interviews with top money managers and securities analysts that contain an enormous amount of useful information about specific stocks. *Business Week* and *Fortune* are useful if you want to keep up with company stories and industry trends. Both also contain a certain amount of material that would interest an aspiring stock picker. For general personal finance and investing information, **MONEY** (my own magazine) and *Smart Money* are worthwhile.

Once you start looking for stock-picking ideas, you'll be surprised how many different places they turn up; lots of newspapers and magazines nowadays have at least a couple of columns or departments devoted to stocks and investing. I can't stress too highly, though, that rankings and ratings and lists of best picks should all be taken with a grain of salt. Successful investors buy and sell only a few times a year. Newspapers and magazines have to publish daily or weekly or monthly. If you follow their advice slavishly, you'll trade too much and the only one who will get rich is your broker.

RESEARCH SOURCES

Three companies stand out as sources for stock analysis. Standard & Poor's in New York City (800-221-5277 or 212-208-8000) tracks more than 5,500 common and preferred stocks. The company's research reports cover most of the stocks on the New York Stock Exchange and American Stock Exchange as well as a broad cross section of NASDAQ and over-the-counter stocks. Subscribing to the stock reports, which can run more than $3,000 a year, is too expensive for most small investors, but you may be able to find them in your local library. S&P does package the information in annuals and other more affordable forms. The firm's popular stock guide, for example, costs $135 a year. And its weekly newsletter, *The Outlook,* is $298.

The Value Line Investment Survey in New York City (800-833-0046 or 212-907-1500) follows about 1,700 stocks. Although the coverage is more limited than Standard & Poor's, Value Line does track most of the common stocks small investors would be interested in. The service is also cheaper at $525 a year. Most important, Value Line does make forecasts for the shares it follows and ranks them for both Timeliness and Safety on scales ranging from one to five. It's also impressive to note that the Value Line Timeliness Ranking System is one of the few that has proved able to beat the market much of the time. If I could subscribe to only one source of stock information, without question I would choose Value Line.

There's also an up-and-coming stock-rating service you should know about for future reference. Morningstar in Chicago (800-876-5005 or 312-696-6000) chiefly follows mutual funds, but the firm has been expanding its common stock coverage in the past few years. Currently the firm has a first-rate service for foreign shares that trade in the United States and another for closed-end funds. And I wouldn't be surprised to see Morningstar extend its franchise further.

NEWSLETTERS

For specific stock recommendations and other specialized investing information, newsletters are immensely helpful. Among the

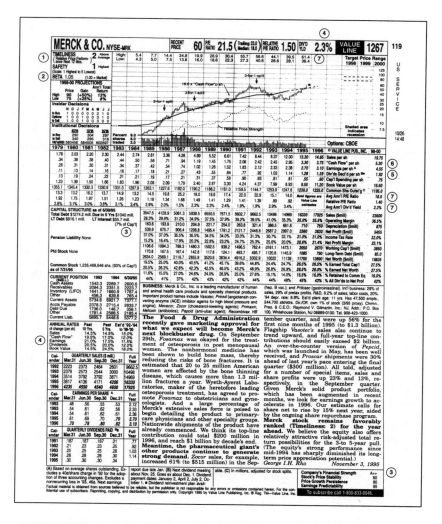

HOW TO READ A PAGE FROM *THE VALUE LINE INVESTMENT SURVEY*

The stock profiles in *The Value Line Investment Survey* contain just about all the data a small investor would need to evaluate a stock. As an example, here is some of the important information you could learn about the leading drug company Merck:

1. The Timeliness Rank of 2 (on a scale of 1 to 5, with 1 the best) means that Value Line considers the stock a better than average buy for the coming six to 12 months.

2. The beta of 1.05 (with the market equal to 1.00) shows that Merck is about 5% more volatile than the overall stock market.

3. Debt that is less than 20% of capital and an A++ financial strength rating confirm that the company is very strong financially.

4. Projected earnings growth of 11.5% plus a 2.3% yield indicate that Merck's long-term total return could be nearly 14% (11.5% plus 2.3%) a year, on average.

5. The projected dividend gives you an idea of what the stock's future dividend yield might be. In this case, the 1996 yield would be 2.3% ($1.39 divided by $60).

6. Cash flow per share allows you to calculate the price/cash-flow ratio, an alternative way of valuing the stock besides its price/earnings ratio. In this case, Merck's 16 P/CF ratio ($60 divided by $3.75) is well above average, confirming that the 21.5 P/E is quite high.

7. The stock's range over the past three years shows that it's pricey on a short-term basis. However, the average annual P/Es and dividend yields over the past 16 years suggest that the shares are still below their potential peaks.

general letters I like, S&P's weekly *The Outlook* (800-221-5277 or 212-208-8000; $298 a year) is worthwhile. Apart from offering market analysis, the newsletter profiles individual stocks and carries stock rankings that rate more than 1,000 companies on a scale of one to five. *Richard C. Young's Intelligence Report* (800-848-2132 or 401-849-2137; $99 a year) includes an economic forecast and recommendations for common stocks, preferreds, convertibles, bonds, and mutual funds. Young's approach is based on core holdings and low portfolio turnover, and his advice is particularly helpful for investors managing their retirement savings. I also like Geraldine Weiss's *Investment Quality Trends* (619-459-3818; $275 a year).

Elsewhere in this book I've mentioned newsletters that cover areas of special interest, and I'll repeat the information here. Investors interested in dividend reinvestment plans (DRIPs) can subscribe to Charles B. Carlson's monthly *DRIP Investor* (219-931-6480; $59 a year). The AAII also offers an annual guide to such plans for $4 (free for members of the AAII).

Among publications that cover convertibles, you can choose *The Value Line Convertibles Survey* (800-833-0046 or 212-907-1500; $625 a year). For closed-end funds, I like *Morningstar Closed-End Funds* (800-876-5005 or 312-696-6000; $195 a year) and *The Scott Letter* (800-356-3508 or 804-741-8707; $150 a year).

For readers who are active enough to want analysis of the overall market, here are the newsletters I would recommend: *Market Logic* (800-442-9000 or 305-563-9000; $95 a year), the *InvesTech Market Analyst,* and the *Mutual Fund Adviser* (800-955-8500 or 406-862-7777; $160 a year). These newsletters offer a wealth of fascinating historical data on the economy and the stock market as well as insightful analysis of market trends.

COMPUTER SOFTWARE AND
ON-LINE SERVICES

In the world of personal computers, investing is one of the most popular subjects for software and on-line services. At the simplest level, you can check stock quotes and news stories on companies that interest you through leading on-line services such as CompuServe or America Online. But that's only the beginning. You can also trade stocks with discount commissions, manage your own portfolio, analyze specific companies, and track market trends—all with an ordinary personal computer.

More than a dozen software packages (typically costing less than $75) allow you to buy and sell individual stocks. Leading discount brokerages—including Charles Schwab, Fidelity, and Quick & Reilly—have their own versions of this software. These packages, as well as software by some independent producers, generally operate through one or more of the on-line services.

In addition to software for buying and selling, programs are available for managing your stock holdings (as well as bonds, mutual funds, and so on). Among their functions: updating all your stocks to current prices; keeping track of dividends and interest; recording commissions; and figuring your portfolio's overall value. Many of these software packages will also help you with more complex calculations, such as analyzing your asset allocation or monitoring the performance of the various stocks you own. Such software ranges in cost from as little as $40 to more than $200. Members of the American Association of Individual Investors, however, can obtain discounts of 10% or more on many programs.

Computer software is also ideal for investors interested in technical analysis, which requires charting enormous amounts of share price and trading volume data. More than a dozen such technical programs are available that are aimed at small investors. Prices range from less than $200 to nearly $1,000, but discounts of as much as 50% are available to AAII members. These software packages will make graphs of stock prices in a variety of different ways, search for trends and patterns, and adjust all the data for splits, interest costs, and brokerage commissions. Unlike the old-time technicians, who were wont to plot incomprehensible charts on dog-eared graph paper with three different colors of ink, today's cybergeeks can chart their way to profits with nothing more than a mouse.

CHAPTER 15

YOUR QUESTIONS ANSWERED:

Here Are Quick Explanations of 18 Money Matters

In this book I've outlined all the essentials you need to know if you want to be a successful small investor. Equally important, I've omitted a lot of flummery that you don't have to worry about. My goal in the previous 14 chapters has been to give you precisely the tools required to manage long-term investments every bit as well as a pro—without wasting any of your time or getting caught up in pointless academic debates.

Nonetheless, a number of other investing topics are worth a brief discussion. So in this final chapter I'll provide quick explanations of some additional money matters. Here are the answers to 18 frequently asked questions:

1. Should I invest in savings bonds?

Millions of Americans do. In fact, U.S. savings bonds are the world's most widely held security. That shouldn't come as a surprise, given savings bonds' advantages. Among them: The bonds are fully backed by the U.S. government. They can be bought at most banks and are often available through payroll deduction plans. You can invest as much as $15,000 a year in amounts as small as $25. The most common type—a EE bond—pays no cash interest; instead the interest accrues and the bonds rise in value until you cash them in. You can redeem bonds after six months or hold them for as long as 30 years.

Best of all is the tax treatment of interest on the bonds. First, the interest is exempt from state and local income taxes. Second, it isn't subject to federal income tax until you sell your bonds. Finally, if your taxable income is low enough, your interest may be fully or partly exempt from tax if the bond is cashed to pay college tuition for the bond's owner or a dependent. The interest rate itself—which is 85% of the yield on five-year Treasury securities if you hold the bond for five years or longer—is usually competitive with short-term yields.

2. How risky are junk bonds?

Theoretically they aren't all that risky. The argument for junk is that while roughly 3% of the bonds default, they offer yields at least four percentage points higher than those on riskless government securities. Therefore, if you bought a widely diversified collection of junk bonds, the added return would more than make up for any losses you suffered—especially since some of the junk bonds that defaulted would eventually recover part of their value. In addition, junk bonds aren't particularly volatile—their high yields make them less sensitive than usual to changing interest rates.

Generally speaking, junk bonds get badly hurt only in two sets of circumstances. First, a recession can make investors worry about companies with weak balance sheets, and that can depress the prices of low-grade bond issues even if the firms are making all their interest payments on time. Second, during periods of easy money, companies can borrow too much and the overall default rate can start to climb. But as a rule, the yields on junk bonds are more than high enough to offset their risk.

Nonetheless, I still don't think junk bonds are particularly appealing investments. First, the whole argument for junk works only if you own a well-chosen assortment of bonds. If you invest in six issues, say, a default puts quite a hole in your portfolio. For all practical purposes, that means you need to own junk bonds through a mutual fund.

The problem there is that it's hard to assess a fund's holdings. Funds do list the bonds they own in documents they are required to make public. But evaluating a junk bond portfolio is impossible for most small investors. The real risk you face, therefore, is that a fund will buy a bunch of awful bonds to boost the yield it can advertise. So you end up investing in a pig in a poke.

Moreover, even good junk funds get hurt in a recession, just as stocks do—but they don't offer the upside potential of stocks. The bottom line is that I'd rather own stocks unless I'm going to get the safety of a top-quality bond. If you disagree and decide that junk bonds are a worthwhile compromise between risk and return, be sure to buy an established fund that avoids the cruddiest issues and has a long track record of outperforming the average junk fund.

3. I can afford to buy only a single tax-exempt municipal bond. Is that safe?

Ideally you need to own at least half a dozen municipal issues to be well diversified. But there are a couple of circumstances in which you can get by with just a single tax-exempt bond. First, if you have a broad portfolio diversified among a variety of assets—such as U.S. blue chips, small stocks, money funds, and so on—and you live in a high-tax state, I could see putting 5% or so of your money in a single muni. In that case you should consider buying a general obligation bond issued by the state government of the state in which you reside. Reason: Such state

GOs are less likely to default than are bonds issued by county, city, or other local governments or bonds connected with state-sponsored projects, such as a hospital.

As an alternative, you can buy so-called pre-refunded bonds. These issues come into existence when interest rates fall and a muni issuer is able to save money on interest payments by issuing new bonds and using the proceeds to buy Treasury issues to secure the old bonds. Since such pre-refunded bonds are backed by U.S. government securities, they effectively have the highest possible credit rating. You may be wondering why the states and municipalities don't simply pay off the old bonds when they issue the new ones. The answer is they can't: generally munis run for 10 years or so before they can be called (redeemed ahead of schedule). In the interim, the best the issuer can do is pre-refund the bonds. Obviously this means that when bonds are pre-refunded, they generally have less than 10 years to go before they either mature or can be called.

4. Do giant mutual funds perform as well as smaller funds?

It's conventional wisdom that giant mutual funds can't perform as well as smaller, more nimble funds. However, that truism turns out to be false. Generally, the largest funds have been outpacing the average mutual fund for more than a decade. The key reason is that since 1984, blue chips have led the stock market most of the time. And since the largest funds tend to focus on big-company stocks, they've naturally been invested in the most promising issues. Moreover, giant funds are at no disadvantage to their smaller rivals when it comes to investing in multibillion-dollar companies.

However, if other investments were outpacing U.S. blue chips, the results would almost certainly be different. Small funds do have an advantage when it comes to investing in issues that are hard to buy and sell: Quite simply, they don't need as many shares as a bigger fund would to have a significant position. So the next time the shares of small growth companies or foreign stocks in emerging markets are the best performers, you can expect to see small funds topping the rankings.

5. Should technology stocks sell at higher prices than the shares of companies in other businesses?

In theory the answer is no. According to the dividend–discount model, the current value of a stock is based on its prospects for future earnings growth and the confidence that those earnings will come through as expected. No brownie points are given for technology; money earned by a restaurant franchise counts for just as much as money earned on computer chips. And no one who has watched the ups and downs of high–tech firms can possibly believe that they are less risky than growth stocks in more mundane businesses.

Nonetheless, history shows that investors are often willing to pay a premium for technologically based growth, irrational as that may be. Since 1979 the technology premium has varied from nothing to as much as 80%. The norm is in the 30% to 40% range. In the past few years the premium has often been very low—below 10% until the boom in technology stocks in early '95. That suggests that even though technology stocks have recently been strong performers, they still have room to outpace the rest of the market between now and the year 2000. You should therefore consider any pullback in high–tech stocks to be a potential buying opportunity.

6. How much money should I invest in foreign stocks?

There's a theoretical argument that an ideal stock portfolio should mirror the global distribution of capital. In other words, if the U.S. market accounts for 40% of the world's equity, you would invest 40% of your money in U.S. stocks. The reasoning here is that the amount of money in any particular stock market reflects the balance between risk and return that it offers. And if you're smart, you'll split up your money the same way big global investors do—with roughly 40% of your money in the United States, 25% in Japan, 20% in Europe, and 15% in emerging markets.

However valid this theory may be, few people want to invest 60% of their money overseas. And in fact, there's a reason to favor the good old U.S. of A. If you live here, what you really care about is your profit in U.S. dollars. And international markets present extra risk because they operate in foreign currencies. Therefore, whenever you consider an investment overseas, it not only has to offer a better return than comparable U.S. alternatives; the extra return has to be big enough to offset currency risk.

So what is the optimum global equity mix? A recent Smith Barney study of international stocks over the past decade concludes that if you look only at developed countries' stock markets, the best trade-off between return and risk (including currency risk) came from a portfolio that is 60% U.S. and 40% foreign. If you include riskier emerging markets, the best mix was 70/30. Even having 30% of your money in foreign stocks may seem like a lot. Typical investors have at most 10% of their money overseas, if they have any. Don't feel you have to go to the limit; there's nothing wrong with keeping all your cash in the United States if you really want to. But don't be afraid to increase your share in foreign stocks; odds are you're not being venturesome enough. Remember, however, that all these percentages refer only to the money you have in stocks. If you keep your money split 60/40 between stocks and income investments, 30% of your stockholdings would be only 18% of your total assets (30% times 60%).

7. Does ethical investing make sense?

Denying capital to a business you don't approve of is a perfectly reasonable political act. Such an ethically motivated decision would make sense if you were putting money directly into a new business, for example. However, when it comes to buying existing shares, refusing to buy a stock usually doesn't deny anything to the company you disapprove of. For one thing, money you invest in an existing stock goes to the previous shareholder, not to the company. Further, whenever you avoid a stock for a reason that isn't economic, you simply make the stock more attractive to other investors. Here's why: Imagine that there are two stocks with the same yield. For ethical reasons, you decide to buy one rather than the other. By purchasing the stock you approve of, you bid up its price, which in turn makes its yield slightly lower. At that point, other investors who don't share your political point of view will all gravitate toward the stock you don't like because of its yield advantage. You may say that your investment is too small to effect the share price. In that case, however, it would also be too small to have any other practical effect.

What about looking at the question the other way around? Ethical investing may not have any political impact but might affect your results. Theory suggests that socially responsible investing ought to underperform the market slightly, because you are passing up some attractive investments. Socially conscious types counter by arguing that progressive companies will get better results from their workforce over the long term. The actual evidence, however, is mixed: sometimes ethical investments beat the market, often they don't. Basically, when alcoholic beverage, tobacco, and defense stocks aren't performing well, ethical investors look like geniuses. But when times are tough for high-tech and service companies, which tend to be overweighted in socially conscious portfolios, progressive investors look like mush-heads.

Even if you accept the idea that ethical investing probably won't help your performance and might hurt it, you may still want to consider the approach. First, there are a few cases where socially conscious investing does make a difference. For example, the boycott of South Africa was so widespread that it did have a real effect on that country's economy. Further, ethical investing may make you feel better. You could have more of an impact on a company's policy by writing letters to the CEO and do more for the poor by tossing a quarter in a Salvation Army bucket at Christmas. But if it would bother you to own a tobacco company's stock because smoking is icky, don't do it. After all, it's your money—and you can invest it any way you want.

8. Should I belong to an investment club?

Thousands of Americans join investment clubs every month. These clubs typically consist of a dozen or so relatively inexperienced investors, and each club member antes up $25 a month or so. Contributions are used to buy a pool of high-quality stocks that is held in common. Over the long term, successful clubs earn 10% to 12% a year—and sometimes more. At that rate, a club member's $25 a month could grow to more than $70,000 over 30 years.

   Those are fine results, but the fact is that you could do just as well by yourself if you added $25 a month to an S&P 500 index fund. The real benefit of belonging to an investment club is not that it improves your results, but that it offers a social way to learn about managing money. Even more important, a club helps reinforce the discipline needed to build a long-term portfolio of blue chips. If you're interested in joining or starting such a club, one helpful source of information is the National Association of Investors Corp. (810-583-6242).

TRUE FACT

Stocks earn an average of only 6% annually in the first two years of a president's term but more than 13% annually in the last two years.

Source: Chris R. Hensel and William T. Ziemba, *Financial Analysts Journal,* March–April 1995

---

9. Does the stock market do better when the president is a Democrat or a Republican?

You easily might think that the stock market does a lot better during Republican administrations than it does under Democrats. After all, the Dems put people before profits, while the GOP does the reverse. Well, don't bet money on it. A comprehensive study of stock and bond prices from 1928 to 1993 by Chris R. Hensel and William T. Ziemba (*Financial Analysts Journal,* March–April 1995) found that big-company stocks do about the same under both parties—generally in the 9.5% to 11% range. The Republicans have an edge if you start in 1937, but if you go back to 1929 and include the Great Crash, the Democrats come out clearly ahead. On balance, though, corporate America can rest easy no matter which party is in power. Of course, Jesse Jackson could have told you that.

There are, however, substantial differences in the way assets other than blue-chip stocks perform, depending on which party controls the presidency. Here are the results the study found, along with my own explanations for why the different asset groups may have performed the way they did.

It turns out that as far as the stock and bond markets are concerned, the key difference between the parties is their attitude toward inflation. Because the Republicans are tough inflation fighters, they do a better job of preserving the value of cash and all types of bonds. Under Republicans, for example, long-term bonds returned 7% to 8%, on average. Democrats managed bond returns of only 1% to 3%.

By contrast, the Democrats favor easy money to help keep unemployment down even if it means higher inflation. Commodities traders, needless to say, love liberals. But they aren't the only ones. Easy money and low interest rates also help small firms, which often have trouble getting adequate financing. The result: Small-company shares can thrive. Since 1937, in fact, small stocks have earned an average of 16.5% when the Democrats were in power and only 9.2% under the Republicans.

10. Would a cut in capital-gains taxes be good for stocks?

There's an excellent case that profits on capital investments ought to get a tax break; in fact, some economists would argue that there shouldn't be any capital-gains taxes at all. Their reasoning: Unlike other uses for money, capital spending creates the capacity to produce new wealth—and, in the process, permanent jobs. In a sense, then, capital spending has already paid its dues to society. Why should it pay a second time in the form of taxes? Looked at purely in pragmatic terms, it's in society's interest to encourage as much capital spending as possible. And the best way to do that is through favorable tax treatment. Periodically, politicians buy into this line of thinking and cut capital-gains taxes. Most recently, taxes were reduced in 1978 and 1981. And today many Republicans would like to see another substantial cut— from 28% to less than 20%.

What would such a tax reduction mean for investors and the stock market? Obviously it's beneficial for stock investors, since the part of their profits that comes from capital gains (as opposed to dividends) would be taxed at a lower rate. For the stock market, though, it's a mixed blessing. Over the long term, lower taxes would attract more money to stocks, helping to buoy prices. But the short-term effects are more complicated.

Once investors begin to think that a capital-gains tax cut is fairly likely, they start bidding up share prices to reflect the improved long-term outlook. They also try to avoid selling; after all, why take profits now and pay full taxes when you could postpone the sale for a few months and pay significantly less? The net result: Share prices rise in the six months before a tax cut. Once the cut takes effect, however, all the investors who have postponed selling start dumping their stock. And that can depress prices. In fact, the last two times capital-gains taxes were cut, the Dow industrials lost more than 12% in two months.

11. Does it help a stock to be in an index like the Dow or the S&P 500?

Just being in such an index probably doesn't have much effect, but numerous studies show that stocks go up when they are added to a major index and go down when they are dropped. That's not at all hard to understand. A number of money managers and mutual fund pros try to keep up with the market by matching their holdings to an important stock index (this strategy is known as **indexing**). As a result, these managers buy a stock when it joins an index and dump it if it is removed. One study found that this buying and selling was great enough to move share prices by as much as 3%.

Similar patterns occur when a stock is listed on the New York Stock Exchange for the first time or when the ratings of shares are raised or lowered by *The Value Line Investment Survey.* However, there is one striking fact about all these cases: The share prices make almost all of their moves before news of the change is reported or within a day after the announcement. One study of stocks joining the New York Stock Exchange discovered that they rose as much as 5% in the three months prior to listing. Other research has found that stocks go on to lag the market after they list. One recent study concluded that shares can underperform by as much as 6% in the three years after they list on the NYSE.

12. Does it mean anything when the Dow crosses a 1000 mark?

Basically, no. Investors are apt to think it's a positive sign whenever the stock market sets a record high. And that small psychological effect is magnified when the Dow's new high involves crossing a 1000 mark. In actuality, though, round numbers on the Dow are arbitrary. They don't have any more meaning than a year like 1900 that ends in two zeros. People tend to think that the end of one century and the start of another has some special significance, but years are essentially arbitrary numbers based on an incorrect date for the birth of Jesus. And you don't need to be much of a historian to know that optimism based on leaving the fin de siècle behind is often misplaced: it was only 12 years after the beginning of the nineteenth century that Napoleon invaded Russia and 14 years after the start of the twentieth that Serbian posturing in Bosnia ignited World War I.

You should also reject the ridiculous but popular argument that the stock market is going up faster than it used to because it crosses 1000 marks more quickly. From the 1929 Crash, it may have taken 43 years for the Dow to cross the 1000 mark, 14 to reach 2000, four years to 3000, three years, 10 months to 4000, and a mere nine months to 5000. But that doesn't prove anything except that the 1000 marks get closer together as the Dow gets higher. From 1000 to 2000 is a 100% gain, while from 2000 to 3000 is only 50%. This simple mathematical fact applies to short-term market gains and losses as well. The media make a fuss whenever the Dow is up or down more than 100 points in a single day. But with the Dow above 5000, those fluctuations are less than one-sixth the size in percentage terms that they were back in 1982 when the Dow was at 800.

13. How much are stock prices likely to fluctuate in a year?

Stock prices have been remarkably steady over the past few years. In both 1993 and 1994 the difference between the market's high for the year and its low was less than 10%. In 1995 the swing was more than 20%, but since the low was set in early January, all of the volatility came from share price increases. And few investors will complain about fluctuations that bring higher prices.

In fact, since World War II, the stock market's normal yearly range from high to low has been 21.9%. Investors should be aware, however, that on occasion stock prices can swing twice that much. Moreover, years of exceptionally high volatility are often dismal for shareholders. The years with the two biggest swings, for example, were 1987 and 1974. In both those years the difference between the market's annual high and low was more than 40%. Unfortunately, both those years were abnormally high because of enormous market declines—1987 was the year of the crash, while 1974 included the final collapse in the worst bear market since 1937.

14. Is a recent buy recommendation from an analyst better than an old one?

As a general rule, new buy recommendations are much better than old ones. The reason is simple common sense. Analysts don't like to keep changing their ratings on stocks, so they normally wait until they are sure that shares are unquestionably underpriced before they issue a new buy rating. Then, if they are right and the stock price moves up, the analysts are inclined to continue to carry the stock as a buy rather than downgrading it to a hold (which might be interpreted as a negative comment on the company rather than simply a reflection of the shares' price appreciation).

Unfortunately, most investors pay no attention to how stale a buy recommendation may be. If you want to avoid this mistake, try to find out where a stock was trading when the analyst first issued his or her buy. If the shares have risen since then, compare their price increase to the company's earnings growth and the change in the overall market. If, for example, earnings are up 10% since the buy was issued, it's quite reasonable for the stock to be up 10% to 15%. Similarly, if the market is up 20%, then a comparable increase in the stock price may be okay. But if the shares have greatly outpaced both the company's earnings and the broad market, you should look carefully to see if the stock has additional value that hasn't been recognized yet. If it doesn't, think twice. You don't want to buy the stock right before analysts downgrade their buy recommendations to holds.

It's also possible, of course, that the share price won't have risen—or even that it may have fallen. In that case, you might have a terrific opportunity. Or, the weak price might be a sign that the analyst was fundamentally wrong. Be skeptical—but don't dismiss the recommendation out of hand. If you can analyze the stock yourself or get a fresh analyst's opinion, you might find you have a chance to scoop up a great bargain.

15. Are stock splits good for shareholders?

It's generally thought that a split is a sign that a stock has bright prospects. And several studies confirm this belief even though it isn't completely logical. When a stock is split two-for-one, for example, an investor who formerly owned 100 shares ends up with 200. But since all shareholders have double the number they had before, nothing changes but the number of pieces of paper. Everyone's percentage ownership remains the same, and the company still has the same earnings and assets.

TRUE FACT

Splitting a stock can boost its return by four to five percentage points over the following year.

Source: Ford Investor Services

Nonetheless, several academic studies have shown that splitting a stock can improve its performance. Analysts cite several possible explanations. For starters, managers decide to split a stock because they think its price is so high that it might be out of the reach of some potential investors. This problem usually arises when the stock has risen considerably over the previous year or two. More important, the company's executives wouldn't split the stock if they thought it might go back down. As a result, a split indicates that top managers believe a strong stock will continue to appreciate.

Further, the evidence shows that the benefits of a split go beyond signaling the opinions of insiders. First, dividends are often rounded up, which gives the yield a boost. In the case where a stock paying 75¢ a quarter splits two-for-one, each post-split share might pay 40¢. Second, the fact that more shares are trading makes the stock easier for large investors to buy. Finally, since splits lower the share price, they make a stock more affordable for investors who want to buy in round lots of 100 shares and have limited funds. The bottom line is that splits are unquestionably a positive sign. One recent study by Ford Investor Services in San Diego found that stocks split two-for-one outperformed the overall stock market by more than four percentage points over the following year.

16. What do I need to do with the cards that companies send me?

Those cards, known as **proxies,** are absentee ballots for shareholders' meetings. If you don't send the cards back, you'll be deprived of your say in important corporate issues—from the makeup of the company's board of directors to its environmental policies. To be completely honest, corporate democracy has about as much to do with real democracy as military music does with music. Most of the time your votes will be meaningless because management has great latitude in what it allows to come to a vote. Further, many shareholders automatically side with management or allow top executives to vote their shares.

Send the cards back anyway. Top managers often watch such votes the way politicians listen to polls. If even 10% of the shareholders vote against some corporate policy, top executives will often consider changing it to head off future bad publicity. Most important, votes at shareholders' meetings occasionally can have a major impact on the value of your shares. For example, if your company is involved in a takeover battle, a fight concerning board membership, a rights offering, or some similar corporate event, the vote will be contested seriously and the outcome will likely affect the stock price. You should make sure your voice will be heard.

17. I have an old stock certificate, but I can't find the company listed anywhere. Is there a way to find out if my certificate is worth anything?

It very well may be. If the firm that issued your certificate was taken over by another company, you may be able to exchange your old certificate for cash or for shares in the acquirer. And even if your certificate has no value as an investment, it may be worth something as a collectible. Some 20,000 people in the

United States collect old stocks and bonds (a hobby known as **scripophily**), and certificates can go for anywhere from $10 to more than $1,000. One has even sold for as much as $30,000. To find out whether your old stock has any value as a collectible, you can contact dealers and auction houses that handle such items. Two prominent firms: George H. LaBarre Galleries in Hollis, N.H. (603-882-2411), and R. M. Smythe & Co. in New York City (212-943-1880).

18. What other books on investing are worth reading?

Given the thousands of investing books that have been published over the years, it's difficult to narrow down the list. So let me tick off a sampling in four categories, and don't assume a book isn't worthwhile just because I omit it.

For starters, there's a group of classics from before World War II. I'm not sure these books actually tell you anything useful about stock picking, but they do get across an attitude that will help keep you from losing your shirt. Among these classics are Charles Mackay's *Extraordinary Popular Delusions & the Madness of Crowds* (Random House), a nineteenth-century compendium of great historical fiascoes, many of which have a financial dimension; Edwin Lefèvre's *Reminiscences of a Stock Operator* (Wiley), loosely based on the career of a 1920s stock trader named Jesse Livermore; and Fred Schwed Jr.'s *Where Are the Customers' Yachts?* (Wiley), a book of amusing but sound financial advice that debunks the investment business in a marvelously relaxed way. The basic message of these books is that the market is more powerful than you are, and if you think you can beat the system, you're a sucker. The point is well taken.

Next up are the contemporary classics. Among these, I would select John Train's *Money Masters* (HarperCollins), which consists of profiles of great investors (Train also wrote a sequel called *New Money Masters*); David Dreman's *The New Contrarian Investment*

Strategy (Random House), which makes a compelling case for investing in stocks with low price/earnings ratios; and Gerald Loeb's *The Battle for Investment Survival* (Fraser). Reading these three books will go a long way toward making you a value-conscious investor.

As far as investment theory is concerned, Benjamin Graham and David L. Dodd's *Security Analysis* (McGraw-Hill) is practically a sacred text. However, the book is hard going, and no one I know has actually read it. Instead you might want to look at Graham's *The Intelligent Investor* (HarperCollins). Burton G. Malkiel's *A Random Walk Down Wall Street* (Norton) is the classic statement of the efficient market argument, which basically says that no one can consistently beat the market. This theory, which was once academic dogma, has been proven wrong—at least in its extreme form. Even so, Malkiel's lucid presentation of the efficient market view is a bracing reminder that opportunities to beat the market are rare and you have to make the most of them when they arise.

Finally, I'd recommend books by or about three great investment figures of the past decade: Robert G. Hagstrom's *The Warren Buffett Way* (Wiley), about the man generally considered the best living investor; Peter Lynch's *Beating the Street* (Simon & Schuster), by the former manager of Fidelity's fabulously successful Magellan fund; and *Bogle on Mutual Funds* (Irwin) by John C. Bogle, the former chairman of the Vanguard Group of mutual funds.

That makes 13 books altogether. To avoid that unlucky number, I'd also like to include *Gaining on the Market* (Little, Brown) by Charles J. Rolo and Robert J. Klein. Charles was my predecessor as Wall Street editor at **MONEY** magazine.

INDEX

INDEX

INDEX

273

INDEX